# NEW DEVELOPMENTS IN STATISTICS FOR PSYCHOLOGY AND THE SOCIAL SCIENCES

## VOLUME TWO

EDITED BY

## P. LOVIE AND A. D. LOVIE

# New Developments in Statistics for Psychology and the Social Sciences

## VOLUME TWO

Edited by

### P. LOVIE
*Lecturer in the Department of Mathematics*
*University of Keele*

### A. D. LOVIE
*Lecturer in the Department of Psychology*
*University of Liverpool*

The British Psychological Society and
Routledge, London and New York

The British Psychological Society and
Routledge, London and New York

© The British Psychological Society, 1991

First edition published in 1991 by BPS Books (The British Psychological
Society), St Andrews House, 48 Princess Road East, Leicester LE1 7DR, in
association with Routledge Ltd, 11 New Fetter Lane, London EC4P 4EE, and
in the USA by Routledge, Chapman and Hall Inc., 29 West 35th Street, New
York, NY 10001.

British Library Cataloguing in Publication Data

New developments in statistics for psychology and the social
sciences.
Vol. 2
1. Statistical mathematics
I. Lovie P.(Patricia)  II. Lovie A. D. (Alexander D)
519.5

ISBN 1-85433-017-9

Library of Congress Cataloging in Publication Data Available

ISBN 1-85433-017-9

Printed in Great Britain by BPCC Wheatons Ltd, Exeter

# Of Exactitude in Science

. . . In that Empire, the craft of Cartography attained such Perfection that the Map of a Single province covered the space of an entire City, and the Map of the Empire itself an entire Province. In the course of Time, these Extensive maps were found somehow wanting, and so the College of Cartographers evolved a Map of the Empire that was of the same Scale as the Empire and that coincided with it point for point. Less attentive to the Study of Cartography, succeeding Generations came to judge a map of such Magnitude cumbersome, and, not without Irreverence, they abandoned it to the Rigours of sun and Rain. In the western Deserts, tattered Fragments of the Map are still to be found, Sheltering an occasional Beast or beggar; in the whole Nation, no other relic is left of the Discipline of Geography.

From *Travels of Praiseworthy Men* (1658)
by J. A. Suárez Miranda

In Jorge Luis Borges, *A Universal History of Infamy*

To the memory of
L.

# Contents

PREFACE        ix

CHAPTER 1    **Nonparametric Methods for Complex Data Sets**    1
Chris Leach, *Department of Clinical Psychology,*
*Dewsbury Health Authority*

CHAPTER 2    **Graphical Methods for Exploring Data**    19
Alexander D. Lovie, *Department of Psychology, University*
*of Liverpool*
Patricia Lovie, *Department of Mathematics, University of*
*Keele*

CHAPTER 3    **Computationally Intensive Statistics**    49
Christopher C. Robertson, *Department of Statistics and*
*Modelling Science, University of Strathclyde*

CHAPTER 4    **Classification Trees**    81
David J. Hand, *Faculty of Mathematics, The Open*
*University*

CHAPTER 5    **Regression Diagnostics: A rough guide to safer**    95
**regression**
Patricia Lovie, *Department of Mathematics, University of*
*Keele*

CHAPTER 6    **Unbalanced Designs**    135
Ranald R. Macdonald, *Department of Psychology,*
*University of Stirling*

CHAPTER 7    **Repeated Measures: Groups × Occasions Designs**    155
Alan J. B. Anderson, *Department of Mathematical*
*Sciences, University of Aberdeen*

CHAPTER 8    **Time Series**    174
Christopher J. Skinner, *Department of Social Statistics,*
*University of Southampton*

CHAPTER 9    **Latent Variable Methods**    199
David J. Bartholomew, *Department of Statistics, London*
*School of Economics and Political Science*

CHAPTER 10    **Compositional Data Analysis**                    214
John Aitchison, *Department of Mathematics, University of Virginia*

CHAPTER 11    **A Short History of Statistics in Twentieth Century**   234
**Psychology**
Alexander D. Lovie, *Department of Psychology, University of Liverpool*

INDEX                                                          251

# Preface

This book brings together another selection of reviews of contemporary statistics of interest to researchers and students in the social sciences. As in the previous volume (see Lovie (ed.), 1986), we have mixed treatments of traditional areas (suitably updated) with discussions of more recent topics, and ended with a tutorial essay.

In the Introduction to the first volume, one of us pointed to *lacunae* in the areas covered; we have attempted, in the present text, to fill some of these voids, particularly in aspects of regression and the linear model. This new volume, like its predecessor, also reflects general trends in the discipline, including the headlong computerization of statistics, and the ever growing invasion of Exploratory Data Analysts bearing aloft well-thumbed copies of Tukey (1977).

We have also taken the opportunity to continue the saga of what we feel is one of the more appealing features of modern statistics, its love affair with graphical methods. Thus readers will find a separate chapter devoted to the topic (Chapter 2) and liberal doses of plots and displays in several of the others, in particular, the chapters on computer intensive methods, classification trees, regression diagnostics and time series (Chapters 3, 4, 5 and 8 respectively).

Another enduring theme is the computer and its central role in modern data analysis. One chapter, therefore, has the explicit brief of marrying the computer to statistics (Chapter 3).

However, since many of the technologies discussed in the other chapters are so completely dependent upon the offspring of Turing's little toys, it is not too fanciful to claim that they could not have been created without the computer. In particular, the computational demands of compositional data analysis (Chapter 10), classification trees (Chapter 4), time series (Chapter 8) and regression diagnostics (Chapter 5) are so considerable that they would not have existed either absolutely or in their current form without the parallel existence of powerful number crunching machinery.

A subsidiary trend is the increasing ability of the microcomputer to run even the most demanding and sophisticated of statistical packages – for instance, SAS, BMDP and SPSS running on IBM PC kit. In fact, a recent survey lists well over two hundred data analytical programs and packages of varying complexity for such cheap desk top units (Woodward *et al.*, 1988).

This increasing diffusion of (statistical computing) power is to be welcomed almost unreservedly, with the usual side warnings of 'garbage-in, garbage-out', 'don't run before you can walk', and 'never buy a pig (or any statistical output) in a poke'!

We now hasten from such domestic and rural saws to introduce our chosen topics in a little more detail.

## Chapter 1 – Nonparametric Methods

The late lamented Samuel Johnson (of the Dictionary fame, and the butt of Boswell's stab at biography) was probably the first member outside the Vienna Circle to coin an operational definition. He defined a classic work of literature as one which lasted. By this admittedly rather basic criterion, Sidney Siegel's *Nonparametric Statistics for the Behavioral Sciences* (1956) is up there with *Macbeth, David Copperfield* and Mrs. Beeton's *Book of Household Management*. It has indeed passed the test of time (and umpteen reprintings). However, excellent as the book is (and it is), nonparametric statistics has moved on since 1956, although (with one or two worthy exceptions, for example, Leach, 1979) coverage of this new material for the social scientist has been conspicuously absent.

Although the recent upgrade of Siegel by Castellan (Siegel & Castellan, 1988), and the equally welcome undergraduate text by Sprent (1988), have both added to the areas that Siegel made his own, yet there is less well known but equally relevant work by people like Hettmansperger (1984) and Lehmann (1975) just waiting to be presented. Chris Leach's chapter is all about this newer material, particularly the nonparametric analysis of complex experiments and the extension of such methods to the treatment of regression and the linear model.

## Chapter 2 – Graphical Methods

We have deliberately kept a low mathematical profile in our joint chapter, since we feel that in the best spirit of Exploratory Data Analysis the pictures should tell the story. In addition, we have chosen the well marked trail originally blazed by Cleveland and others (see his 1985 text) which moves from the representation and analysis of univariate data samples to the treatment of multivariate/ multivariable ones, emphasizing (in our perambulations) the *joint* operation of plots and data transformations in making sense of increasingly complex situations.

All of this means a great many quantile plots and scatterplots. Other more gaudy novelties are not, however, ignored; for example, we advocate an effects and box plot error display for the informal analysis of multifactor structures.

Finally, the displays would not have been possible without a particular PC statistics package. Our chapter makes this dependence abundantly plain!

## Chapter 3 – Computationally Intensive Statistics

Chris Robertson also worships at the same silicon altar since his chapter covers those growing areas of statistics which could never have existed prior to the computer. The classic problems of estimation and inference are addressed in the chapter, with the added twist that the procedures depend minimally upon statistical theory and maximally upon the number of computer operations that you can force out of your hardware.

Thus the bootstrap and the jackknife may employ literally thousands of simple calculations to estimate (with varying amounts of bias) a full range of parameters. The inferential side is represented by permutation/randomization tests and Monte Carlo simulations, both of which use the computer to generate empirical sampling distributions, often for more realistic hypotheses than the usual run. There is something of a link, therefore, between this chapter and Chapter 1 where the model specification is equally liberal.

## Chapter 4 – Classification Trees

David Hand writes about one of the less familiar topics in the book, but the widespread adoption of such dynamic, multi-level decision trees has produced substantial practical payoffs in such fields as medical and psychiatric diagnosis, biological taxonomy and pattern recognition.

In their simplest guise, classification trees are cascaded choice structures which offer the user a binary alternative at each descending choice point. The statistical interest is that since such trees formalize essentially uncertain choice, they can be described by extensions of the linear model, familiar to the users of regression analysis and ANOVA. Building such trees, therefore, is a nontrivial exercise in the multistage exploration of complex situations, hence their actual and potential interest to the social sciences.

The chapter offers a nontechnical, graphically based introduction to a subject which many statisticians also view as one of their more useful contributions to knowledge based expert systems.

## Chapter 5 - Regression Diagnostics

The first editor's chapter is devoted to a topic which, fifteen years ago, was no bigger than a human hand but now threatens to blot out the entire sky. Heroic attempts to diagnose and treat all the ills that least squares is heir to have been driven by the important insight that regression is both an analytical procedure and an empirical exploration of the complex relationships which typically exist between variables.

The strategy adopted by recent work has been to explore those aspects of the data and variables which disturb the pristine nature of the (assumed) underlying linear model. In particular, this chapter considers three such challenges: nonlinearity, discrepant data values which exert too much influence on the fitted model, and the lack of independence (collinearity) between the predictor variables. Practical tests and sovereign remedies for these complaints are suggested (analytic, empiric and graphical), and their merits for the applied worker assessed.

## Chapter 6 – Unbalanced Designs

The chapter by Ranald Macdonald is concerned with an abiding problem in the analysis of multifactor designs, that is, where there are unequal numbers of readings in the cells. The experimenter stuck with such a situation will frequently be unable to estimate any interactions involving these unequally sampled factors.

Although typically this has been ascribed either to bad luck or bad management on the part of the researcher (one of whose many priorities is supposed to be the maximization of statistical power by ensuring equal readings), Ranald Macdonald argues that this ignores the problem of naturally occurring inequalities.

Thus the chapter outlines the difficulties in applying the standard unequal $n$ treatments to such inherently unbalanced data sets and suggests a way of separately describing (and differentially treating) both artificial and naturally occurring unbalanced designs. This, in practice, leads to easily implemented modifications to the standard ANOVA for unequal $n$.

## Chapter 7 – Repeated Measures

So widely employed are repeated measures designs in psychology and other social sciences, and so varied have been the consequent statistical developments in their treatment that it is more appropriate today to talk about a repeated measures 'movement' than a solitary repeated measures 'analysis'. It is not surprising, therefore, that the chapter by Alan Anderson deploys a wide range of methods from the univariate to the multivariate, concluding with a final commendation for trend based analyses.

Although repeated measures designs include those whose *raison d'être* is primarily subject economy, the present chapter argues that the name 'repeated measures' should only be applied to studies where changes over time are central to the experimenter's concerns, for example, learning or training. Consequently, the chapter also provides a useful introduction to alternative analyses for the subject of the next chapter.

## Chapter 8 – Time Series

The chapter by Chris Skinner concentrates on the treatment of individual sequences of responses sampled over time, rather than on the more traditional topic of grouped or aggregate time series. Thus the material covered is particularly appropriate in the analysis of psychophysiological data where one is typically faced with a large amount of time-referenced information from a single subject.

Such an approach is also valuable in situations where the aim is primarily to model the changes over time rather than using the data to predict the future course of events, as is often the case with aggregate time series. As in the previous chapter, therefore, changes over time are seen here as central features of interest to the researcher.

Readers are also introduced to many of the currently available statistical alternatives, including Box-Jenkins ARIMA methods, transfer functions and dynamic factor modelling.

## Chapter 9 – Latent Variable Methods

Most social sciences have long supported the view that they must dig well below the mere appearance of events in order to understand these appearances. Although the first attempts to do this formally resulted in the birth (and subsequent adolescence) of factor analysis, several investigations around the time of the Second World War looked into alternative ways of accomplishing the same end.

One of the more successful of these (christened latent structure analysis by Lazarsfeld, one of its pioneers) is the subject of the present chapter by David Bartholomew. This surveys recent trends in what has proved to be a less controversial way of looking below the surface than classical factor analysis.

Initially, the chapter offers a way of regularizing the relationships between factor analysis and latent variable methods so as to unify both in a common latent framework. The properties of this more general description are then explored in greater detail, with sections devoted to modelling, and estimation and inference. The chapter closes with a discussion of the reliability of estimated latent components.

## Chapter 10 – Compositional Data Analysis

There are many situations in social science where one has to make comparative judgements between events on the basis of proportions of their occurrence. An example would be the proportion of time that children in a play area spent on different activities in a fixed time period, or the proportional frequency with which they handled various toys. (There is an obvious animal behaviour analogue here.) Another would be where the number of times each subject predicted a particular suit in a multiple-draw card guessing task were converted into proportions for each of the four suits.

John Aitchison points briefly to the problems that earlier data analysts have encountered when attempting to devise suitable methods for these situations. This is followed by an outline of his own work in the area, drawing on a worked example of the proportion of time allocated by university teachers to different academic and other activities.

In particular, he develops an alternative sampling space for the distribution of ratios of proportions and uses this to build a graphical display of the complex relationships between the events. This leads to a way of modelling the structure of these relationships (and those between subsets of the events), and a sequential strategy for testing different versions of the model which parallels that in log linear modelling (see Upton, 1986).

## Chapter 11 – A Short History of Statistics in Psychology

Suffice to say that the second editor's chapter touches on most of the central issues in psychological statistics which have arisen over the first fifty years of this century. These include comparisons between two or more samples, the link between design and analysis, and the rise of factor analysis.

If there is one simple message from the chapter, it is that one can indeed say new things about the past!

Pat Lovie and Sandy Lovie
Keele and Liverpool
April 1990

## Acknowledgements

We are grateful to all our contributors for their excellent chapters. In addition, their ready and cheerful acquiescence to our editing 'suggestions' and the speed with which they returned their revised material made our job that much easier.

We would also like to thank Joyce Collins of the British Psychological Society and members of the BPS's Books and Special Projects Group for their continuing support, including, of course, Chris Leach, our long suffering copy editor.

## References

CLEVELAND, W.S. (1985). *The Elements of Graphing Data*. Monterey, CA.: Wadsworth.

HETTMANSPERGER, T.P. (1984). *Statistical Inference Based on Ranks*. New York: Wiley.

LEACH, C. (1979). *Introduction to Statistics: A Nonparametric Approach for the Social Sciences*. Chichester: Wiley.

LEHMANN, E.L. (1975). *Nonparametrics: Statistical Methods Based on Ranks*. San Francisco: Holden-Day.

LOVIE, A.D. (Ed.) (1986). *New Developments in Statistics for Psychology and the Social Sciences*. London: The British Psychological Society & Methuen.

SIEGEL, S. (1956). *Nonparametric Statistics for the Behavioral Sciences*, 1st ed. New York: McGraw-Hill.

SIEGEL, S. & CASTELLAN, N.J. (1988). *Nonparametric Statistics for the Behavioral Sciences*, 2nd ed. New York: McGraw-Hill.

SPRENT, P. (1988). *Applied Nonparametric Statistical Methods*. London: Chapman & Hall.

TUKEY, J.W. (1977). *Exploratory Data Analysis*. Reading, Mass.: Addison-Wesley.

UPTON, G.J.G. (1986). Cross-classified Data. In A.D. Lovie (Ed.), *New Developments in Statistics for Psychology and the Social Sciences*. London: The British Psychological Society and Methuen.

WOODWARD, W.A., ELLIOT , A.C., GRAY, H.L., and MATLOCK, D.C. (1988). *Directory of Statistical Microcomputer Software*. New York: Dekker.

# 1
# Nonparametric Methods for Complex Data Sets

## CHRIS LEACH

This chapter looks at some non-standard nonparametric approaches that might be considered either in preference to, or in conjunction with, classical approaches for relatively complex designs. The first section covers tests appropriate for block designs where matched groups are compared on two or more treatments or where there are repeated measures across individuals. The techniques used build on simple well-known techniques like the Wilcoxon Rank-Sum/Mann-Whitney Test, the Wilcoxon Signed-Rank Test, the Sign Test, the Kruskal-Wallis Test and the Friedman Test. In the second section, multivariate extensions of the Signed-Rank, Sign and Rank-Sum Tests are introduced. In the third section, a brief introduction to the use of rank tests in the general linear model is given. The first two sections should be comprehensible to anyone with a working knowledge of basic nonparametric techniques, as available in applied texts such as Leach (1979), Siegel & Castellan (1988), Neave & Worthington (1988) or Sprent (1988), although a smattering of matrix algebra is assumed for the multivariate section. A simple knowledge of matrix algebra is also assumed in the final section. Throughout, the applied use is stressed and technical details are kept to a minimum. The chapter is intended as an introduction to the more technical accounts available in Lehmann (1975) and Hettmansperger (1984). Where possible, the notation and terminology in Leach (1979) has been used.

## BLOCK DESIGNS

### Two treatments

Table 1 shows the results from a study reported by Meddis (1975) investigating the incorporation of external stimuli into dreams. The data are arousal thresholds on waking classified according to whether or not the arousing stimulus was incorporated into the subject's dream report. A common strategy for dealing with the unequal cell frequencies in such a design is to calculate averages for each condition and carry out a Signed-Rank or a Sign Test or a *t*-test. This strategy ignores potentially important information about variability within conditions. Two generally useful techniques that incorporate such within condition variability are outlined below.

1

**Table 1.** Arousal thresholds (sound intensity, dBA) from dreaming sleep for eight subjects woken a variable number of times (data from Meddis, 1975) plus calculations for Combined $S$ Test

| Subject | Stimulus incorporated I | Stimulus not incorporated II | Subject means | $S_i/n_i$ | $\mathrm{Var}S_i/n_i^2$ | $n_i$ |
|---------|---------|---------|---------|---------|---------|---------|
| 1 | 59 | 54, 54, 72 | 59.75 | 0.25 | 0.3125 | 4 |
| 2 | 63 | 52, 54, 56 | 56.25 | 0.75 | 0.3125 | 4 |
| 3 | 53, 66, 76 | 48, 52, 57 | 58.67 | 1.17 | 0.5833 | 6 |
| 4 | 70 | 50, 51, 51, 66 | 57.60 | 0.80 | 0.3200 | 5 |
| 5 | 62, 64, 86 | 66 | 69.50 | −0.25 | 0.3125 | 4 |
| 6 | 70, 82 | 68 | 73.33 | 0.67 | 0.2963 | 3 |
| 7 | 68, 77 | 62, 64, 64, 77 | 68.67 | 0.83 | 0.5185 | 6 |
| 8 | 69, 73, 73, 77 | 56, 64, 79 | 70.14 | 0.57 | 0.6537 | 7 |
| Treatment means | 69.88 | 59.86 | | $\mathcal{J}^* = 4.79$ | $3.3087 = \mathrm{Var}\mathcal{J}^*$ | |

**Combined $S$ Test.** The simplest strategy for making use of all the data is to find a test statistic that captures the difference between conditions or treatments separately for each subject and then to combine these statistics across subjects. The strategy is quite general and can be used when the blocking variable is subjects, as here, or when it is matched pairs or groups, or when it is results from different experiments that are to be combined (see Leach, 1979, Chapter 7; or Lehmann, 1975, Chapter 3, for a range of examples). In this case, the two conditions for each subject can be compared using a Rank-Sum Test to give a statistic $S$ reflecting the size of the difference between conditions. $S$ is a centred form of the Mann-Whitney statistic $U$, with values close to zero indicating no difference between conditions. One method of calculation first ranks the data and finds $R$, the sum of the ranks associated with one of the conditions. For example, Subject 1's four scores of 54, 54, 59 and 72 have ranks 1.5, 1.5, 3 and 4 (using midranks for tied values), so the rank-sum for Condition 1 is 3. $S$ is then given by $S = 2R - t_2(n + 1)$, where $t_2$ is the size of the smaller sample (1 in this case), $t_1$ is the size of the larger sample (3 here) and $n = t_1 + t_2 = 4$ is the size of the combined sample, so $S = 2 \times 3 - 1 \times 5 = 1$, the positive value indicating that Condition 1 has larger ranks, a small difference in this case. As the subjects produce differing amounts of data, it is usually better to work with the statistic $S/n$ before combining across subjects. Table 1 shows the value of $S/n$ for each subject, together with the Combined $S$ statistic, $\mathcal{J}^* = \Sigma S_i/n_i$, where $S_i$ and $n_i$ are the values of $S$ and $n$ for the $i$th subject. Values of $\mathcal{J}^*$ close to zero indicate no group difference between conditions. In this case, all but one of the $S_i$ are positive, so $\mathcal{J}^*$ is relatively large and positive, again indicating higher ranks for Condition 1, suggesting higher arousal scores after dreams in which the stimulus has been incorporated. A test of significance is obtained by using the asymptotic normality of the statistic

$$z^* = \mathcal{J}^*/\sqrt{\mathrm{Var}\mathcal{J}^*},$$

$$\text{where } \mathrm{Var}\mathcal{J}^* = \Sigma \ \mathrm{Var}S_i/n_i^2,$$

$$\text{and } \mathrm{Var}S_i = t_{i1}t_{i2}(n_i+1)/3,$$

with $t_{i1}$ and $t_{i2}$ the sample sizes for the $i$th subject and $n_i = t_{i1} + t_{i2}$. $\mathrm{Var}S$ is just the usual formula for the variance of $S$ in the Rank-Sum Test. For Subject $1$, $S_1/n_1 = 1/4 = 0.25$ and $\mathrm{Var}S_1 = 1 \times 3 \times 5/3 = 5.00$. Table 1 shows the relevant calculations for $\mathrm{Var}\mathcal{J}^*$, giving $z^* = 4.79/\sqrt{3.3087} = 2.63$, a value significant at the 0.01 level (two-tailed) when compared with normal distribution critical values. The normal approximation improves rapidly with both increasing sample size for each subject and increasing numbers of subjects being combined. It can be improved by incorporating a correction for ties and, in some cases, a continuity correction (see Leach, 1979, for details).

The Combined $S$ Test is a generalization of a comparison based on pairs of scores. It is easy to see that, in this extreme case, when $t_1 = t_2 = 1$ for all subjects, the test reduces to the Sign Test. It inherits the advantage of simple calculation from the Sign Test, so it can be used in cases where only the ranks of the data for each subject are available, or where there are worries about the distribution of the data. However, it also inherits the relatively low power of the Sign Test, particularly when the sample sizes are low.

On the other hand, with more than two treatments, the Combined $S$ Test generalizes immediately to provide a powerful test when there is a natural order for the treatments or when an ordinal rather than an omnibus prediction is to be tested. See Leach (1979, Chapter 7) for details and examples.

**Hodges-Lehmann Aligned Rank Test.** A simple way of increasing the power of a combined test is to make more use of the numerical information when this is available and fairly well-behaved, in much the same way as the Signed-Rank Test improves on the Sign Test. The Hodges-Lehmann test generalizes the Signed-Rank Test to cases where there are one or more scores per condition for each subject (or block). The first stage is to remove an estimate of the subject effect from each score, in an attempt to make all scores throughout the study comparable, to produce a set of aligned observations. In Table 2, the subject means have been subtracted from the scores so, for example, Subject $1$'s original scores are replaced by $(59 - 59.75)$, $(54 - 59.75)$, $(54 - 59.75)$ and $(72 - 59.75)$. In Table 3, all 39 aligned observations have been ranked, from the lowest $(-14.14)$ to the highest $(17.33)$, using midranks in the case of ties. The simplest combined statistic to work with is $R^*$, the sum of the ranks in one of the conditions. Here $R^* = 436.5$, focusing on Condition I. This is, effectively, the sum of the individual rank-sums for each subject and, in much the same way

**Table 2.** Sleep example. Aligned observations

| Subject | I | II |
|---|---|---|
| 1 | −0.75 | −5.75, −5.75, 12.25 |
| 2 | 6.75 | −4.25, −2.25, −0.25 |
| 3 | −5.67, 7.33, 17.33 | −10.67, −6.67, −1.67 |
| 4 | 12.40 | −7.60, −6.60, −6.60, 8.40 |
| 5 | −7.50, −5.50, 16.50 | −3.50 |
| 6 | −3.33, 8.67 | −5.33 |
| 7 | −0.67, 8.33 | −6.67, −4.67, −4.67, 8.33 |
| 8 | −1.14, 2.86, 2.86, 6.86 | −14.14, −6.14, 8.86 |

**Table 3.** Sleep example. Ranks of aligned observations plus calculations for Hodges-Lehmann Aligned Rank Test

| Subject | I | II | $\bar{k}_i$ | $\bar{R}_i$ | VarR$_i$ |
|---|---|---|---|---|---|
| 1 | 23 | 10.5, 10.5, 36 | 20.00 | 20.00 | 111.3750 |
| 2 | 28 | 17, 20, 25 | 22.50 | 22.50 | 18.2500 |
| 3 | 12, 30, 39 | 2, 5.5, 21 | 18.25 | 54.75 | 312.5625 |
| 4 | 37 | 3, 7.5, 7.5, 33 | 17.60 | 17.60 | 206.1400 |
| 5 | 4, 13, 38 | 18 | 18.25 | 54.75 | 155.1875 |
| 6 | 19, 34 | 14 | 22.33 | 44.67 | 72.222 |
| 7 | 24, 31.5 | 5.5, 15.5, 15.5, 31.5 | 20.58 | 41.17 | 141.1222 |
| 8 | 22, 26.5, 26.5, 29 | 1, 9, 35 | 21.29 | 85.14 | 247.1225 |
| | $R^* = 436.5$ | 343.5 | 340.58 = $\bar{R}^*$ | | 1263.9819 = VarR$^*$ |

as the Combined $S$ Test, an overall normal approximation can be obtained by calculating, for each subject, a mean and variance for this rank-sum statistic. The overall $R^*$ has mean and variance given by the sums of the individual means and variances. The relevant calculations are shown in Table 3, and can be illustrated with Subject $I$'s data. The ranks assigned to Subject $I$'s data are $k_1 = 23$, $k_2 = 10.5$, $k_3 = 10.5$, $k_4 = 36$, the average being $\bar{k} = 20.00$. The average rank-sum for Condition I, $\bar{R}$, is then given by $\bar{R} = t_1\bar{k}$, where $t_1$ is the sample size for Condition I, so here $\bar{R} = 1 \times 20.00$. The variance of $R$ for Subject $I$ is given by

$$\text{Var}R = \frac{t_1 t_2}{n(n-1)} \Sigma \, (k_j - \bar{k})^2 = 111.3750.$$

Summing across subjects gives $\bar{R}^* = \Sigma \, \bar{R}_i$ and VarR$^* = \Sigma$ VarR$_i$, giving an overall normal approximation of

$$z^* = (R^* - \bar{R}^*)/\sqrt{\text{VarR}^*}$$
$$= (436.5 - 340.58)/\sqrt{1263.9819}$$
$$= 2.70,$$

**Table 4.** Data and calculations for the Friedman Test and Aligned Test. (Data from Damaser, Shore and Orne (1963), Physiological effects during hypnotically requested emotions, *Psychosomatic Medicine*, 25, 334–343.)

(a) Data: Measurements of skin potential (mV), adjusted for initial level, when different emotions were requested during hypnosis.

| Subject | 1 | 2 | 3 | 4 | 5 | 6 | 7 | 8 | means |
|---|---|---|---|---|---|---|---|---|---|
| *Fear* | 23.1 | 57.6 | 10.5 | 23.6 | 11.9 | 54.6 | 21.0 | 20.3 | 27.83 |
| *Happiness* | 22.7 | 53.2 | 9.7 | 19.6 | 13.8 | 47.1 | 13.6 | 23.6 | 25.41 |
| *Depression* | 22.5 | 53.7 | 10.8 | 21.1 | 13.7 | 39.2 | 13.7 | 16.3 | 23.88 |
| *Calmness* | 22.6 | 53.1 | 8.3 | 21.6 | 13.3 | 37.0 | 14.8 | 14.8 | 23.19 |
| means | 22.725 | 54.400 | 9.825 | 21.475 | 13.175 | 44.475 | 15.775 | 18.750 | |

(b) Ranks used in Friedman Test

| Subject | 1 | 2 | 3 | 4 | 5 | 6 | 7 | 8 | $R_i$ | $R_i^2$ |
|---|---|---|---|---|---|---|---|---|---|---|
| *Fear* | 4 | 4 | 3 | 4 | 1 | 4 | 4 | 3 | 27 | 729 |
| *Happiness* | 3 | 2 | 2 | 1 | 4 | 3 | 1 | 4 | 20 | 400 |
| *Depression* | 1 | 3 | 4 | 2 | 3 | 2 | 2 | 2 | 19 | 361 |
| *Calmness* | 2 | 1 | 1 | 3 | 2 | 1 | 3 | 1 | 14 | 196 |
| | | | | | | | | | | $\Sigma R_i^2 = 1686$ |

(c) Aligned Observations

| Subject | 1 | 2 | 3 | 4 | 5 | 6 | 7 | 8 |
|---|---|---|---|---|---|---|---|---|
| *Fear* | 0.375 | 3.200 | 0.675 | 2.125 | −1.275 | 10.125 | 5.225 | 1.550 |
| *Happiness* | −0.025 | −1.200 | −0.125 | −1.875 | 0.625 | 2.625 | −2.175 | 4.850 |
| *Depression* | −0.225 | −0.700 | 0.975 | −0.375 | 0.525 | −5.275 | −2.075 | −2.450 |
| *Calmness* | −0.125 | −1.300 | −1.525 | 0.125 | 0.125 | −7.475 | −0.975 | −3.950 |

(d) Ranks (or midranks in case of ties) of aligned observations

| Subject | 1 | 2 | 3 | 4 | 5 | 6 | 7 | 8 | $R_i$ |
|---|---|---|---|---|---|---|---|---|---|
| *Fear* | 21 | 29 | 24 | 27 | 10 | 32 | 31 | 26 | 200.0 |
| *Happiness* | 18 | 11 | 16.5 | 7 | 23 | 28 | 5 | 30 | 138.5 |
| *Depression* | 15 | 13 | 25 | 14 | 22 | 2 | 6 | 4 | 101.0 |
| *Calmness* | 16.5 | 9 | 8 | 19.5 | 19.5 | 1 | 12 | 3 | 88.5 |
| $C_i$ | 70.5 | 62.0 | 73.5 | 67.5 | 74.5 | 63.0 | 54.0 | 63.0 | |

with the same conclusion as reached by the Combined $S$ Test.

It is not necessary to use subject means to produce the aligned observations. Other measures of location, such as the median, could be used. The statistic $z^*$ tends to the normal distribution provided the scores for each subject (or block) include, after alignment, at least one positive and one negative score. Lehmann (1975) shows that this condition is always satisfied when the scores are aligned on the block mean or median. When $t_1 = t_2 = 1$, the Hodges-Lehmann Test reduces to a form similar (although not identical) to the Signed-Rank Test, the two tests being asymptotically equivalent in this case.

## More than two treatments

Table 4a shows data from a study of the effectiveness of hypnosis, analysed by Lehmann (1975). During hypnosis, the emotions of fear, happiness, depression and calmness were requested from each of eight subjects, with skin potential recorded under each condition.

The standard analysis is to carry out a Friedman Test, with relevant calculations given in Table 4b. Because there are repeated measures, ranking is done within each subject's data to take account of likely variability between subjects. The Friedman statistic is

$$Q = -3n(k+1) + 12 \; \Sigma \; R_i^2/nk \; (k+1),$$

where $n$ is the number of subjects (or blocks), $k$ is the number of treatments, and $R_i$ is the sum of the ranks for the $i$th treatment. Here, $n = 8$, $k = 4$, and $\Sigma R_i^2 = 1686$, so $Q = 6.45$. $Q$ is approximately distributed as $\chi^2$ with $k - 1$ degrees of freedom. $\chi^2_{0.05} (3) = 7.82$, so the obtained value is not significant at the 0.05 level.

Like the Combined $S$ Test, the Friedman Test is a generalization of the Sign Test, to which it reduces when $k = 2$. For small $k$, the Friedman Test inherits the Sign Test's lack of power. By ranking only within blocks, only a small amount of the numerical information in the data is used, particularly when $k$ is small.

**Hodges-Lehmann Aligned Rank Test.** Some of the power loss can be recaptured by using aligned observations to make the data more comparable across blocks by removing the effect of subject variability. The most straightforward way of doing this is to subtract subject means or medians from the original data. In Table 4c, subject means have been removed so, for example, Subject $1$'s aligned observations are given by $(23.1 - 22.725)$, $(22.7 - 22.725)$, $(22.5 - 22.725)$ and $(22.6 - 22.725)$. All 32 scores have been ranked in Table 4d. Under the null hypothesis of no treatment effect, it is argued that each subject would have obtained the same scores, but the assignment of scores to treatments is random, so all 4! permutations of the scores are equally likely. This carries through to the aligned ranks, with the four ranks assigned to each subject being those that would have been assigned anyway, but not necessarily in that order. This leads to the derivation of a statistic $Q^*$, similar, but not identical, to those used in the Friedman and Kruskal-Wallis Tests (see Lehmann, 1975, pp. 271–272, for details of the derivation). $Q^*$ is approximately distributed as $\chi^2$ with $k-1$ degrees of freedom and is given by

$$Q^* = (k-1) \frac{[\Sigma R_i^2 - kn^2 (kn+1)^2/4]}{\Sigma A_i^2 - \Sigma C_j^2/k} ,$$

where $k$ is the number of treatments,
   $n$ is the number of subjects (or blocks),
   $\Sigma R^2_i$ is the sum of the $k$ row rank sums,
   $\Sigma C_i^2$ is the sum of the $n$ column rank sums, and
   $\Sigma A_i^2$ is the sum of the squares of all $nk$ ranks.
When there are no ties, $\Sigma A_i^2$ simplifies to $kn/(kn+1)$ $(2kn+1)/6$. For the ranks in Table 4d, $k=4$, $n=8$, $\Sigma R_i^2 = 77\ 215.5$, $\Sigma C_i^2 = 35\ 177$, and $\Sigma A_i^2 = 11\ 439$, so

$$Q^* = 3(77\ 215.5 - 69696)/11\ 439 - 8794.25) = 8.53,$$

which exceeds the $\chi^2_{0.05}(3)$ critical value of 7.82. Note that this conclusion is different from that resulting from the Friedman Test.

## Generalizing the Friedman Test

The Friedman Test can be straightforwardly generalized to cover cases in which there is more than one score per cell or where some of the data are missing. We shall cover just two cases.

**Friedman Test with $m$ observations per cell.** The generalization to the case of $m$ observations per cell is very simple. It would apply, for example, if $m$ observations instead of just one had been collected from each subject for each of the four emotions in the study above. In this case, the test statistic

$$Q^* = -3n(mk+1) + \frac{12}{nkm^2 (mk+1)} \Sigma R_i^2 ,$$

is approximately distributed as $\chi^2$ with $k-1$ degrees of freedom, where $k$ is the number of treatments, $n$ is the number of subjects (or blocks), $m$ is the number of observations per cell, and $R_i$ is the sum of the ranks for the $i$th treatment, with ranking done within the $mk$ observations for each subject (or block). For more information, see Benard & van Elteren (1953).

**Balanced incomplete block designs.** One important special case of missing data arises when it is not possible to assign all subjects to all treatments. Balanced incomplete block designs (BIBDs) help in the design of such studies to allow comparisons across all treatments to be made. This occurs frequently when preference data are obtained, with subjects asked to rank order a number of conditions. With a large number of conditions, it becomes difficult for subjects to rank the total set, so just a subset is presented to each subject, and the overall preference ranking for the group is obtained. In a BIBD, each condition is presented an equal number of times across subjects, as is each pair of conditions. Cochran & Cox (1957) give a list of BIBDs to simplify the design of such studies. For example, when $t = 10$ conditions are compared, the BIBD shown below compares $k = 4$ conditions at a time.

| | | | | | | Block | | | | | | | | |
|---|---|---|---|---|---|---|---|---|---|---|---|---|---|---|
| *1* | *2* | *3* | *4* | *5* | *6* | *7* | *8* | *9* | *10* | *11* | *12* | *13* | *14* | *15* |
| 1 | 1 | 1 | 1 | 1 | 1 | 2 | 2 | 2 | 2 | 3 | 3 | 3 | 4 | 4 |
| 2 | 2 | 3 | 4 | 5 | 6 | 3 | 4 | 5 | 7 | 5 | 6 | 4 | 5 | 6 |
| 3 | 5 | 7 | 9 | 7 | 8 | 6 | 7 | 8 | 8 | 9 | 7 | 5 | 6 | 8 |
| 4 | 6 | 8 | 10 | 9 | 10 | 9 | 10 | 10 | 9 | 10 | 10 | 8 | 7 | 9 |

Here, $n = 15$ subjects are required, with each subject asked to rank only the four conditions labelled. For example, the first subject ranks only conditions 1, 2, 3 and 4, while the second subject ranks conditions 1, 2, 5 and 6. This design has each condition presented a total of $r = 6$ times and each pair presented $\lambda = 2$ times.

When using these designs, the treatments are assigned randomly to each of the $t$ treatment labels, and the subjects are assigned randomly to each of the $b$ blocks. Any BIBD satisfies the requirement that $nk = tr$, with $\lambda = r(k-1)/(t-1)$. Because of this restriction, not all combinations of $n$, $k$, $t$, and $r$ are available. For example, there is no BIBD which would allow presentation of $t = 10$ treatments $k = 7$ at a time, although there are such designs for all other values of $k$ when $t = 10$.

The version of the Friedman statistic appropriate for BIBDs is given by

$$Q^* = \frac{-3r(t-1)(k+1)}{k-1} + \frac{12(t-1)}{rt(k^2-1)} \sum R_i^2,$$

where $t$ is the total number of treatments,
$\quad\quad k$ is the number of treatments for each subject (or block),
$\quad\quad r$ is the number of times each treatment is presented, and
$\quad\quad R_i$ is the sum of the ranks for the $i$th treatment, with ranking carried out within the $k$ treatments for each subject. $Q^*$ is approximately distributed as $\chi^2$ with $k-1$ degrees of freedom.

As a simple example, suppose that, in the hypnosis study, only two observations could be collected from each subject and yet it was still required to compare all four emotions. From Cochran & Cox (1957), there is a BIBD with $t = 4$, $k = 2$, $r = 3$, $b = 6$, and $\lambda = 1$, given by

| | Block | | | | |
|---|---|---|---|---|---|
| *1* | *2* | *3* | *4* | *5* | *6* |
| 1 | 3 | 1 | 2 | 1 | 2 |
| 2 | 4 | 3 | 4 | 4 | 3 |

This requires $b = 6$ subjects and some example data and ranks are given in Table 5. For these data,

$$Q^* = -\frac{3 \times 3 \times 3 \times 3}{1} + \frac{12 \times 3 \times 82}{3 \times 4 \times 3} = 1.00.$$

This example is too small to refer to the approximating $\chi^2$ (1) distribution, but the small value of $Q^*$ suggests little difference between the four emotions. For more information, see Durbin (1951) and van Elteren & Noether (1959).

**Table 5.** Analysis of Balanced Incomplete Block Design for hypnosis example (ranks in brackets)

| Subject | *1* | *2* | *3* | *4* | *5* | *6* | $R_i$ | $R_i^2$ |
|---|---|---|---|---|---|---|---|---|
| *Fear* | 23.1(2) | | 10.5(1) | | 11.9(1) | | 4 | 16 |
| *Happiness* | 22.7(1) | | | 19.6(1) | | 47.1(2) | 4 | 16 |
| *Depression* | | 53.7(2) | 10.8(2) | | | 39.2(1) | 5 | 25 |
| *Calmness* | | 53.1(1) | | 21.6(2) | 13.3(2) | | 5 | 25 |
| | | | | | | | $\Sigma R_i^2 = 82$ | |

## MULTIVARIATE ONE AND TWO SAMPLE TESTS

The tests in this section are straightforward multivariate extensions of the standard univariate Sign and Wilcoxon Signed-Rank one sample and Wilcoxon Rank-Sum/Mann-Whitney two sample tests. Like these univariate approaches, the multivariate extensions mirror their classical counterparts working with ranks rather than the original scores and relaxing the assumptions somewhat. The tests considered here are however only asymptotically nonparametric and their behaviour with small data sets is not well researched (unlike their truly nonparametric univariate counterparts). For more information, see Hettmansperger (1984).

### One sample multivariate tests

Table 6 shows the scores for ten women on two measures collected at the beginning and end of a group for adult survivors of child sexual abuse run by

10    *Chris Leach*

**Table 6.** Before and After scores on the BDI and Self-Esteem Scale for ten survivors of sexual abuse, together with calculations relevant for Sign and Signed-Rank Tests. (Unpublished data from Ainscough & Toon, 1989)

| | BDI | | Diff | Self-Esteem | | Diff | $Sgn(X_1)\times$ | SR | SR | $SR(X_1)\times$ |
|---|---|---|---|---|---|---|---|---|---|---|
| Subject | Before | After | $X_1$ | Before | After | $X_2$ | $Sgn(X_2)$ | $(X_1)$ | $(X_2)$ | $SR(X_2)$ |
| 1 | 24 | 63 | −39 | 20 | 17 | −3 | 1 | −10 | −2 | 20 |
| 2 | 2 | 3 | −1 | 61 | 62 | 1 | −1 | −1 | 1 | −1 |
| 3 | 6 | 3 | 3 | 30 | 54 | 24 | 1 | 2 | 9 | 18 |
| 4 | 15 | 11 | 4 | 35 | 41 | 6 | 1 | 3 | 3 | 9 |
| 5 | 6 | 0 | 6 | 34 | 63 | 29 | 1 | 4 | 10 | 40 |
| 6 | 10 | 0 | 10 | 48 | 63 | 15 | 1 | 5 | 6 | 30 |
| 7 | 32 | 18 | 14 | 17 | 24 | 7 | 1 | 6 | 4 | 24 |
| 8 | 23 | 1 | 22 | 31 | 41 | 10 | 1 | 7 | 5 | 35 |
| 9 | 36 | 8 | 28 | 22 | 41 | 19 | 1 | 8 | 7 | 56 |
| 10 | 31 | 2 | 29 | 22 | 44 | 22 | 1 | 9 | 8 | 72 |
| | | | 8 | | | 9 | 8 | 44 | 53 | 303 |
| | | | $N+$ | | | $N+$ | $nv_{12}$ | $W+$ | $W+$ | $n(n+1)^2v_{12}$ |

Carolyn Ainscough and Kay Toon in Wakefield, together with some of the calculations necessary for carrying out Sign and Signed-Rank Tests. Difference scores are calculated, with positive scores indicating improvement. All but two of the women show improvement on the Beck Depression Inventory (BDI) and all but one show improvement in self-esteem by the end of the group. There is one extreme outlier on the BDI and she is also the woman with decreased self-esteem. Interestingly, she felt stuck in a rut during the group, seeing the other women improve. Shortly after the end of the group, she confronted her abuser for the first time and her depression and self-esteem improved dramatically. Testing the two scales separately, two-tailed univariate Sign and Signed-Rank Tests both suggest no reliable change on the BDI ($\alpha = 0.05$) but a reliable improvement in self-esteem. With the outlying score of −39 removed, both tests indicate reliable improvement on the BDI. The Hodges-Lehmann estimate of size of effect (see Leach, 1979) is 8.5 on the BDI and 11 in self-esteem score.

The multivariate extensions of these tests consider all the variables simultaneously. The test statistics are very straightforward to compute, with a particularly simple form in the bivariate case, as in this example. All that is required is a vector of test statistics (one for each variable) together with a variance-covariance matrix, **V**.

**Multivariate Sign Test.** For the Sign Test, the vector of test statistics, **N**, is given by calculating, for each variable,

$$N = N+ - N-,$$

where $N+$ and $N-$ are the number of positive and negative difference scores, respectively. $N+$ is the usual univariate Sign Test statistic (Leach, 1979). In the multivariate case, it is more convenient to use the symmetric form of the statistic, $N$, since this simplifies the calculation of the variance-covariance matrix. For the example, $N+$ and $N-$ are 8 and 2 for the BDI and 9 and 1 for self-esteem, so $\mathbf{N}' = (6, 8)$.

The variance-covariance matrix, $\mathbf{V}$, has diagonal entries, $v_{ii}$, equal to 1, and off-diagonal entries given by

$$v_{ij} = 1/n \sum_{t=1}^{n} \text{sgn}\,(X_{it})\,\text{sgn}\,(X_{jt}),$$

where $X_{it}$ is the difference score for the $t$th subject on the $i$th variable, $n$ is the number of differences, and $\text{sgn}(x) = -1$ if $x < 0$, 0 if $x = 0$, and $+1$ if $x > 0$. For the example, the calculations are shown in the eighth column of Table 6, giving $v_{12} = 8/10$. Under the null hypothesis that the population medians for each variable are all 0, the statistic

$$N^* = \mathbf{N}'(n\mathbf{V})^{-1}\mathbf{N}$$

is asymptotically distributed as $\chi^2(p)$, where $p$ is the number of variables. In this case, $p = 2$, $\mathbf{N}' = (6, 8)$ and

$$n\mathbf{V} = \begin{bmatrix} 10 & 8 \\ 8 & 10 \end{bmatrix},$$

so

$$(n\mathbf{V})^{-1} = \begin{bmatrix} 0.2778 & -0.2222 \\ -0.2222 & 0.2778 \end{bmatrix},$$

giving $N^* = 6.44$. This exceeds 5.99, the 0.05 critical value of $\chi^2(2)$, indicating reliable improvement for the group when both variables are considered together.

When $p = 2$, as in this case, it is not necessary to go through these calculations, since a much simpler method of calculating $N^*$ is available. Simply draw up a two way table of the signs on each variable:

|  |  | $X_2$ | |
|---|---|---|---|
|  |  | $<0$ | $>0$ |
| $X_1$ | $<0$ | a | b |
|  | $>0$ | c | d |

$N^*$ is then given by

$$N^* = \frac{(a-d)^2}{a+d} + \frac{(b-c)^2}{b+c}.$$

In this case, with BDI as $X_1$ and self esteem as $X_2$, the table is

$$
\begin{array}{ccc}
 & \multicolumn{2}{c}{X_2} \\
 & <0 & >0 \\
X_1 \quad <0 & 1 & 1 \\
\phantom{X_1} \quad >0 & 0 & 8 \\
\end{array}
$$

giving $N^* = 49/9 + 1/1 = 6.44$, as before.

**Multivariate Signed-Rank Test.** Like its univariate counterpart, the multivariate Signed-Rank Test makes fuller use of the data, but requires an additional assumption of symmetry in the underlying distribution. The vector of test statistics, $\mathbf{W}$, is given by calculating, for each variable separately,

$$W = (W+ \; - \; W-)/(n+1),$$

where $W+$ and $W-$ are the usual signed-rank statistics (Leach, 1979), obtained by ranking the absolute values of the difference scores and summing the ranks attached to positive and negative differences, respectively. For the example, $W+$ and $W-$ are 44 and 11 for the BDI and 53 and 2 for self-esteem, giving $\mathbf{W}' = (33/11, 51/11)$.

The variance covariance matrix, $\mathbf{V}$, has diagonal entries given by

$$v_{ii} = (2n+1)/(6(n+1))$$

and off-diagonal entries given by

$$v_{ij} = \left[ \sum_{t=1}^{n} \mathrm{SR}(X_{it}) \; \mathrm{SR}\,(X_{jt}) \right] \Big/ [n(n+1)^2],$$

where $n$ is the number of difference scores, and $\mathrm{SR}(X_{it})$ is the rank of the absolute value of the $t$th difference score on the $i$th variable with sign attached, i.e., the final stage in the calculation of $W$. The relevant calculations are illustrated in the last three columns of Table 6.

From these, the test statistic $W^*$ is given by

$$W^* = \mathbf{W}'(n\mathbf{V})^{-1}\mathbf{W}.$$

This is asymptotically distributed as $\chi^2(p)$, where $p$ is the number of variables.

For the example, the diagonal cells of $\mathbf{V}$ are given by $v_{11} = v_{22} = 21/66 = 0.31818$. The off-diagonal cells are $v_{12} = v_{21} = 303/(10 \times 121) = 0.25041$, giving

$$n\mathbf{V} = \begin{bmatrix} 3.1818 & 2.5041 \\ 2.5041 & 3.1818 \end{bmatrix},$$

$$(n\mathbf{V})^{-1} = \begin{bmatrix} 0.8257 & -0.6499 \\ -0.6499 & 0.8257 \end{bmatrix},$$

and $W^* = 7.10$, which exceeds the 0.05 critical value of $\chi^2(2)$, giving the same conclusion as the Sign Test

Again, for the bivariate case, $p = 2$, a simpler way of calculating $W^*$ is available. First, calculate $v_{11}$ and $v_{12}$, as above, giving $v_{11} = 0.31818$ and $v_{12} = 0.25041$. Then calculate $c = n(v_{11}^2 - v_{12}^2) = 0.38533$, $a = v_{11}/c = 0.82573$ and $b = v_{12}/c = 0.64985$. Then $W^* = a(W_1^2 + W_2^2) - 2bW_1W_2$, where $W_1$ and $W_2$ are the two entries of the test statistic vector $\mathbf{W}$, in this case 33/11 and 51/11. So $W^* = 0.38533(9 + 21.4959) - 2 \times 0.64985 \times 3 \times 4.6364 = 7.10$, as before.

To estimate size of effect, simply report the vector of Hodges-Lehmann estimates, as calculated by considering each variable separately (see Leach, 1979, Chapter 3). In this case, the vector is (8.5, 11), which is interpreted as the difference between before and after scores being a decrease in BDI by 8.5 points and an increase in self-esteem by 11 points.

## Two sample multivariate test

Table 7 shows the scores on the General Health Questionnaire (GHQ) and the Impact of Events Schedule (IES) for 23 police officers immediately after the Hillsborough Football Stadium disaster in 1989. Twelve of the officers (Group H) were directly involved in the disaster. The other eleven (Group S) form a comparison group of officers from the same force not directly involved. These data are a random sample from a larger set of data collected by Douglas Duckworth to assess the immediate impact of the disaster on the officers involved. It

**Table 7.** GHQ and IES scores for two groups of police officers. (Unpublished data from Duckworth, 1989)

### Group H

| GHQ: | 32 | 34 | 49 | 33 | 42 | 49 | 17 | 48 | 37 | 48 | 37 | 22 |
|------|----|----|----|----|----|----|----|----|----|----|----|----|
| IES: | 38 | 17 | 49 | 45 | 41 | 49 | 29 | 43 | 51 | 48 | 32 | 51 |

### Group S

| GHQ: | 13 | 13 | 11 | 21 | 8 | 24 | 28 | 9 | 24 | 22 | 11 |
|------|----|----|----|----|---|----|----|---|----|----|----|
| IES: | 6 | 14 | 13 | 36 | 0 | 23 | 19 | 0 | 34 | 7 | 5 |

**Table 8.** Ranks of the police data

### Group H

| GHQ: | 14 | 16 | 22.5 | 15 | 19 | 22.5 | 7 | 20.5 | 17.5 | 20.5 | 17.5 | 9.5 |
|------|----|----|------|----|----|------|---|------|------|------|------|-----|
| IES: | 15 | 8 | 20.5 | 18 | 16 | 20.5 | 11 | 17 | 22.5 | 19 | 12 | 22.5 |

### Group S

| GHQ: | 5.5 | 5.5 | 3.5 | 8 | 1 | 11.5 | 13 | 2 | 11.5 | 9.5 | 3.5 | $R_1 = 74.5$ |
|------|-----|-----|-----|---|---|------|----|---|------|-----|-----|------|
| IES: | 4 | 7 | 6 | 14 | 1.5 | 10 | 9 | 1.5 | 13 | 5 | 3 | $R_2 = 74.0$ |

is clear that both GHQ and IES scores are higher in Group H, an observation easily confirmed by carrying out univariate Wilcoxon Rank-Sum/Mann-Whitney tests on each variable separately. Both variables can be considered together by carrying out a simple multivariate extension as follows.

First, rank the combined sample on each variable separately, as in Table 8. This is the same procedure as would be followed using the univariate test on each variable. The vector of test statistics, $\mathbf{U}$, is given by calculating, for each variable,

$$U_i = R_i/(N+1) - n/2,$$

where $R_i$ is the sum of ranks in the smaller group on the $i$th variable, $N$ is the size of the combined sample and $n$ is the size of the smaller group. From Table 8, $R_1 = 74.5$, $R_2 = 74.0$, $N = 23$ and $n = 11$, so $U_1 = -2.40$ and $U_2 = -2.42$. ($U_i$ is another centred version of the rank-sum statistic, which is more convenient to work with in this case than $S$, used in the first section of this chapter.)

The variance-covariance matrix, $\mathbf{V}$, has diagonal entries given by

$$v_{ii} = mn/(12N(N+1))$$

and off-diagonal elements given by

$$v_{ij} = \frac{mn}{N^2(N-1)(N+1)^2} \left( \sum_{i=1}^{N} R_{it} R_{jt} - N(N+1)^2/4 \right),$$

where $m$ and $n$ are the sizes of the two groups, $N = m + n$ is the size of the combined sample, and $\Sigma R_{it} R_{jt}$ is the sum of the cross products of the rankings on each pair of variables across the combined sample.

For the example, $\Sigma R_{it} R_{jt} = 4104.5$, $m = 12$, $n = 11$ and $N = 23$, so $v_{11} = v_{22} = 0.01993$, and $v_{12} = v_{21} = 0.01561$. Under the null hypothesis that the differences in the population medians for each variable are all 0, the statistic

$$U^* = \mathbf{U}' \, (N\mathbf{V})^{-1} \mathbf{U}$$

is asymptotically distributed as $\chi^2(p)$, where $p$ is the number of variables. In this case, $p = 2$, $\mathbf{U}' = (-2.40, -2.42)$, and

$$N\mathbf{V} = \begin{bmatrix} 0.45839 & 0.35903 \\ 0.35903 & 0.45839 \end{bmatrix},$$

so

$$(N\mathbf{V})^{-1} = \begin{bmatrix} 5.643887 & -4.420525 \\ -4.420525 & 5.643887 \end{bmatrix},$$

giving $U^* = 14.2$. This exceeds 13.81, the 0.001 critical value of $\chi^2(2)$, indicating a reliable difference between the two groups when both variables are considered together.

When $p = 2$, as in this case, a simpler method of calculating $U^*$ is available. First calculate $v_{11}$ and $v_{12}$, as above, giving $v_{11} = 0.01993$ and $v_{12} = 0.01561$. Then calculate $c = N(v_{11}^2 - v_{12}^2) = 0.0035313$, $a = v_{11}/c = 5.64389$ and $b = v_{12}/c = 4.42053$. Then $U^* = a(U_1^2 + U_2^2) - 2bU_1U_2$. In this case, $U_1 = -2.40$ and $U_2 = -2.42$, so $U^* = 5.64389(5.7600 + 5.8564) - 2 \times 4.42053 \times 2.40 \times 2.42 = 14.2$, as before.

To report size of effect, simply calculate the vector of Hodges-Lehmann estimates, as calculated by considering each variable separately (see Leach, 1979, Chapter 2). In this case, the vector is (22.5, 29), which is interpreted as the difference between the two groups of police officers being 22.5 GHQ points and 29 IES points. Those involved in the disaster thus had substantially higher scores on both variables.

## RANK TESTS IN THE LINEAR MODEL

This section gives a very brief introduction to the use of rank tests and estimates in the general linear model. The general linear model provides a framework which can accommodate simple and multiple regression, analysis of variance and analysis of covariance. Nonparametric approaches have recently become available. These mirror the classical approaches, but focus attention on the ranks of the scores rather than the scores themselves. Except in some of the simpler models, hypothesis testing and estimation is computationally complex, but can be straightforwardly carried out within the MINITAB computing package using the RANK REGRESSION routine. As with the multivariate techniques, this approach provides techniques that are only asymptotically nonparametric.

This section introduces one of a number of approaches in the context of a multiple regression model. For further information on the more general usage and discussion of alternative approaches, see Hettmansperger (1984, Chapter 5).

### The general linear model

The general linear model works with a vector of independent observations, $Y' = (Y_1, \ldots, Y_N)$. Each $Y_i$ is considered to be a linear function of $p$ given, independent variables, $x_{i1}, \ldots, x_{ip}$, together with an error component, $e_i$, so that

$$Y_i = x_{i1}\beta_1 + \ldots + x_{ip}\beta_p + e_i.$$

The coefficients $\beta_1, \ldots, \beta_p$ are unknown parameters. The model is more conveniently expressed in matrix form as

$$Y = X\beta + e,$$

where $Y$ is the vector of $N$ independent observations, $X$ is the matrix of independent variables, also known as the design matrix, $\beta$ is the parameter vector, and **e** is the vector of residuals, assumed to be independent, identically distributed random variables.

If we let **X** be an $N \times 1$ vector of ones, we obtain the one sample location model,

$$Y_i = x_i\beta + e_i .$$

To obtain the two-sample location model (i.e., a single factor analysis of variance comparing two groups),

$$Y_i = x_{i1}\beta_1 + x_{i2}\beta_2 + e_i, \text{ for the first } n \text{ scores, and}$$

$$Y_i = x_{i1}\beta_1 + e_i, \text{ for the } N - n \text{ remaining scores,}$$

we let

$$\mathbf{X} = \left[ \begin{matrix} \mathbf{1} & \begin{matrix} 1 \\ 0 \end{matrix} \end{matrix} \right],$$

where the first column contains $N$ ones and the second column contains $n$ ones and $N - n$ zeros. Here, the hypothesis of no treatment effect is $H_0$: $\beta_2 = 0$, with $\beta_1$ being considered a nuisance parameter. Other more complex designs can be obtained by varying the entries in the design matrix, **X**.

The general model provides a framework within which the unknown parameters, **$\beta$**, can be estimated, and hypotheses concerning these parameters (e.g., $\beta_2 = 0$) can be tested. The approach to estimation is to find the value **$\beta$** which minimizes some function of $(\mathbf{Y} - \mathbf{X}\beta)$. In the standard approach, estimates are obtained using least-squares procedures, so that outliers may be highly influential. In the rank approach, the function minimized is a linear function of the ranks of $(\mathbf{Y} - \mathbf{X}\beta)$, which reduces the influence of outliers, making the estimates and related hypothesis tests more robust.

**Multiple regression example.** To illustrate the general approach, we consider the multiple regression model. The example is one analyzed using rank procedures and compared with other approaches by Hettmansperger (1984). Full accounts of the standard least-squares analysis for this example and its problems are available in Draper & Smith (1981) and Daniel & Wood (1980). The data, given in Table 9, consist of 21 observations on a response variable and three independent variables $x_1$, $x_2$, and $x_3$, obtained from a manufacturing plant that oxidizes ammonia to nitric acid. The response variable, $Y$, is a measure of the amount of ammonia lost up the stack in the process, and is a measure of the inefficiency of the process. The interest centres on the contribution of the independent variables to the inefficiency.

The multiple regression model considers the equations

$$Y_i = \beta_0 + x_{i1}\beta_1 + x_{i2}\beta_2 + x_{i3}\beta_3 + e_i, \quad i = 1, \ldots, 21.$$

The least-squares analysis can be carried out by regressing the data in the $Y$

**Table 9.** Stack loss data

| Run no. | Air flow $x_1$ | Cooling water inlet temp. $x_2$ | Acid concentration $x_3$ | Stack loss $Y$ |
|---|---|---|---|---|
| 1 | 80 | 27 | 89 | 42 |
| 2 | 80 | 27 | 88 | 37 |
| 3 | 75 | 25 | 90 | 37 |
| 4 | 62 | 24 | 87 | 28 |
| 5 | 62 | 22 | 87 | 18 |
| 6 | 62 | 23 | 87 | 18 |
| 7 | 62 | 24 | 93 | 19 |
| 8 | 62 | 24 | 93 | 20 |
| 9 | 58 | 23 | 87 | 15 |
| 10 | 58 | 18 | 80 | 14 |
| 11 | 58 | 18 | 89 | 14 |
| 12 | 58 | 17 | 88 | 13 |
| 13 | 58 | 18 | 82 | 11 |
| 14 | 58 | 19 | 93 | 12 |
| 15 | 50 | 18 | 89 | 8 |
| 16 | 50 | 18 | 86 | 7 |
| 17 | 50 | 19 | 72 | 8 |
| 18 | 50 | 19 | 79 | 8 |
| 19 | 50 | 20 | 80 | 9 |
| 20 | 56 | 20 | 82 | 15 |
| 21 | 70 | 20 | 91 | 15 |

column on the three $x$ variables using, for example, the RREGRESS command in MINITAB. The rank regression is carried out in the same way, but using the RREGRESS command. The resulting regression equations are

$$y = -39.9 + 0.72x_1 + 1.30x_2 - 0.15x_3$$

for the least-squares analysis, and

$$y = -40.1 + 0.82x_1 + 0.89x_2 - 0.12x_3$$

for the rank analysis.

Plotting the residuals against the fitted values shows evidence of four outliers which affect the estimates provided by the least-squares approach more than those of the rank approach. Tests of significance for the $\beta$ coefficients can also be obtained by making use of the standard errors produced by MINITAB. For the rank test, the standard errors are 0.13 for $\beta_1$, 0.35 for $\beta_2$, and 0.15 for $\beta_3$. For example, to test for the significance of $\beta_3$, calculate the test statistic

$$B^* = (\beta_3 \text{ estimate}/\beta_3 \text{ standard error})^2$$

and compare this with the critical value of the $F$ distribution with 1 and $N - p - 1$

degrees of freedom. In this case $B^* = (-0.12/0.15)^2 = 0.64$ is not significant when compared with the $F_{0.05}(1,17)$ critical value of 4.45, so the acid concentration variable, $x_3$, could be removed from the analysis.

This same approach generalizes straightforwardly to other designs. The main requirement is to specify the design matrix, $X$. For examples of design matrices appropriate for a number of different designs, see, for example, Hettmansperger (1984) or Draper & Smith (1981).

## Acknowledgements

I am grateful to Kay Toon, Carolyn Ainscough and Douglas Duckworth for permission to use their unpublished data.

## References

BENARD, A. & van ELTEREN, P. (1953). A generalization of the method of *m* rankings. *Indagationes Math.*, 15, 358–369.

COCHRAN, W.G. & COX, G.M. (1957). *Experimental Designs*, 2nd ed. New York: Wiley.

DANIEL, C. & WOOD, F.S. (1980). *Fitting Equations to Data*, 2nd ed. New York: Wiley.

DRAPER, N.R. & SMITH, H. (1981). *Applied Regression Analysis*, 2nd ed. New York: Wiley.

DURBIN, J. (1951). Incomplete blocks in ranking experiments. *British Journal of Psychology (Statistical Section)*, 4, 85–90.

van ELTEREN, P. & NOETHER, G.E. (1959). The asymptotic efficiency of the $\chi^2$-test for a balanced incomplete block design. *Biometrika*, 46, 475–477.

HETTMANSPERGER, T.P. (1984). *Statistical Inference Based on Ranks*. New York: Wiley.

LEACH, C. (1979). *Introduction to Statistics: A Nonparametric Approach for the Social Sciences*. Chichester: Wiley.

LEHMANN, E.L. (1975). *Nonparametrics: Statistical Methods Based on Ranks*. San Francisco: Holden-Day.

MEDDIS, R. (1975). A simple two-group test for matched scores with unequal cell frequencies. *British Journal of Psychology*, 66, 225–227.

NEAVE, H.R. & WORTHINGTON, P.L. (1988). *Distribution-Free Tests*. London: Unwin Hyman.

SIEGEL, S. & CASTELLAN, N.J. (1988). *Nonparametric Statistics for the Behavioral Sciences*, 2nd ed. New York: McGraw-Hill.

SPRENT, P. (1988). *Applied Nonparametric Statistical Methods*. London: Chapman & Hall.

# 2

# Graphical Methods for Exploring Data

SANDY AND PAT LOVIE

## EDA AND ALL THAT

The meteoric rise of Exploratory Data Analysis (EDA) has dragged many statistical technologies and philosophies winking and blinking into the harsh light of the late twentieth century. One has only to see, for instance, how regression analysis and robust methods have flourished to realize the profound and far-reaching changes wrought by the work of John Tukey. Indeed, the mimeographed form of his book *Exploratory Data Analysis* (finally published in 1977) became the bible of many in the statistical underground of the early 1970s.

One traditional area to have benefited especially from EDA's kiss of life is, of course, graphical methods. Having languished for decades on a frugal diet of indigestible histograms and stale pie-charts, this proved to be the ideal vehicle for spreading the word of Tukey, albeit subtly re-expressed by the missionaries of EDA to avoid the neologistic excesses of the original.

This is not to suggest that, in Tukey's vision of the world, EDA should stand as an alternative to the more formal processes of statistical hypothesis testing (or confirmatory data analysis (CDA), to use Tukey's phrase). Rather, in the seminal 1977 text, one reads of the complementary nature of the two faces of data analysis, with EDA providing the inductively derived hypotheses for the deductive processes of CDA. Both were seen as necessary parts of the knowledge gathering mechanism of science since, if one or other were missing, the data analyst was either stuck with the classical problem of induction, or deprived of new hypotheses to evaluate.

Thus, EDA promotes risky inductions because it draws attention to the novel and surprising aspects of the data, that is, findings not predicted by the analyst. Ideally, therefore, EDA should suggest new directions for research and new hypotheses for testing. The particular importance of graphical methods here is that, properly designed, they should not only summarize results but should also highlight in a direct fashion any anomalous data or pattern of results.

Of course, the analytical and graphical aspects of data analysis do not exist in water-tight compartments. For example, the effectiveness of data transformations is often evaluated by plotting. In addition, the graphical form or pattern of

19

a sample of data is frequently translated into more formal mathematical terms, perhaps as an intermediate stage in the journey from exploration to confirmation, or as a quick method of observing the fit of data-to-model. These latter plots are especially useful in modern regression analysis (see Chapter 5), where problems can be detected and fixes evaluated.

However, there are those amongst the practitioners of EDA who have argued that a well chosen plot can replace more formal inference (Chambers *et al.*, 1983). Interestingly, this seems to echo earlier claims made by those working in multivariate statistics that some data sets are so complex that getting a handle on the structure is only possible through plotting (see, for example, Gower & Digby, 1981). Our position is rather less radical than that of Chambers *et al.*, although it is clear that three hundred metres of indigestible tables printed out by your favourite statistical package are no substitute for a nicely rounded plot.

In short, EDA encourages conceptual risk-taking of the inductive kind but should, ideally, interface smoothly with CDA. The major roles of graphical methods in EDA are to emphasize the novel and the worthwhile in data by means of perceptually unambiguous plots. They should act, in other words, as reliable guides in the traverse of unknown and unpredictable lands. It is in this spirit that we offer a small survival pack of graphical amulets, wampum, bottle openers, things to remove stones from equine hooves and black boxes for this journey into *terra incognita*. We begin our expedition clutching that classic of EDA – the box plot.

## THE BOX PLOT

A box plot is a compact graphical summary of a set of data which gives a quick impression of its main features, that is, location, spread, shape and the presence of unusually large or small values (Tukey, 1977; see also Seheult, 1986). Since the plot was evolved in the philosophical context of EDA, so its components are designed to be reasonably robust and resistant (see Mosteller & Tukey, 1977). What this means in practice is that important aspects of the data should show up reliably whatever the particular underlying distribution, even in the presence of a few stray observations.

The time data in Figure 1 are taken from a human factors study reported briefly by Moore & McCabe (1989). A group of right handed subjects were asked to use their right hands to set a pointer to a fixed position by turning a control knob which had either a right or left turning thread on its shank. One boxplot summarizes the subjects' times (in seconds) with the right turning knob, the other for their left turning times. Showing multiple box plots on the same display allows direct comparisons to be made between data sets.

The numerical building blocks for the box plot are most easily accessed when the data are sorted into size order. From this ordered set, we can extract the sample median and the upper and low quartiles (which cut off the top and

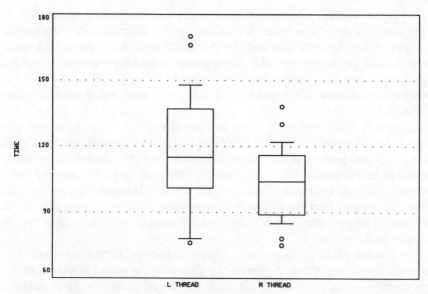

**Figure 1.** Standard side by side box plots. Data are times (in seconds) to turn left and right threaded knobs. *Source:* Moore & McCabe (1989), page 532.

bottom 25% of the ordered sample), as well as picking out other quantities used in certain variants of the basic display. It is worth noting that we can usually make do with approximate values of these measures rather than needing to find exact percentiles, although these are required for certain plots we consider later.

The 'box and whisker' plot is a rectangle (the box) with filaments (the whiskers) extending from the top and bottom of the box (Tukey, 1977). The top and bottom of the box mark the positions of the upper and lower quartiles along the data scale. The midspread, which is the range of the middle 50% of the data, corresponds to the length of the box; a line drawn across the box shows the position of the median. Although in the original box plot, the whiskers ran to the two extreme data values, rules for defining their end points have proliferated. No single one is generally accepted: the choice is largely dependent on what aspects of the data are of most interest. For instance, the whiskers on Figure 1 mark off the top and bottom 10% of the data, that is, they cover 80% of the data; data points in the tails are plotted individually. In this display, the behaviour of the main body of the data (location, spread, shape) is emphasized but, with 20% of the data points lying beyond the whiskers, we might find it harder to pick up strays in a large data set.

Another method (not illustrated here), uses a rule of thumb to isolate stray data points by setting the ends of the whiskers at 1.5 midspreads above and below the box; any values caught outside these boundaries are treated as suspicious, that is, as potential outliers (see Lovie, 1986). (A roughly equivalent notion is that a 'good' observation in normally distributed data falls within so many standard deviations either side of the mean.) Extending the whiskers in this way, while scarcely diminishing the plot's ability to convey a general impression of the data set, turns it into a useful visual early warning system for outliers and also offers some check of normality. Note that if all the data fall within the boundaries, the whiskers end at the minimum and maximum values of the set.

Looking in detail at Figure 1, we can see that left hand adjustments take longer, since the medians are higher for this sample than for right turns. This is not exactly unexpected, as the group claimed to be right handed. In addition, the spread in the data for left turns is greater than right turns, whether we make the comparison on the range of the data, the distance between the whisker ends or the box length. Finally, although there is some evidence of skewness in the direction of longer times, none of the data points in the upper or lower tails is likely to be an outlier.

The data for the single box plot in Figure 2 are the differences between left and right turn times for each subject. By retaining the paired structure of the experiment, we can see that right hand turns are easier for most subjects (positive differences). But there are negative scores too, which suggest that some subjects might actually be ambidextrous or even left hand dominant.

We have selected one of the box plot variants for Figure 3, which shows the male and female suicide rates (per 100 000 of the population) in 1971 for people between the ages of 25 and 34, drawn from a selection of mainly European

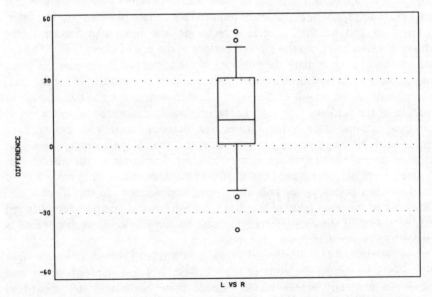

**Figure 2.** Single box plot. Data are differences in paired times from Figure 1.

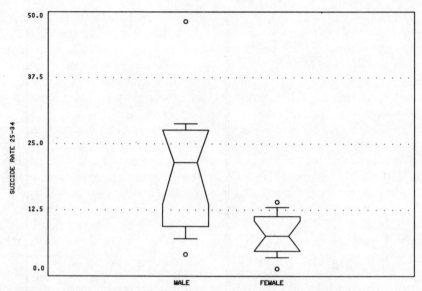

**Figure 3.** Notched box plots. Data are 1971 suicide rates (per 100 000) for 25 to 34 year old males and females. Adapted from data in Erickson & Nosanchuk (1979), page 14; originally from *World Health Statistics Annual 1971* (1974).

countries. The display is called a notched box plot for rather obvious reasons; the distance between the top and bottom of the notch represents an approximate 95% confidence interval about the median.

If the notches on side by side box plots do not overlap, then there is evidence for a significant difference between the two medians; if they overlap, then the evidence is less strong. Figure 3 shows that although the boxes overlap, the notches do not; hence we have some reason for arguing that there is a real difference in the rates, with males having a significantly higher rate than that for females. As with regular box plots, we can also say something about the spreads of the samples: thus the male sample seems much more variable than the female one since, for instance, the box is longer for males than for females. A possible upper outlier seems to be responsible for the marked asymmetry in the male data.

## THE ALL-PURPOSE SCATTERPLOT

We have chosen the relatively familiar topic of scatterplots in regression to introduce our discussion.

The data in Figure 4 are the admission rates (per 100 000 of the population) into Scottish psychiatric hospitals and units and the number of clinical psychologists employed (again, per 100 000) by each of the fifteen health boards (*Scottish Health Statistics*, 1983, 1984). Figure 4a is a simple scatterplot showing

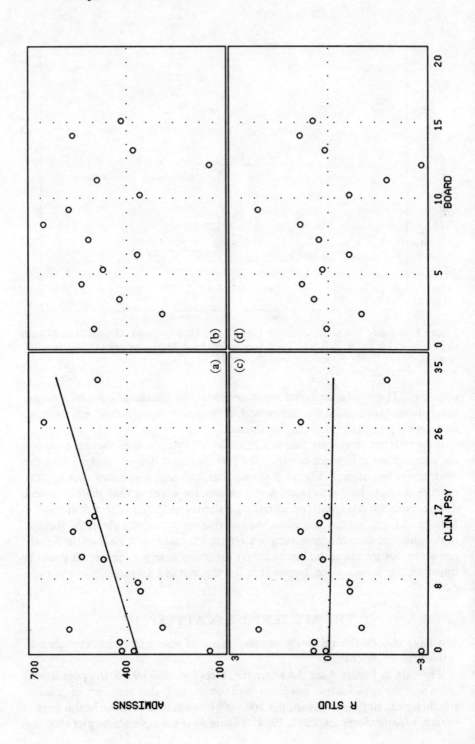

the relationship between admission rates and the number of clinical psychologists. The solid line on the plot is the ordinary least squares (OLS) line for the simple regression of admissions rates on clinical psychologists. Although there seems to be a positive association between the two variables, this simple regression line is perhaps not an ideal fit to the data.

The second display, Figure 4b, is an index plot of the admission rates for each of the fifteen health boards, taken in alphabetical order. An index plot is useful in a case by case analysis of data, particularly where the index values (ordered or nominal) reflect a substantive aspect of the situation such as the time of the observation, socio-economic class or, as in this case, a named health board. From this index plot, we can see that there is considerable variation in admission rates over the boards, with board 8 (Greater Glasgow) having the highest and board 12 (Orkney) the lowest.

Our regression analysis continues in Figure 4c with a plot of the OLS residuals against the number of clinical psychologists (the predictor or explanatory variable). An OLS best fit line has also been drawn on the graph. The residual values (the differences between observed and predicted admission rates) have been studentized, that is, scaled by independent estimates of the standard errors. The pattern of raw residuals, however, would have been similar.

If a linear model is a reasonable fit to the data, then the residuals should be small, without any obvious pattern, and an OLS line through them should have zero slope (see Chapter 5 on regression diagnostics). Little by way of systematic behaviour can be detected and the slope of the OLS line is scarcely different from zero. Nevertheless, there are three large residuals (in the top left, bottom left and bottom right of the plot) which might indicate that all is not well; two boards have much lower admission rates than one would predict from the number of clinical psychologists alone, whereas more admissions are made by the third. On balance, therefore, we would not conclude that a simple linear regression is an adequate model for these data.

The final graph for these data (Figure 4d) is an index plot of the studentized residuals over health boards. Scanning across from Figure 4c to 4d, we can easily identify the three largest residuals as corresponding to boards 9 (Highlands), 11 (Lothian) and 12 (Orkney). We also notice now that Highlands,

---

**Figure 4.** Scatterplots for regression analysis. Data are admission rates (per 100 000) to Scottish psychiatric hospitals and units, and the number of clinical psychologists employed (per 100 000) in the 15 health boards, 1983.
(a) standard scatterplot of admissions by number of clinical psychologists;
(b) index plot of admissions by health board;
(c) studentized residuals from regression in Figure 4a by number of clinical psychologists;
(d) index plot of studentized residuals by health board.
*Source: Scottish Health Statistics* 1983, Table 9.3, and 1984, Table 4.8.

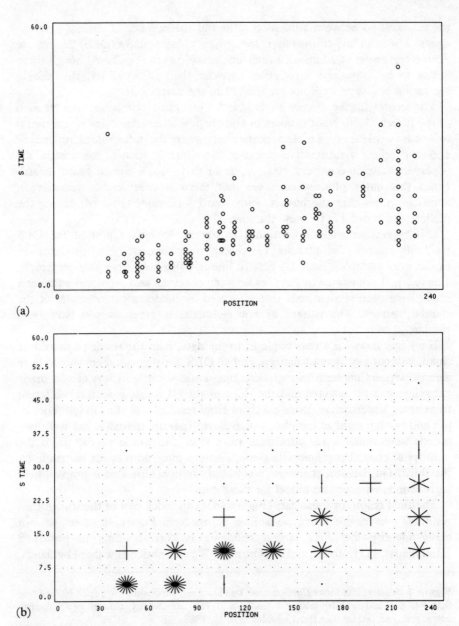

**Figure 5.** Sunflower plots as density displays. Data are search times (in seconds) for a target by the target's position in a list (a Neisser search task).
(a) standard scatterplot;
(b) sunflower plot, grid size 8 × 8;
(c) sunflower plot, grid size 4 × 4.
*Source:* Student practical.

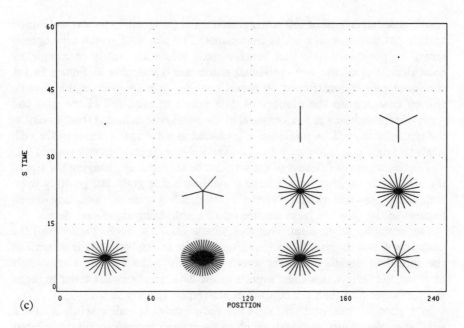

(c)

whose admission rate seems unremarkable, is actually admitting patients at a higher rate than expected from the size of its complement of psychologists. On the other hand, although board 8 (Greater Glasgow) has the highest admission rate, it is actually admitting at about the 'correct' rate. This has happened because the residuals are conditional upon the predictor, that is, the number of clinical psychologists employed, and Greater Glasgow recruits more clinical psychologists than the Highlands region.

This is, of course, only a preliminary analysis which by no means exhausts the possibilities of the data or the problem! For instance, how should we deal with the three boards who employ no clinical psychologists? Would additional or alternative explanatory variables or a respecified model lead to a better fit?

### Sunflower Plots

Standard scatterplots can give a misleading impression of the local structure and density of a large data set, particularly as the separate identities of nearby or repeated readings frequently become lost in the 'data-ink' (Tufte, 1983). One answer to this is to jitter the points by adding random noise to one or both variables (Chambers *et al.*, 1983). A solution which requires less computation and, to our minds, has a bigger visual impact is the sunflower plot which uses different plotting symbols to designate different densities (Chambers *et al.*, 1983; Cleveland, 1985).

Figures 5a, b and c compare a regular scatterplot with a sunflower plot of the same data. The data were obtained from four subjects on a standard Neisser search task and consist of 160 target search times (in seconds) for a vowel buried at different positions in a list of consonants. The plot is of search time against target list position. (Note that because some values are nearly or completely coincident, not all the 160 individual points are discernible in Figure 5a.) A sunflower plot is constructed by superimposing an $n \times n$ grid on the plotting region, counting up the number of data points in each cell of the grid and representing each one as a ray or petal of the sunflower radiating from a point at the centre of the cell. A single point is plotted as a dot at the centre of the cell, while two data points are shown as two vertical lines (petals) from a central dot.

The coarseness or fineness of the plot can be adjusted by changing the size of the $n$ in the $n \times n$ grid, with a large $n$ yielding a fine grain but possibly over-complex display and a small $n$ giving a plot which is clear on the strong overall features of the plot but lacks any means of highlighting significant detail.

For example, in the sunflower plot with a grid size $8 \times 8$ (Figure 5b), the clumping of search times for early positions in the search list, and the increase in the spread of times as subjects search further into the list, are immediately obvious. We believe that these aspects of the data are somewhat easier to see in the sunflower plot than the equivalent scatterplot (Figure 5a).

In Figure 5c, the grid size of $4 \times 4$ reduces the overall resolution of the sunflower plot. Thus, although much of the overall pattern is still discernible, just about all of the detail is lost, as a comparison between Figures 5b and c will reveal.

## Smoothed Plots

Smoothing, that is, reducing the impact of local variations in a data sequence in order to reveal any underlying pattern, has had a long history in time series analysis. However, although we illustrate the application of two recent data smoothing techniques, median smoothing and lowess, within a time series context (Figures 6a and b), neither of these methods is exclusively a tool for such problems. They can be applied wherever interest centres on the overall pattern of one quantitative variable over the ordered values of another. In this context, therefore, fitting a regression line or curve can be thought of as a smoothing operation.

Both the smoothing methods described here chart a path through a point cloud by finding a sequence of 'middle points' of the y values on the vertical axis corresponding to a predetermined number of adjacent points (x values) along the horizontal axis. This number describes the size of the 'smoothing window'.

In median smoothing (Tukey, 1977), a series of running medians for a chosen smoothing window size provides the initial set of middle points. These running medians are then refined by techniques for removing local variations in the data. Exactly how this is achieved depends on which of the many smoothing procedures is chosen (see Tukey, 1977, or Velleman & Hoaglin, 1981, for a discussion of some of the alternatives).

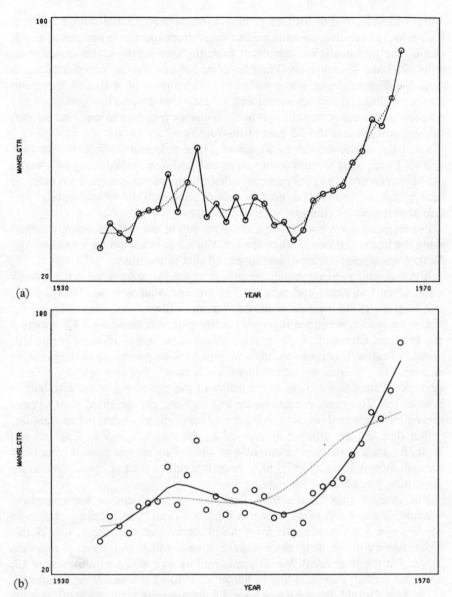

**Figure 6**. Smoothed plots. Data are the number of convictions for manslaughter in England and Wales for the years 1935 to 1966.
(a) median and lowess smoothed plots, smoothing window size 3;
(b) median and lowess smoothed plots, smoothing window size 10.
Key: median – dotted line
    lowess – solid line
*Source:* Bartholomew & Bassett (1971), page 269; originally from *Annual Abstract of Statistics* (1947, 1956, 1967).

For example, in the 3RSSH routine used to produce the dotted curve in Figure 6a, the running medians are calculated from successive samples of size 3, that is, the first median is calculated from the first 3 values, the second from points 2, 3 and 4, and so on. These medians are now the smoothed data values corresponding to the middle $y$ values in each triple, with a special 'end-point rule' providing the two smoothed end values. This process is repeated on the medians until there are no changes in the sequence from run to run, that is, until convergence. This is the 3R part of the routine.

Small flat spots, caused by a pair of adjacent identical medians, are then split (S) by applying the end point rule to each and resmoothed using 3R – again, until convergence. SS in the name says that this operation is carried out twice. A final polish is given by a process called hanning (H) which replaces the smoothed values by running weighted averages.

For simplicity, we have taken a situation where the data are equally spaced along the horizontal axis. If they are not, the $x$ values should be smoothed too. As they are already ordered, hanning is all that is required.

Although this perhaps sounds complicated, median smoothing is possible by hand, given time, care and patience (for worked examples, see Tukey, 1977, and McNeil, 1977). Lowess is another matter entirely.

Lowess (locally weighted regression scatterplot smoothing – see Chambers *et al.*, 1983 and Cleveland, 1985) also takes successive sets of adjacent points but, instead of calculating medians, fits a weighted least squares line to the points in each set. The weights are determined from a weight function which decreases smoothly from 1 at the point in the centre of the smoothing window to 0 at its boundaries. To ensure robustness against outliers, the weighted least squares procedure is repeated (iterated) until the values of the smoothed points stabilize.

Our data are the number of convictions for manslaughter in England and Wales for each of the years from 1934 to 1966. This set was used originally by Bartholomew & Bassett (1971) to demonstrate one of the traditional time series smoothing procedures – the moving average.

The median smoothed (dotted) and lowess (solid) curves for smoothing windows of size 3 and 10 are shown in Figures 6a and b, respectively. Although window size 3 is probably the most useful for median smoothing, it is clearly unsatisfactory for lowess since only a single value will have a non-zero weight.On the other hand, lowess comes into its own with a window size of 10, while the median smoothed line no longer looks like a reasonable representation of the data. Indeed, what Figures 6a and b demonstrate is the trade-off possible between the particular smoothing method's ability to capture detail (with a small window size) and show the underlying picture (when the window is large), a strategy akin to the one that can be employed over the selection of grid size with a sunflower plot (see Figures 5a and b).

Taking the median smoothed curve (window size 3) in Figure 6a and the lowess curve (window size 10) in Figure 6b, we can see an initial rise in

convictions for manslaughter to a low peak in about 1943, a slow decline until
the mid 1950s and a steep rise thereafter.

## Difference-Average Plots

At first sight, the difference-average plot in Figure 7 is perhaps less obviously a
member of the scatterplot clan than others we have seen so far. Nevertheless, it
is a plot which depicts the relationship between two quantities, in this case
comparing the differences between paired observations with their averages (or,
equivalently, their sums). Such plots are useful for showing whether the
variability in paired samples changes over the range of the data. A recent
application of the difference-sum graph is in the analysis of $2 \times 2$ cross-over
designs where the effects of treatment order need to be distinguished from those
of the treatments themselves (see Jones & Kenward, 1989).

Figure 7, which is a difference-average plot of the left and right knob turning
data in Figures 1 and 2, shows that there is a tendency for differences in turning
times to rise as overall times increase, that is, the disparity between times to turn
a left and right threaded knob is likely to be greater for people who are generally
slower at the task. This connection between magnitude and differences is lost in
the box plot in Figure 2. Moreover, we can see also that the 'non-conforming'
cases are spread over the whole range of overall times.

An alternative exploratory plot for paired data, which combines a scatterplot
with box plots, is discussed in a recent article by Rosenbaum (1989).

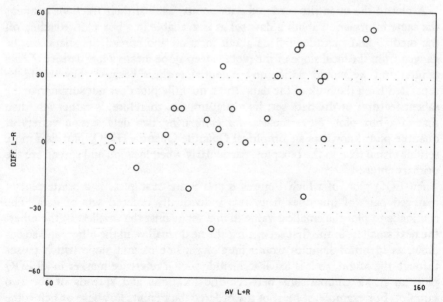

**Figure 7.** Difference-average plot. Data as in Figure 1.

## Quantile and Empirical Quantile Quantile Plots

Figures 8 and 9 (and some later ones, particularly Figures 10b, 11b and 12b) illustrate a very useful class of scatterplots, those based upon the quantiles of either a sample or a population. The data for the first plot, Figure 8, are from a study reported in Hardyck & Petrinovich (1969). They are the response times of two independent groups of subjects on a task involving either spatially compatible or incompatible arrangements of lights and reaction keys. The data plotted in Figure 9 are the same male versus female suicide rates shown as box plots in Figure 3.

Before looking at the two displays in detail, we discuss some of the more general features of quantiles. A quantile is the value of a variable which cuts off a fixed proportion of either an ordered data set (an empirical distribution) or a theoretical distribution. For example, the empirical 0.5 quantile, which is the median, is the cutoff point on the data scale such that half of the observations are smaller than it and half are larger. Incidentally, a percentile differs from a quantile only in specifying a percentage, rather than a proportion, of the data set or distribution.

In fact, every value in an ordered data set is a particular quantile, although exactly which fraction it corresponds to depends on the number of data points. Consequently, it is not always possible to obtain a particular quantile from a sample and interpolation is sometimes needed to elicit important quantiles like the median and quartiles (0.25 and 0.75 quantiles). Rules for determining the quantile fraction and for interpolation can be found in Chambers *et al.* (1983).

A plot of the quantiles (ordered data points) against their fractions contains the same information about a data set as is available in a box plot. Reading off the median and quartiles tell us about location and spread; its shape can be gauged from the local slope of the plot (a steep slope means a low density of data points) and we would notice any potential outliers because they would be separated from the bulk of the data. But a quantile plot does not summarize the salient features of the data set; its visual impact, therefore, is rather less than that of a box plot. Nevertheless, for comparing two data sets, a variety of quantile plot, known as an Empirical Quantile Quantile (EQQ) plot, is a more serious visual rival to the box plot, particularly when location and spread are the primary interest.

An EQQ plot, of which Figures 8 and 9 are examples, is a scatterplot of matched pairs of quantiles from two individually ordered sets of data. The routine is to plot the smallest value in one set against the smallest in the other, the next smallest in the first set against the next smallest in the other, and so on. Now, as identical samples would lie along a line of unit slope which passes through the origin, so it is usual to include such a reference marker in all EQQ plots to make comparisons between the locations and spreads of the two samples. For example, if most of the ordered data points lie above or below the reference line, this suggests that the locations of the two samples are different.

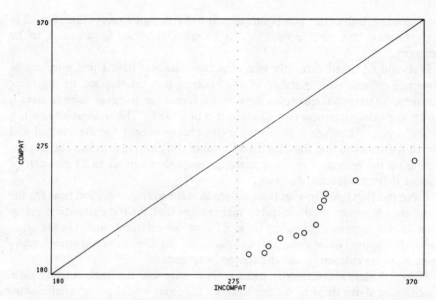

**Figure 8.** Empirical Quantile Quantile (EQQ) plot: location different, same spread. Data are reaction times for tasks with compatible and incompatible arrangements of stimuli and responses. *Source:* Hardyck & Petrinovich (1969), p. 230 (slightly modified).

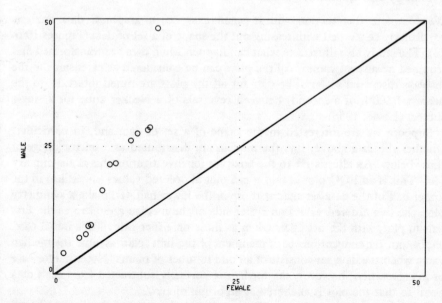

**Figure 9.** Empirical Quantile Quantile plot: location and spread different. Data as in Figure 3.

Furthermore, unless the data points appear to lie along a straight line parallel to the reference line, the spreads of the samples also can be assumed to be different.

It should be noted that only when the two data sets have equal numbers of observations will each member of the ordered pair correspond to the same quantile; interpolated quantiles have to be found for unequal sample sizes – which is a fiddly business (see Chambers *et al.*, 1983). The final point also is a practical one. Although it is customary to choose ranges for the vertical and horizontal scales so that the data fill up most of the plotting area in a scatterplot, setting up the reference line and making comparisons in an EQQ plot can be trickier if the ranges are different.

From the EQQ plot in Figure 8, we see that the average reaction time for the incompatible group is considerably higher than that for the compatible group since all the ordered data points lie well below the reference line. On the other hand, they appear to lie along a straight(ish) line parallel to the reference line, so there is little evidence of any difference in spreads.

Figure 9 shows a different picture. Not only are the male suicide rates consistently above those of the females, but they are also far more variable since the ordered data points are not parallel with the reference line. Also, the single point in the top left quadrant looks suspicious. This is, of course, exactly the story told by the box plots in Figure 3.

### Symmetry and Quantile Quantile Plots

We complete this section with a small exercise in graphical data analysis particularly concerned with teasing out the shape of a set of data (Figures 10 to 13). The study also illustrates what can happen when data are transformed and trimmed of suspect values. All the plots can be considered as extensions to the displays discussed so far. The data for all the plots are timed intervals (to the nearest 1/100th of a second) between reversals of a Necker cube for a single subject (Lovie, 1986).

Suppose we are interested in the shape of a set of data and, in particular, whether the data above, say, the median are distributed as a mirror image of those below. An alternative to the box plot for investigating this is a symmetry plot. This is an EQQ plot in that it is a plot of ordered values (quantiles) in the upper half of the data set against those in the lower half. To make a symmetry plot, the two ordered values on either side of the median are taken as the first pair to plot, with the next pair taken as those on either side of this initial pair, and so on. By convention, both members of the first 'pair' assume the median value when the data set consists of an odd number of points. Note that for ease of interpretation, however, the median is normally subtracted from each data point so that the plot is anchored at an origin of zero.

The symmetry plot in Figure 10a shows a very long tail of slow inter-reversal times and a cluster of faster times around the median. The box plot labelled

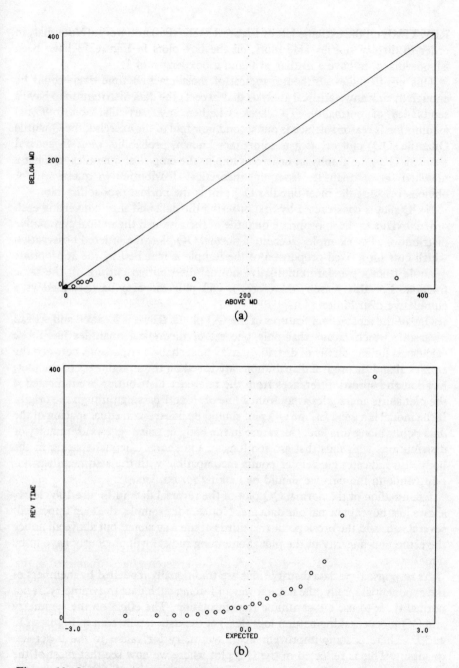

**Figure 10.** Symmetry and Quantile Quantile (QQ) plots. Data are times (in 1/100th second) between reversals of a Necker cube.
(a) symmetry plot; (b) normal QQ plot.
*Source:* Lovie (1986), page 63.

REV TIME on the extreme left of Figure 13 tells the same story. (Note that, in order to display side by side plots, all the box plots in Figure 13 have been 'standardized' to have a median at 0 and a box length of 1.)

This positive skew, although typical of most reaction time data, could be enough to sink any statistical analysis that expects the data distribution to have a semblance of normality. To check whether any particular distributional assumption is reasonable needs our second new tool of the exercise, the Quantile Quantile (QQ) plot or, as it is sometimes known, probability plot. In general terms, a QQ plot graphs an ordered sample (the empirical quantiles) against a matched set of quantiles from the theoretical distribution in question. For obvious reasons, the most popular QQ plot is the normal probability plot.

A QQ plot is constructed by first ordering the data and then converting each ordered value to the appropriate quantile of the assumed theoretical cumulative distribution. For example, to create a normal QQ plot, the ordered observation which cuts off a fixed proportion of the sample is matched by the appropriate quantile from a standard cumulative normal distribution cutting off the same fraction. For this reason, therefore, a QQ plot can also be described as a cumulative distribution plot.

One of the most useful features of the QQ plot is that it is location and spread invariant, which means that only one set of theoretical quantiles has to be calculated for any family of distributions. Thus, shape comparisons between the empirical and theoretical distributions are based on the straightness of the plot; location and spread differences from the reference distribution are indicated if the plot shifts and angles away from a line of slope 1 passing through the origin. If the model is a good fit, the QQ plot should be linear, with equal spacing of the data points along this line. Curvature in the body or tails suggests asymmetry or distributions with tails that are too long or too short. Unequal spacing in the body also indicates clusters of points incompatible with the assumed distribution, while in the tails we should be looking for outliers.

Examination of the normal QQ plot of the reversal data in Figure 10b clearly shows just how abnormal our data are. Notice, for example, the long upper tail, several gaps and the break point two thirds of the way along; but above all notice the acute non-linearity of the plot. Something radical will obviously have to be done!

As response time data distributions are traditionally modelled by members of the exponential family, the natural way of forcing such data to symmetry, if not normality, is to use a logarithmic transformation. The effect on the symmetry and QQ plots of taking natural logs ($\log_e$) of the data can be seen in Figures 11a and b. There is some improvement in symmetry for values in the lower left quadrant. This is reflected in the QQ plot where we now see that most of the curvilinearity is confined to the tails. Compare this with the QQ plot for the unlogged data (Figure 10b).

An earlier outlier analysis of these data suggested that the largest value was an

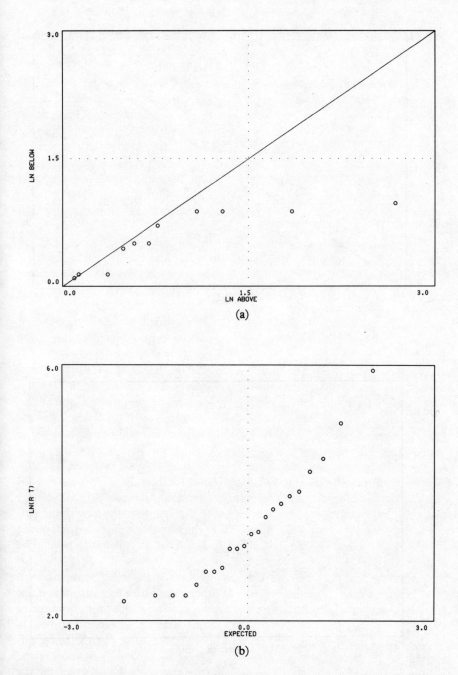

**Figure 11.** Symmetry and Quantile Quantile plots. Natural logarithms of data in Figure 10.
(a) symmetry plot; (b) normal QQ plot.

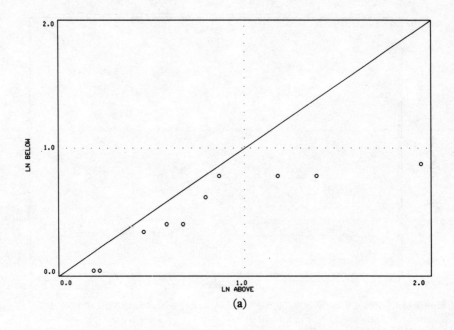

(a)

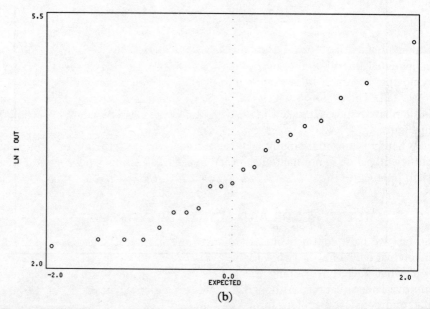

(b)

**Figure 12.** Symmetry and Quantile Quantile plots: Data are as in Figure 11 with one upper value trimmed.
(a) symmetry plot; (b) normal QQ plot.

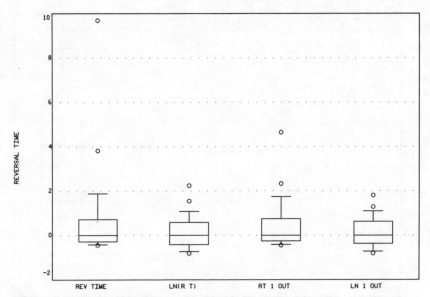

**Figure 13.** Side by side box plots, standardized to have median at 0 and a box length of 1. Data are from Figures 10 to 12.
Key: REV TIME, LN(R T) – original and logged data
    RT 1 OUT, LN 1 OUT - original and logged data with 1 trimmed value.

exponential outlier, that is, an outlier if the data were generated from an exponential distribution (Lovie, 1986). As we can see in Figures 12a and b, removing the largest value slightly improves the overall symmetry, except in the lower tail. The extent to which transforming the data and removing the upper outlier have reduced the skew in the data can also be clearly seen in the box plots in Figure 13.

Whether we would happily take these transformed and trimmed data to be sufficiently close to normality for formal hypothesis testing is not something we shall pursue.

## MULTIFACTOR AND MULTIVARIATE DISPLAYS

So far, we have confined our attention to the graphical analysis of data sets involving only one or two variables. However, modern data analysts are, somewhat gingerly, grasping the nettle of devising plots for more complex multivariable situations. Although existing techniques, such as the box plot and the traditional scatterplot, form the building blocks for many of the new methods, the multivariate challenge has also generated some rather more radical responses.

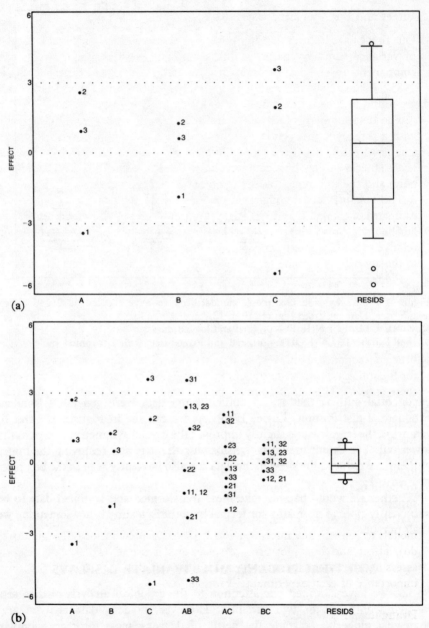

**Figure 14.** Effects and box plot error display for ANOVA. Data are from a three factor design with three levels per factor.
(a) main effects only; (b) main and interaction effects.
Key: Labels are numbered levels or level combinations.
*Source:* Winer (1971), page 477.

## Effect and Box Plot Error Displays

Our first plots, Figures 14a and b serve as semi-graphical analogues of analysis of variance summary tables in the sense that they are parallel plots of the components involved in fitting a linear model in a designed experiment (Cook, 1985). Estimates of the main and interaction effects and the residuals (errors) are found in exactly the same way as for an analysis of variance.

The data for both plots (taken from Winer, 1971) are from an experiment with a three-way independent groups design and a single observation per cell (the $n = 1$ case); the three factors, which are assumed to be fixed, have three levels apiece. Our analysis considers both the reduced model (main factor effects only) and the full model (all six main and interaction effects).

The residuals are summarized on the display by a single box plot, while estimates of the main and, where appropriate, interaction effects are shown as labelled dot plots. The range of the estimated effects for a factor or interaction relative to the box length (midspread) of the residual plot provides a rough guide to the contribution made to the model fit by that factor or interaction.

Figures 14a and 14b show the effects and box plot error displays for the reduced and full model analyses, respectively. Direct comparisons between these displays are easy because the vertical scales and plotting regions are the same. Comparing the effect estimates and the residuals in Figure 14a, we see that factor C and then factor A contribute most to the model fit, while B is of little consequence. However, on moving to Figure 14b which shows the picture for the full model, we note the marked reduction in the midspread and range of the residuals. This is, of course, the result of extracting the three interaction effects from the reduced model residual. Accordingly, these much diminished residuals increase the relative importance of the main effects to the extent that, for example, factor B is now a factor of some significance. The ranges of the AB and AC interaction effects relative to the residuals' box length indicate the importance of these interactions also. Only the BC interaction contributes little to the fit of the model. Naturally, we conclude that the full model gives us a far superior fit.

Although analyses of variance should be carried out on the reduced and full models to confirm any interpretation of the plots (which, for our example, they do), effect and box plot error displays are a useful exploratory device for assessing the adequacy of a proposed model and for gauging the relative importance of each experimental variable.

## Draughtsman's Display

Our second plot in this section (Figure 15) is one of the earliest attempts to overcome the problems of representing multidimensional data in the two-dimensional space of a graph. It is called a draughtsman's display, because it lays out two-dimensional views of a cloud of data points in plan form. The

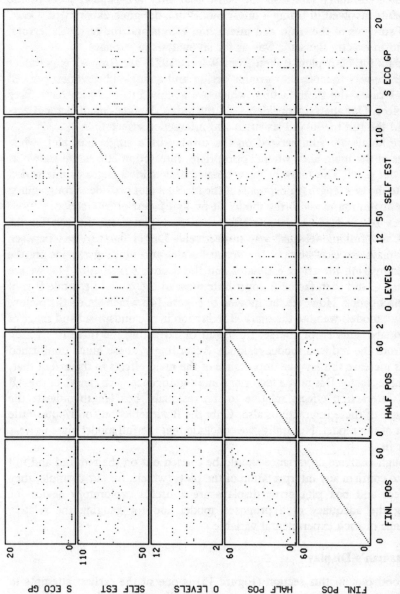

**Figure 15.** Draughtsman's display. Data are measurements on five variables used for assessment in a technician training programme.

Key: FINL POS - final position in class    HALF POS - halfway position in class    O LEVELS - number of 'O' levels
SELF EST - self esteem score    S ECO GP - socio-economic group of father

*Source:* Student dissertation.

display consists of an array of scatterplots for all the variables taken in pairs, arranged so that a row or column consists of the individual scatterplots for any one variable against all the others. The draughtsman's display can be thought of as a graphical analogue of an intercorrelation table. However, if the variables are plotted against themselves (as in Figure 15), the plots along the main diagonal show up as straight lines. In this case, experience suggests that the display is easier both on the eye and to interpret if the leading diagonal is allowed to run from lower left to upper right, rather than in the conventional upper left to lower right direction of a correlation matrix.

The data for the draughtsman's display in Figure 15 are measurements of five variables (extracted from a larger set) on 55 students enrolled on a technician training programme. The variables are: position in the class at the end of the course, position half way through the course, number of 'O' levels obtained prior to entry, self esteem and socio-economic class of father.

As we scan along the rows (or columns) of scatterplots of all pairs of these variables, it is easy to see that the only evidence of a systematic relationship is between the final and half way position scores. Note, of course, that as the variables socio-economic group and number of 'O' levels have discrete values, their plots appear as vertical or horizontal lines similar to point or dot graphs (Cleveland, 1985).

## Casement Plots

Casement plots (Figure 16) follow a similar principle to the draughtsman's display in that they reduce data in three dimensions to a series of scatterplots. For this display, however, the scatterplots depict the relationship between two of the variables after the data have been partitioned according to each of the (discrete) values of a third variable. Obviously, some care is needed in choosing the number of discrete values to use – scatterplots with too few data points will not be particularly informative.

The casement display in Figure 16 allows us to investigate the relationship between search time and target vowel position for each of the four subjects whose labours provided the data for Figure 5. Starting at the top left of Figure 16, the five scatterplots show how search time varies with target position, first for all four subjects together, then for each of the four subjects S1 to S4 separately. We see that, for every subject, the spread of search times increases as the target vowel is located further down the list, although this is less marked in S1's case. We can also identify S3 and S4 as generators of the most extreme search times visible on the combined plot.

## Chernoff Faces

The scatterplot methods described earlier, and their various enhancements, all attempt to reflect the overall multidimensional structure of the data. How they

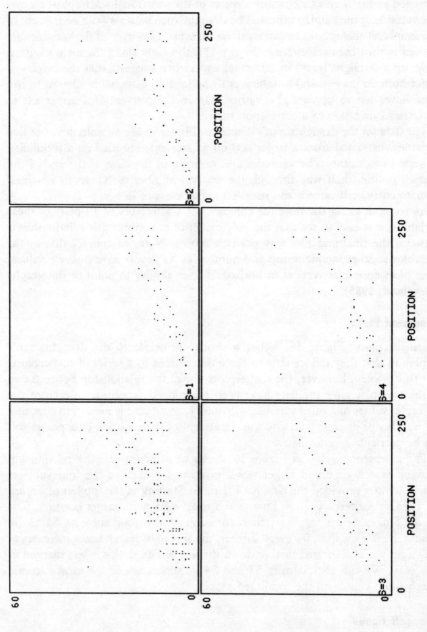

**Figure 16.** Casement plot. Data are the times for the Neisser search task, as in Figure 5, split by subject ($S = 1, 2, 3, 4$).

try to get to grips with this task is necessarily more and more piecemeal and contrived as the number of variables increases. An alternative approach, which effectively frees the display from an obligation to provide a grand overview, is to concentrate on the set of measurements for an individual case as the basic data set. Consequently, all variables are represented simultaneously in a separate two-dimensional plot or profile for each case. Once the set of profile plots has been generated, it is then up to the analyst to try to group the cases in some meaningful fashion in order to infer relationships between the variables, check for outliers, and so on.

Many 'casewise' techniques have been mooted over the years, of which plots sporting names or attributions like Trees, Castles, Stars, and Andrews' plots are just a few of the contenders (see, for example, Chambers *et al.*, 1983, Tufte, 1983). Probably the best known (or perhaps the most notorious), is the Chernoff Faces plot (Chernoff, 1978) in which a particular facial characteristic is associated with each variable, the size or orientation of this feature reflecting the score on that variable. A different face will be produced for each unique case. The aim, as we have said, is to attempt to cluster cases on several variables taken together, or perhaps identify outliers.

For a display to have good face validity (we were unable to resist that one!), care is needed in choosing appropriate facial characteristics for the variable, in relating changes in this feature to changes in the variable, and in combining features effectively. For example, for the five variables of the technician training study used for Figure 15, we assigned final position score to the mouth, so that a smile indicates that an individual has done well, whereas poor performers will scowl. A V-shaped slant to the eyebrows is a sign of a poor half way score, whereas an upside down V says that the student was well placed. Large-eared people come from backgrounds high on the socio-economic scale; those with the deepest foreheads have the most 'O' levels; long noses go with high self esteem. (Yes, we do know about the problems of illusory correlation!)

Figure 17 shows the face plots for 24 of the students on the technician training course. Student number 15 was top of the class at the end of the course and at the half way point, has 7 'O' levels, comes from a high socio-economic background, and has an average self esteem score. On the other hand, number 20, who belongs to the highest socio-economic group, performed very badly despite having a reasonable number of 'O' levels and a high self esteem score. Number 23 is about average on most variables. It is left to the reader to fill in the stories for the rest.

Finally, what Figure 17 illustrates rather too well (because it also shows up the limitations of the software we used) is the problem of spatial interaction in Chernoff faces. For instance, cases 10 and 17 are scarcely credible as faces because the nose stays anchored in the same position even though the forehead depth is increased.

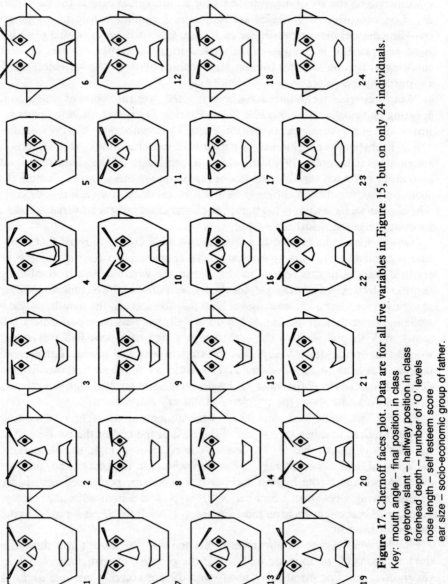

**Figure 17.** Chernoff faces plot. Data are for all five variables in Figure 15, but on only 24 individuals.

Key: mouth angle – final position in class
     eyebrow slant – halfway position in class
     forehead depth – number of 'O' levels
     nose length – self esteem score
     ear size – socio-economic group of father.

## ENDPOINTS

Naturally, the main consideration in choosing the displays for this chapter was that they should be effective communicators. However, there seemed to be little point in including those which need expensive software, special computer equipment or vast expenditure of time. Most of the plots in this chapter could have been drawn by hand, although we generated them (in most cases exactly as you see them in the text) using a relatively cheap package called NCSS which runs on an IBM PC compatible microcomputer. Regrettably, though, few of the popular statistical packages are geared up to generate the sort of graphics needed for EDA, or to carry out procedures such as smoothing, without much ingenuity and a great deal of fuss. Some of the packages which do fit the bill are MINITAB release 7, variants on S ('the' package for EDA), and, of course, NCSS.

By restricting ourselves in this way, we have ignored colour completely, even though it can be an effective plotting device. For example, a different colour for the scores of each of the subjects in the Neisser search task would have done much the same job as the casement display, but on a single scatterplot. Colour monitors are common: access to colour printers or plotters for a hard copy of one's endeavours is likely to be more problematic.

Nor have we touched upon the exciting field of dynamic graphics which can give, quite literally, a new dimension to the humble scatterplot (see Cleveland & McGill, 1988; Cook & Weisberg, 1989). NCSS, for instance, has some interactive routines for scatterplot brushing (essentially a way of deleting, labelling and highlighting selected points throughout a scatterplot matrix) and for rotating point clouds. Although these are extremely helpful in exploratory work, we immediately hit the problem of how to make a permanent record of what we have gleaned from the computer screen; a dynamic display is just that – and a two-dimensional snapshot is unlikely to impress!

When books are 'printed' on video disks, or whatever is invented next, the story could be very different.

## References

*Note:* Citations within the chapter are usually to one or more of the excellent books on modern graphical methods. These contain references to the original journal articles as well as further reading.

*Annual Abstract of Statistics No. 84* (1947). London: H.M.S.O.
*Annual Abstract of Statistics No. 93* (1956). London: H.M.S.O.
*Annual Abstract of Statistics No. 104* (1967). London: H.M.S.O.
BARTHOLOMEW, D.J. & BASSETT, E.E. (1971). *Let's Look at the Figures*. Harmondsworth: Penguin.
CHAMBERS, J.M., CLEVELAND, W.S., KLEINER, B. & TUKEY, P.A. (1983). *Graphical Methods for Data Analysis*. Monterey, CA: Wadsworth.
CHERNOFF, H. (1978). Graphical representation as a discipline. In P.C.C. Wang (Ed.), *Graphical Representation of Multivariate Data*. New York: Academic Press.

CLEVELAND, W.S. (1985). *The Elements of Graphing Data.* Monterey, CA: Wadsworth.
CLEVELAND, W.S. & McGILL, M.E. (Eds). (1988). *Dynamic Graphics for Statistics.* Belmont: Wadsworth & Brooks/Cole.
COOK, N.R. (1985). Three-way analyses. In D.C. Hoaglin, F. Mosteller & J.W. Tukey (Eds), *Exploring Data Tables, Trends, and Shapes.* New York: Wiley.
COOK, R.D. & WEISBERG, S. (1989). Regression diagnostics with dynamic graphics. *Technometrics,* **31,** 277–291.
ERICKSON, B.H. & NOSANCHUK, T.A. (1979). *Understanding Data.* Milton Keynes: The Open University Press.
GOWER, J.C. & DIGBY, P.G.N. (1981). Expressing complex relationships in two dimensions. In V. Barnett (Ed.), *Interpreting Multivariate Data.* Chichester: Wiley.
HARDYCK, C.D. & PETRINOVICH, L.F. (1969). *Introduction to Statistics for the Behavioral Sciences.* Philadelphia: Saunders.
JONES, B. & KENWARD, M.G. (1989). *Design and Analysis of Cross-Over Trials.* London: Chapman & Hall.
LOVIE, P. (1986). Identifying outliers. In A.D. Lovie (Ed.), *New Developments in Statistics for Psychology and the Social Sciences.* London: The British Psychological Society & Methuen.
McNEIL, D.R. (1977). *Interactive Data Analysis.* New York: Wiley.
MOORE, D.S. & McCABE, G.P. (1989). *Introduction to the Practice of Statistics.* New York: Freeman.
MOSTELLER, F. & TUKEY, J.W. (1977). *Data Analysis and Regression.* Reading, Mass.: Addison Wesley.
ROSENBAUM, P.R. (1989). Exploratory plots for paired data. *The American Statistician,* **43,** 108–109.
*Scottish Health Statistics 1983* (1984). Edinburgh: H.M.S.O.
*Scottish Health Statistics 1984* (1986). Edinburgh: H.M.S.O.
SEHEULT, A. (1986). Simple graphical methods for data analysis. In A.D. Lovie (Ed.), *New Developments in Statistics for Psychology and the Social Sciences.* London: The British Psychological Society & Methuen.
TUFTE, E.R. (1983). *The Visual Display of Quantitative Information.* Cheshire, Conn.: Graphics Press.
TUKEY, J.W. (1977). *Exploratory Data Analysis.* Reading, Mass.: Addison-Wesley.
VELLEMAN, P.F. & HOAGLIN, D.C. (1981). *Applications, Basics and Computing of Exploratory Data Analysis.* Boston, Mass.: Duxbury.
WINER, B.J. (1971). *Statistical Principles in Experimental Design,* 2nd ed. New York: McGraw-Hill.
*World Health Statistics Annual 1971, vol. 1* (1974). Geneva: World Health Organization.

**Statistical Software**
MINITAB RELEASE 7, Minitab Inc., State College, PA, USA.
NCSS Version 5, Kaysville, Utah, USA.
S, AT&T Bell Laboratories, New Jersey, USA.

# 3

# Computationally Intensive Statistics

CHRIS ROBERTSON

The aim of this chapter is to bring some recent statistical techniques to the attention of psychologists and other social scientists. A unifying theme connecting the techniques is their heavy use of computational procedures with little emphasis on parametric assumptions. This contrasts with the more classical statistical techniques which make assumptions about the underlying probability distribution of the data. In regression analyis, for example, it is common to assume that the errors are normally distributed with zero mean and unknown variance.

The techniques discussed here are the Bootstrap, Jackknife, Randomization methods and Monte Carlo tests. The first three fall into the category of nonparametric procedures. Their uses span the main areas of classical statistical inference; namely, estimation and testing. The bootstrap and jackknife are used primarily in the former area. They are particularly suited to the estimation of bias and variability, and can be used to provide confidence intervals for an unknown parameter. Randomization methods and Monte Carlo tests have uses in the area of significance testing. Randomization tests make minimal assumptions about the data. Monte Carlo tests are appropriate when the null distribution of the test statistic is not known. Diaconis & Efron (1983) provide a discussion of the power of computationally intensive methods in statistics.

In view of the practical nature of the techniques a number of data sets are presented for illustration. The techniques will be described and anyone following them should be able to reproduce the results. All of the data sets are quite small. The reasons for this choice are twofold. Firstly the methods described here are particularly suited to small data sets. In larger data sets the parametric assumptions may not be so crucial. Secondly with the small data sets it is easier to follow through the calculations to check the method. The reader should not go away with the impression that the techniques are only small sample techniques, though, and there are examples of their use in complex studies. Vinod & Raj (1988) use bootstrapping in a regression analysis; Efron & Gong (1983) discuss the bootstrap prediction rule in logistic discrimination; Mosteller & Tukey (1977, Chapter 8) use the jackknife in a discriminant analysis.

The data in Table 1 are taken from a study of reading ability among a sample

**Table 1.** Reading ages (in months) of a sample of primary school children

| | | | | Boys | | | | | |
|---|---|---|---|---|---|---|---|---|---|
| 96 | 72 | 78 | 93 | 90 | 96 | 75 | 69 | 84 | 78 |
| 81 | 84 | 72 | 93 | 84 | 111 | 81 | 93 | 75 | 78 |

| | | | | | Girls | | | | | |
|---|---|---|---|---|---|---|---|---|---|---|
| 117 | 90 | 72 | 81 | 108 | 120 | 78 | 90 | 96 | 93 | 126 |
| 117 | 96 | 72 | 75 | 84 | 96 | 141 | 72 | 75 | 84 | 72 |
| 69 | 105 | 84 | | | | | | | | |

of primary school children. The children were all in primary 4 and were aged between 97 and 108 months. A natural way to begin the analysis of this data and to compare the reading ages of the boys and girls in the class is to calculate summary statistics of the two groups and compare them. One might be tempted to assume that the reading ages are normally distributed, calculate means and standard deviations, and estimate the difference in reading ages using a confidence interval based on the *t*-distribution. Inspection of the histograms of the reading age distributions (Figure 1) suggests that the normal assumption is not completely valid in this instance, with reading ages grouped at 3 month intervals. Also, in view of the large number of observations in the tails it is not likely that a tranformation of the reading ages will result in normality. In any event, transformations to an arbitrary scale will possibly hinder the interpretation and there is a good case for analysing the data in the scale in which it is recorded.

The jackknife and bootstrap are both techniques which can be used to estimate a summary statistic of a distribution, together with an estimate of variability. Later, the use of these techniques in the context of bias reduction will be discussed. Both techniques are similar in that they do not require a distributional assumption to be made and, in a sense, are nonparametric techniques. They have advantages over the classical approach in that reliable estimates can be obtained and inferences made without the necessity of making, possibly invalid, distributional assumptions.

After the discussion of the estimation problem attention will be focused on the testing problem. Randomization tests will be introduced. These tests allow conclusions to be drawn without the necessity of making possibly unrealistic parametric assumptions. The range of application of such tests is not as widespread as their parametric equivalents so at present they are not likely to usurp them. Finally, Monte Carlo tests are discussed. These are parametric tests in that two models are compared. They are of use principally when the distribution of the test statistic under the null hypothesis cannot be evaluated. A major area of application is in likelihood ratio tests based on small samples where the asymptotic results may not be valid.

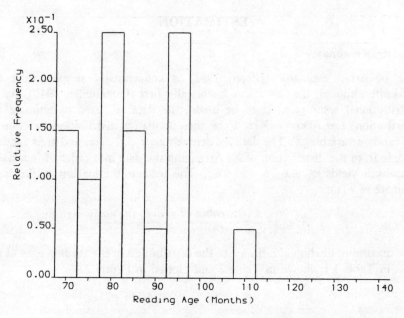

**Figure 1a.** Histogram of the reading ages – boys

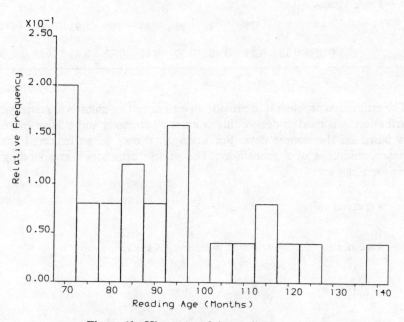

**Figure 1b.** Histogram of the reading ages – girls

# ESTIMATION

## Bootstrap estimator

The bootstrap estimator (Efron, 1982) is conceptually simpler than the jackknife although the latter was historically first (Quenouille, 1949). As no distributional assumption is to be made, the data are used to estimate the distribution. Let $F(x) = P(X \leq x)$ be the cumulative distribution function of the random variable, $X$. The data are denoted $x_1, x_2, \ldots, x_n$ and are a random sample from the distribution of $X$. Arranging the data into order of increasing magnitude yields $x_{(1)} \leq x_{(2)} \leq \ldots \leq x_{(n)}$. This leads to the maximum likelihood estimate of $F(x)$:

$$\hat{F}(x_{(i)}) = \frac{i}{n} = \frac{\text{number of } x_1, \ldots x_n \leq x_{(i)}}{n}.$$

The maximum likelihood estimate of the distribution of the reading ages of the boys in Table 1 is shown in Table 2 and plotted in Figure 2.

**Table 2.** Maximum likelihood estimate of the distribution of reading ages for the boys' data in Table 1

| Ordered observations | | | | | | | | | | |
|---|---|---|---|---|---|---|---|---|---|---|
| $x_{(1)} \ldots x_{(n)}$ | 69 | 72 | 75 | 78 | 81 | 84 | 90 | 93 | 96 | 111 |
| $\hat{F}(x_{(i)})$ | 0.05 | 0.15 | 0.25 | 0.40 | 0.50 | 0.65 | 0.70 | 0.85 | 0.95 | 1.00 |

The estimation problem is to provide an estimate of an unknown quantity of a distribution. $\theta$ is used to denote this unknown parameter and $\hat{\theta}$ is an estimate of $\theta$ based on the sample data. For example, $\theta$ may be an expected value, variance, midrange or a probability. The sample estimates corresponding to these examples are:

expected value $\qquad \hat{\theta} = \bar{x} = \frac{1}{n} \sum_{i=1}^{n} x_i$

variance $\qquad \hat{\theta} = s^2 = \frac{1}{n-1} \sum_{i=1}^{n} (x_i - \bar{x})^2$

mid range $\qquad \hat{\theta} = \frac{1}{2} (x_{(1)} + x_{(n)})$

$P(X \leq x_{(i)}) \qquad \hat{\theta} = i/n$

25% trimmed mean     $\hat{\theta} = \dfrac{2}{n}\,(x_{(n+1/4)} + \ldots + x_{(3n/4)})$

(the mean of the middle 50% of the data)

mid hinge     $\hat{\theta} = \dfrac{1}{2}\,(x_{(n/4)} + x_{(3n/4)})$.

Note that in the latter two cases appropriate modifications need to be made if $n$ is or is not a multiple of 4. (See Mosteller & Tukey (1977), pp.34, 43–48 for a discussion of trimmed means and hinges.)

Bootstrap estimation begins by selecting a random sample of $n$ observations *with replacement* from the distribution, $\hat{F}$. Uniform random numbers between 0 and 1 are generated and the corresponding value of $x$ is then included in the sample. If the random numbers 0.1755, 0.9165, 0.2285 are obtained then the points 75, 96, 75 are included in the sample (see Figure 2). At this stage it is important to use a good random number generator (see Ripley, 1987, p.45).

Let $x_1^*, x_2^*, \ldots, x_n^*$ be the observations in this random sample. Based on this, calculate $\theta^*$ which is the sample estimate of a population parameter $\theta$. Repeating the sampling procedure $B$ times will result in estimates $\theta_i^*$, $i=1, \ldots, B$, of $\theta$. The bootstrap estimate of $\theta$ is

$$\hat{\theta}_B = \frac{1}{B} \sum_{i=1}^{B} \theta_i^*,$$

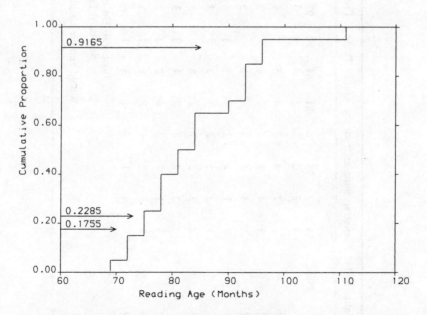

**Figure 2.** Estimated cumulative distribution function

**Table 3.** Ten Bootstrap samples from the data in Table 2. Frequency (*f*) with which each observation is resampled

| Data: f | 69 | 72 | 75 | 78 | 81 | 84 | 90 | 93 | 96 | 111 | mean | median | midrange | midhinge | 25% trimmed mean |
|---|---|---|---|---|---|---|---|---|---|---|---|---|---|---|---|
| 1 | 1 | 2 | 2 | 3 | 2 | 3 | 1 | 3 | 1 | 1 | 83.1 | 81.0 | 91.5 | 81.8 | 80.7 |
| 2 |  | 2 | 4 | 2 | 4 | 3 |  | 3 | 1 | 1 | 82.4 | 79.5 | 90.0 | 81.0 | 80.4 |
| 3 | 1 | 4 | 1 | 4 | 1 | 4 |  | 2 | 3 |  | 81.0 | 78.0 | 84.0 | 81.8 | 78.3 |
| 4 | 1 | 1 | 4 | 5 | 1 | 3 | 1 | 4 | 3 |  | 84.0 | 84.0 | 82.5 | 84.0 | 84.0 |
| 5 | 1 | 2 | 5 | 2 | 3 | 3 |  | 3 | 1 |  | 80.7 | 79.5 | 82.5 | 79.5 | 79.2 |
| 6 | 2 | 3 | 2 | 1 | 2 | 6 |  | 3 | 1 | 2 | 81.2 | 82.5 | 82.5 | 78.8 | 81.0 |
| 7 |  | 2 | 2 | 2 | 3 | 4 | 1 | 3 | 6 | 2 | 85.0 | 84.0 | 91.5 | 85.5 | 84.0 |
| 8 | 3 | 1 | 2 | 2 | 4 | 2 | 1 | 3 | 2 |  | 81.9 | 81.0 | 82.5 | 83.3 | 81.3 |
| 9 | 1 | 2 | 2 | 4 | 2 | 1 | 1 | 5 | 2 |  | 83.4 | 81.0 | 82.5 | 84.8 | 83.4 |
| 10 |  | 3 | 1 | 3 | 1 | 3 | 1 | 4 | 2 | 2 | 86.7 | 84.0 | 91.5 | 85.5 | 85.8 |
| Bootstrap Estimate |  |  |  |  |  |  |  |  |  |  | 83.01 | 81.45 | 86.10 | 82.58 | 81.81 |
| Standard Error |  |  |  |  |  |  |  |  |  |  | 2.03 | 2.13 | 4.37 | 2.41 | 2.39 |
| Whole Sample Estimate |  |  |  |  |  |  |  |  |  |  | 84.15 | 82.50 | 90.00 | 84.75 | 83.10 |

the mean of the estimates from the $B$ random samples. The variance of this estimate is estimated as

$$\hat{\sigma}_B^2 = \frac{1}{B-1} \sum_{i=1}^{B} (\theta_i^* - \hat{\theta}_B)^2.$$

In Table 3 the results of a bootstrap experiment with $B = 10$ are displayed. In this experiment $\theta$ is the mean of the distribution of the reading ages of the boys in Table 1, so that

$$\hat{\theta} = \frac{1}{n} \sum_{1}^{n} x_i.$$

The bootstrap samples are selected with replacement and consequently some of the samples in Table 3 have multiple occurrences of the same observation. Indeed there is no point trying to select a bootstrap sample of size $n$ without replacement as the same sample (namely that data) would be obtained every time. In view of the random sample selection, different values of $\theta_i^*$ are obtained and the bootstrap estimate is $\hat{\theta}_B = 83.01$ months with an estimated standard error of 2.03 months.

In the case of the estimation of the mean of a random variable there is little point in using the bootstrap technique unless the sample size is small or the distribution is markedly non normal. The sample mean, $\bar{x}$, and $s/\sqrt{n}$ provide appropriate estimates of the mean and its standard error. Turning attention to the median, midhinge, midrange and 25% trimmed mean as alternative estimates of location it can be seen that the bootstrap estimates are calculated in a similar fashion to the mean (see Table 3). This shows one of the powerful features of the bootstrap technique, namely its ability to handle a number of different problems within the same unifying approach.

In Table 3 only 10 bootstrap samples were selected as an illustration. In applications usually at least 100 samples are selected and, depending on the parameter of interest, it is sometimes necessary to take a much larger number of samples. This is clearly computationally not feasible without a computer. To an extent the heavy use of computer power is a compensation for the lack of any distributional assumptions. Efron & Tibshirani (1986) and Efron (1987) provide some guidelines for the number of bootstrap replications required.

In Table 4 the effect of increasing the number of bootstrap simulations is investigated on some measures of location. The midrange is omitted in view of its dependence on the extremes and its consequent large variance. The general impression from this Table is that increasing the number of bootstrap samples increases the accuracy of the estimates and their standard errors. The mean and trimmed mean appear to have settled down by 100 samples. A slightly larger number of samples is necessary for the estimates based on one or two order statistics. The standard error of the mean is $s/\sqrt{n} = 2.349$ and the bootstrap estimated standard error of the mean is approaching this value as the number of

**Table 4.** The effect of increasing the number of bootstrap samples

|  | mean | median | midhinge | 25% trimmed mean |
|---|---|---|---|---|
| $\hat{\theta}$ | 84.150 | 82.500 | 84.750 | 83.100 |
| $B = 50$ $\hat{\theta}_B$ | 84.501 | 82.440 | 83.715 | 83.034 |
| $\hat{\sigma}$ | 2.141 | 3.360 | 2.689 | 2.799 |
| $B = 100$ $\hat{\theta}_B$ | 84.553 | 82.110 | 83.543 | 83.550 |
| $\hat{\sigma}$ | 2.375 | 2.928 | 2.615 | 2.940 |
| $B = 500$ $\hat{\theta}_B$ | 84.304 | 82.530 | 83.739 | 83.167 |
| $\hat{\sigma}$ | 2.460 | 3.201 | 2.512 | 2.656 |
| $B = 1000$ $\hat{\theta}_B$ | 84.114 | 82.493 | 83.802 | 83.078 |
| $\hat{\sigma}$ | 2.297 | 3.208 | 2.406 | 2.677 |
| $B = 2000$ $\hat{\theta}_B$ | 84.102 | 82.604 | 83.939 | 83.109 |
| $\hat{\sigma}$ | 2.302 | 3.242 | 2.529 | 2.802 |

samples increases. Only with the smallest number of samples is the estimate bad. If assumptions were made about the distribution of the reading ages then it would be possible to work out the standard errors of the other three estimates and the bootstrap standard errors could be compared to them. This is not attempted here as there is no obvious model for the distribution of reading ages. In view of the outliers (111 in the boys' data and 141 in the girls') the trimmed mean might be used as a robust estimate of location. The median and midhinge are also robust estimates and could be considered further. It is unusual that the standard error of the midhinge is smaller than that of the 25% trimmed mean as it is based on fewer observations. This occurs here as there are local modes at the hinges of the data $76.5 = \frac{1}{2}(75 + 78)$ and 93, but is not expected in general.

### Jackknife estimation

The jackknife, as originally proposed by Quenouille (1949), is a method of reducing the bias of an estimator. Like the bootstrap it relies on taking subsamples from the data. However it is more systematic in that each observation is omitted in turn. Thus the jackknife approach does not place such a heavy burden on computation. Miller (1974) reviews the jackknife and its applications.

The jackknife estimate of a parameter, $\theta$, proceeds as follows. $\hat{\theta}$ is the estimate based on all the data. $\hat{\theta}_{(i)}$ is the estimate based on the data with observation $i$ omitted, $i = 1, 2, \ldots, n$. The $i$th pseudo-value is defined as

$$\tilde{\theta}_i = n\hat{\theta} - (n-1)\,\hat{\theta}_{(i)}.$$

The pseudo-value is a linear combination of the two estimates of $\theta$, one including and the other excluding $x_i$. The coefficients of these estimates, $n$ and $-(n-1)$, are chosen to eliminate bias in the estimator. The jackknife estimate, $\hat{\theta}_{\mathcal{J}}$, of $\theta$ is the mean of the $n$ pseudo-values obtained by deleting each observation in turn. Thus

$$\hat{\theta}_{\mathcal{J}} = \frac{1}{n}\sum_{i=1}^{n}\tilde{\theta}_i = n\hat{\theta} - (n-1)\,\hat{\theta}_{(.)},$$

where

$$\hat{\theta}_{(.)} = \frac{1}{n}\sum_{i=1}^{n}\hat{\theta}_{(i)}.$$

The variance of $\hat{\theta}_{\mathcal{J}}$ is estimated as

$$\hat{\sigma}_{\mathcal{J}}^2 = \left(\frac{1}{n-1}\sum_{i=1}^{n}(\tilde{\theta}_i - \hat{\theta}_{\mathcal{J}})^2\right)\Big/n$$

$$= \frac{(n-1)}{n}\sum_{i=1}^{n}(\hat{\theta}_{(i)} - \hat{\theta}_{(.)})^2$$

on substitution for $\tilde{\theta}_i$ and $\hat{\theta}_{\mathcal{J}}$. In the calculation of the variance of $\hat{\theta}_{\mathcal{J}}$ it is assumed that the pseudo-values behave as if they were independent (Mosteller & Tukey, 1977, p. 135).

In Table 5 the jackknife calculations corresponding to Table 3 are shown. Each of the 20 observations is deleted in turn resulting in 20 separate estimates which are then combined to form the jackknife estimate together with its standard error. The sample mean of the data is 84.15 months with a standard deviation ($s$) of 10.5 months yielding a standard error ($s/\sqrt{n}$) of 2.35 months. This is in complete agreement with the jackknife estimate of the mean. This result is expected in view of the algebraic identity relating the sample mean, $\bar{x}$, to the mean on deletion of observation $i$, $\bar{x}_{(i)}$:

$$\bar{x}_{(i)} = (n\bar{x} - x_i)/(n-1) = \hat{\theta}_{(i)}.$$

On replacing $\hat{\theta}$ by $\bar{x}$ and $\hat{\theta}_{(.)}$ by

$$\frac{1}{n}\sum_{i=1}^{n}\bar{x}_{(i)}$$

in the equation for $\hat{\theta}_{\mathcal{J}}$ above, it can be seen that

$$\hat{\theta}_{\mathcal{J}} = n\bar{x} - \frac{n-1}{n}\sum_{i=1}^{n}\frac{n\bar{x}-x_i}{n-1} = \frac{1}{n}\sum_{i=1}^{n}x_i = \bar{x}.$$

**Table 5.** Jackknife estimates of location for the data in Table 1

| deleted observation | mean | median | $\hat{\theta}_{(i)}$ midrange | midhinge | 25% trimmed mean |
|---|---|---|---|---|---|
| 69 | 84.9 | 84 | 91.5 | 85.5 | 84.0 |
| 72 | 84.8 | 84 | 90.0 | 85.5 | 84.0 |
| 72 | 84.8 | 84 | 90.0 | 85.5 | 84.0 |
| 75 | 84.6 | 84 | 90.0 | 85.5 | 84.0 |
| 75 | 84.6 | 84 | 90.0 | 85.5 | 84.0 |
| 78 | 84.5 | 84 | 90.0 | 84.7 | 83.7 |
| 78 | 84.5 | 84 | 90.0 | 84.7 | 83.7 |
| 78 | 84.5 | 84 | 90.0 | 84.7 | 83.7 |
| 81 | 84.3 | 84 | 90.0 | 84.7 | 83.5 |
| 81 | 84.3 | 84 | 90.0 | 84.7 | 83.5 |
| 84 | 84.2 | 81 | 90.0 | 84.7 | 83.2 |
| 84 | 84.2 | 81 | 90.0 | 84.7 | 83.2 |
| 84 | 84.2 | 81 | 90.0 | 84.7 | 83.2 |
| 90 | 83.8 | 81 | 90.0 | 84.7 | 82.6 |
| 93 | 83.7 | 81 | 90.0 | 84.0 | 82.4 |
| 93 | 83.7 | 81 | 90.0 | 84.0 | 82.4 |
| 93 | 83.7 | 81 | 90.0 | 84.0 | 82.4 |
| 96 | 83.5 | 81 | 90.0 | 84.0 | 82.4 |
| 96 | 83.5 | 81 | 90.0 | 84.0 | 82.4 |
| 111 | 82.7 | 81 | 82.5 | 84.0 | 82.4 |
| $\hat{\theta}$ | 84.2 | 82.5 | 90.0 | 84.7 | 83.1 |
| $\hat{\theta}_J$ | 84.2 | 82.5 | 95.7 | 85.5 | 80.8 |
| $\hat{\sigma}_J$ | 2.35 | 6.54 | 7.34 | 2.42 | 2.87 |

Similarly

$$\hat{\sigma}_{\bar{J}}^2 = \frac{n-1}{n} \sum_{i=1}^{n} \left[ \frac{n\bar{x} - x_i}{n-1} - \frac{n^2\bar{x} - n\bar{x}}{n(n-1)} \right]^2$$

$$= \frac{1}{n(n-1)} \sum_{i=1}^{n} (\bar{x} - x_i)^2 = s^2/n.$$

The equivalence of the jackknife estimates and standard error of a mean to the theoretical results is a property which gives much credence to the jackknife estimator. However, when the other columns of Table 5 are inspected it can be seen that the jackknife is not a particularly satisfactory approach for other estimators. For the median there are only two distinct values for the $\hat{\theta}_{(i)}$, whereas for the midrange and midhinge there are three. This grouping arises because these statistics are based on only one or two of the order statistics of the data. The mean is based on all the data and so could lead to distinct values for $\hat{\theta}_{(i)}$.

The 25% trimmed mean exhibits a behaviour which is between the extremes of the mean and median, as expected.

Mosteller & Tukey (1977, Chapter 8) discuss the use of the jackknife and recommend that it be used both for estimation and to estimate variability. There are problems with its use in cases where there are few distinct pseudo-values and there are also likely to be difficulties if the distribution is long tailed with outliers. The latter difficulty may be overcome by transforming the data.

Comparing the jackknife estimates of location in Table 5 with the bootstrap estimate in Table 4 it is clear that the jackknife is superior in the case of the mean. This is not really a positive advantage for the jackknife as there are standard approaches to assessing the precision of the sample mean, namely, using $s/\sqrt{n}$, the estimated standard error. As regards the trimmed mean, both methods yield a similar estimate of the standard error unlike their estimates of location. The jackknife estimate suggests that there is some bias (see later discussion) whereas the bootstrap does not, as $\hat{\theta} - \hat{\theta}_J = 2.3$ whereas $\hat{\theta}_B - \hat{\theta} = 0.009$. The bootstrap method is superior to the jackknife when using the median, as there are only two distinct pseudo-values and the jackknife variability is larger. For the midhinge both methods yield similar standard errors, though the small number of distinct pseudo-values leads to the bootstrap being preferred. The midrange is again seen to be poor and the influence of the outlier (111) is clearly seen – hence the bias and high standard error.

## Estimation of a difference in location

For the data of Table 1 the main aim is to estimate the difference in location of the two distributions together with an estimate of the variability of the estimate. In view of the outliers it is advisable to use a robust estimate of location and the 25% trimmed mean is used here. This is not the only possibility. Among others, the median or the Hodges-Lehmann shift estimator, which is the median of all possible differences between points in the two samples, could be used (see Sprent, 1988, p. 36ff, p. 96ff).

As the two samples are independent, the bootstrap and jackknife estimates can be calculated separately for each sample. The results are shown in Table 6. There is not much difference between the bootstrap and jackknife estimates of the standard error of the difference in the location; both are around 5.5 months. As previously mentioned the jackknife throws up a suggestion of bias in the estimator which is not present in the bootstrap.

The results are repeated for the sample mean. Although this is not the preferred estimate of location in this instance its use serves as a check on the results. The difference in the sample means has an estimated standard error of $\sqrt{s_g^2/n_g + s_b^2/n_b}$ which is equal to 4.58 and is the value obtained by the jackknife. The bootstrap estimates are similar.

There is a sense in which the separate sampling is wasteful. If the only difference between the distribution of reading ages for the boys and girls is one

**Table 6.** Estimating the difference in location of the reading ages for the boys and girls

| | | 25% trimmed mean | | | mean | | |
|---|---|---|---|---|---|---|---|
| JACKKNIFE | | $\hat{\theta}$ | $\hat{\theta}_J$ | $\hat{\sigma}_J$ | $\hat{\theta}$ | $\hat{\theta}_J$ | $\hat{\sigma}_J$ |
| | Girls | 88.6 | 89.9 | 4.89 | 92.52 | 92.52 | 3.93 |
| | Boys | 83.1 | 80.8 | 2.87 | 84.15 | 84.15 | 2.35 |
| | Difference | 5.5 | 9.1 | 5.67 | 8.37 | 8.37 | 4.58 |
| BOOTSTRAP | | | | | | | |
| *Separate* | | $\hat{\theta}$ | $\hat{\theta}_B$ | $\hat{\sigma}_B$ | $\hat{\theta}$ | $\hat{\theta}_B$ | $\hat{\sigma}_B$ |
| $B=100$ | Girls | 88.6 | 88.61 | 4.89 | 92.52 | 92.32 | 3.83 |
| | Boys | 83.1 | 83.55 | 2.94 | 84.15 | 84.55 | 2.38 |
| | Difference | 5.5 | 5.06 | 5.71 | 8.37 | 7.77 | 4.51 |
| $B=1000$ | Girls | 88.6 | 89.35 | 4.56 | 92.52 | 92.27 | 3.76 |
| | Boys | 83.1 | 83.08 | 2.68 | 84.15 | 84.11 | 2.30 |
| | Difference | 5.5 | 6.27 | 5.29 | 8.37 | 8.16 | 4.41 |
| *Combined* | | | | | | | |
| $B=100$ | Difference | 5.5 | | 5.13 | 8.37 | | 4.82 |
| $B=1000$ | Difference | 5.5 | | 4.75 | 8.37 | | 4.86 |

of location then a better estimate of the distribution function $F(x)$ can be obtained by combining the two samples. If the two samples are denoted $x_1, \ldots, x_n$ and $y_1, \ldots, y_m$ with location estimates $\hat{\theta}_x$ and $\hat{\theta}_y$ respectively, then the combined sample

$$x_1 - \hat{\theta}_x, \ldots, x_n - \hat{\theta}_x, y_1 - \hat{\theta}_y, \ldots, y_m - \hat{\theta}_y$$

will provide a more efficient estimator of $F(x)$ than either of the two separate samples. This combined sample can be used to provide an estimate of the common variability in the two samples and hence will lead to an estimate of the standard error of the estimated difference in location.

The results based on this approach are also presented in Table 6. In both location estimates there are some differences in the combined and separate approaches. The combined approach is based on more stringent assumptions than the separate approach in that it is assumed that the shapes and variances of the two distributions are equal. This does not appear to be valid as the variability is greater for the girls (see also Figure 1 where the shapes can be seen). The combined approach is analogous to using a pooled estimate of variability. If there is indeed only a location difference between the distributions, then the combined approach is likely to be more efficient and should require fewer bootstrap samples for a desired accuracy. Further details are in Efron & Gong (1983).

## Bias estimation

As well as providing estimates of the variability of estimators the jackknife and bootstrap also yield estimates themselves. In the case of the mean, the jackknife estimate and the sample estimate are identical. This is not true for the bootstrap and need not be so for other estimators. This leads to the use of the bootstrap and jackknife in estimating the bias of an estimator.

The bias of an estimator, $\hat{\theta}$, of a parameter, $\theta$, is

$$b(\theta) = \theta - E[\hat{\theta}],$$

where $E[\hat{\theta}]$ is the expected value of $\hat{\theta}$ taken over the distribution of the data $x$. The differences between $\hat{\theta}$ and the bootstrap and jackknife estimators provide an estimate of the bias of an estimator. Specifically the jackknife estimate of bias is

$$\hat{b}_J = \hat{\theta} - \hat{\theta}_J = (n-1)(\hat{\theta}_{(.)} - \hat{\theta})$$

on substituting for $\hat{\theta}_J$. The bootstrap estimate is

$$\hat{b}_B = \hat{\theta}_B - \hat{\theta} = \frac{1}{B} \sum_{i=1}^{B} (\theta_i^* - \hat{\theta}).$$

The sample mean, $\bar{x}$, is an unbiased estimator of the mean of the distribution. The bootstrap and jackknife estimates in Tables 4 and 5 illustrate this. The jackknife estimate of bias is zero and the bootstrap estimate is small ($\hat{b}_B = -0.003$, $B = 2000$). When considering the 25% trimmed mean, $\hat{b}_J = -2.3$ and $\hat{b}_B = 0.009$, which is a considerable difference. This arises as a result of the influence of the groups of observations with the same value (see Table 3).

The common parameters which are estimated with bias are the standard deviation and ratios such as the correlation between two variables. Calculations of bias are illustrated using the boys' data of Table 1.

The sample variance

$$s^2 = \frac{1}{n-1} \sum_{i=1}^{n} (x_i - \bar{x})^2$$

is an unbiased estimate of the variance of the distribution. However, $s$ is not an unbiased estimate of the standard deviation. Table 7 shows that there is some bias in the use of $s$ as an estimator of the standard deviation. However, the bias is small relative to the standard error of the estimator.

**Table 7.** Bias of the standard deviation

| JACKKNIFE | $\hat{\theta}$ | $\hat{\theta}_J$ | $\hat{b}_J$ | $\hat{\sigma}_J$ |
|---|---|---|---|---|
| | 10.50 | 10.70 | −0.193 | 2.01 |
| BOOTSTRAP $B = 100$ | $\hat{\theta}$ | $\hat{\theta}_B$ | $\hat{b}_B$ | $\hat{\sigma}_B$ |
| | 10.50 | 10.22 | −0.287 | 1.96 |

**Table 8.** Reading ages ($R$), Word Test Scores ($W$) and Thurstone's Primary Mental Abilities scores ($T$) for a sample of 20 boys aged 97 to 108 months

| R | W | T |
|---|---|---|
| 96 | 33 | 114 |
| 72 | 4 | 92 |
| 78 | 13 | 118 |
| 93 | 34 | 119 |
| 90 | 20 | 103 |
| 96 | 26 | 89 |
| 75 | 8 | 88 |
| 69 | 8 | 84 |
| 84 | 12 | 108 |
| 78 | 13 | 71 |
| 81 | 15 | 75 |
| 84 | 16 | 91 |
| 72 | 3 | 61 |
| 93 | 26 | 77 |
| 84 | 12 | 101 |
| 111 | 38 | 96 |
| 81 | 16 | 88 |
| 93 | 28 | 89 |
| 75 | 12 | 95 |
| 78 | 13 | 83 |

With this approach the experimenter is able to assess the bias of the estimator. As the standard error of the estimator is also obtained it is possible to compare the bias and the variability. The results from the jackknife and bootstrap are similar in this example. An advantage of the bootstrap approach is that the bias of the estimator can be specified as the parameter of interest and its standard error calculated. Efron & Gong (1983) provide more details of this approach.

The correlation coefficient is widely used in psychology and an example of its use is presented using the data in Table 8, where the scores on a word test for the boys in Table 1 are available. A plot of the two measures of reading ability is given in Figures 3a and 3b and it is clear that there is considerable correlation between the two variables. The Pearson correlation between these variables is $r = 0.936$. In order to attach a standard error to this estimate we can use the jackknife or bootstrap approaches or assume normality and estimate the standard error of the correlation by $(1 - r^2)/\sqrt{n-3} = 0.030$ (Johnson & Kotz, 1970, p.229). In view of the marginal distributions of the two variables, normality is not really a reasonable assumption and the nonparametric approaches are more realistic.

In Table 9 the bootstrap and jackknife results are presented. Both of these methods suggest that there is some slight bias although it is a factor of 10 smaller

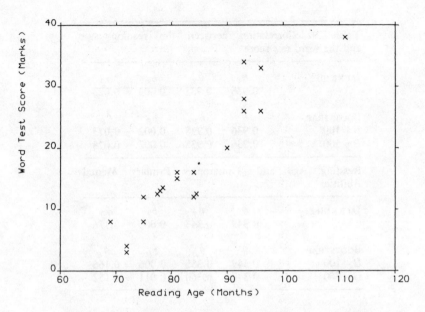

**Figure 3a.** Scatterplot of reading ability and word test score

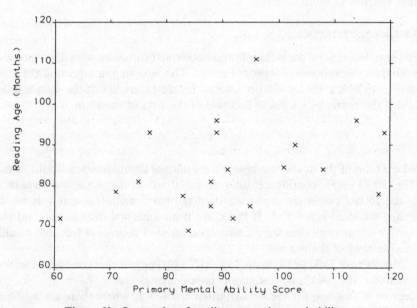

**Figure 3b.** Scatterplot of reading age and mental ability

**Table 9.** Correlation between the reading age and the word test score

| JACKKNIFE | $\hat{\theta}$ | $\hat{\theta}_J$ | $\hat{b}_J$ | $\hat{\sigma}_J$ |
|---|---|---|---|---|
| | 0.936 | 0.933 | 0.003 | 0.023 |
| | | | | |
| BOOTSTRAP | $\hat{\theta}$ | $\hat{\theta}_B$ | $\hat{b}_B$ | $\theta_B$ |
| $B = 100$ | 0.936 | 0.938 | 0.002 | 0.023 |
| $B = 500$ | 0.936 | 0.938 | 0.002 | 0.023 |

Reading Age and Thurstone's Primary Mental Abilities

| JACKKNIFE | $\hat{\theta}$ | $\hat{\theta}_J$ | $\hat{b}_J$ | $\hat{\sigma}_J$ |
|---|---|---|---|---|
| | 0.349 | 0.343 | 0.006 | 0.176 |
| | | | | |
| BOOTSTRAP | $\hat{\theta}$ | $\hat{\theta}_B$ | $\hat{b}_B$ | $a\theta_B$ |
| $B = 100$ | 0.349 | 0.355 | 0.006 | 0.166 |
| $B = 500$ | 0.349 | 0.360 | 0.011 | 0.152 |

than the estimated standard error of the correlation. Again these approaches yield valid estimates of bias and variability and are not subject to the requirement of parametric assumptions regarding the distribution of the random variables. Rasmussen (1989) discusses computer intensive methods of correlation analysis in more detail.

## Confidence Intervals

In previous sections the jackknife and bootstrap estimators were discussed along with their corresponding standard errors. The next step in reporting the results may be to look at the confidence interval for the parameter. If the sample is large and if the estimate is a linear function of the data of the form

$$\frac{1}{n}\sum_{i=1}^{n} w_i x_i,$$

where most of the $w_i$ are non-zero, then a normal approximation would be used. The $100(1-\alpha)\%$ confidence interval for $\theta$ would be $\hat{\theta} \pm z_{\alpha/2}\,\hat{\sigma}$ where $z_{\alpha/2}$ is the $100\alpha/2$ percentile of the standard normal distribution and $\hat{\sigma}$ is the estimated standard error of $\hat{\theta}$. If the $x_i$ are from a normal distribution and if the sample size is small then the $t$-distribution on $n-1$ degrees of freedom would be used instead of the normal.

Mosteller & Tukey (1977, pp.135–137, 140) suggest that confidence intervals based on the jackknife estimator be calculated using $\hat{\theta}_J \pm t_{\alpha/2}\,\hat{\sigma}_J$. The degrees of freedom for the $t$-distribution are $n_J - 1$, where there are $n_J$ distinct pseudo-values, $\bar{\theta}_{(i)}$, or, equivalently, $\hat{\theta}_{(i)}$, $i=1, \ldots, n$. This suggestion is based on an argument which has the pseudo-values as approximately independent. $\hat{\theta}_J$ is a linear combination of the pseudo-values and so might be approximately normally distributed. As can be seen from Table 5, sometimes $n_J$ is very much less than $n$, see especially the median, where $n_J = 2$.

Confidence intervals based upon the bootstrap can be obtained similarly using $\hat{\theta}_B \pm z_{\alpha/2} \; \hat{\sigma}_B$. As there will be at least 100 bootstrap samples there is not usually any need to use the $t$-distribution. This procedure relies on the sampling distribution of the bootstrap estimates being approximately normal. While this is so in many cases, there are instances where the distributions of the $\theta_i^*$ are skew or discrete. Examples of the distributions are given in Figure 4. For the mean the distribution of the bootstrap estimates is roughly normal, but this is not so for the median.

The sampling distribution of $\theta_i^*$, under the repeated resampling from the empirical cumulative distribution function, can be used to calculate bootstrap confidence intervals for $\theta$ directly. The percentile method of calculating an equi-tailed confidence interval is discussed by Efron (1982), Chapter 10. The $\theta_i^*$ are arranged in order to increasing magnitude, $\theta_{(i)}^*$, and the interval $(\theta_{(l)}^*, \theta_{(h)}^*)$ is a $100(1-\alpha)\%$ confidence interval for $\theta$, where $l = \text{int}[\alpha B/2]$ and $h = B + 1 - l$. (int[$y$] is the integer part of $y$; for example, int[3.3] = 3 and int[3.9] = 3). If $B = 1000$ and $\alpha = 0.05$ then $l = 25$ and $h = 976$; thus the 95% confidence interval is obtained by using the 25th smallest and 25th largest values of $\theta_i^*$. These intervals are presented in Table 10 together with the normal based intervals.

All methods are satisfactory as regards the mean of the distribution. The interval based on the jackknife is wider as a result of using the $t$-distribution as opposed to the normal. As the sampling distribution of the $\theta_i^*$ is reasonably normal (see Figure 4a) the percentile method and the normal method are in good agreement. Similar remarks can be made when using the 25% trimmed mean though the percentile method is to be recommended here as the distribution of the $\theta_i^*$ is slightly skew (Figure 4c). Again the jackknife interval is wider than the bootstrap intervals as a result of the grouping of the pseudo-values.

When the correlation between the reading age and the word test score is considered, the distribution of $\theta_i^*$ is skew (Figure 4d) and the normal based intervals are not recommended. If normality is assumed then the transformation $\text{Tanh}^{-1}(r)$, where $r$ is the correlation, would generally be used to calculate the normal based confidence intervals. This is necessary as the distribution of $\text{Tanh}^{-1}(r)$ is approximately normal, whereas the distribution of $r$ is not. The percentile method intervals reflect the skewness in the distribution of the correlation coefficient and are preferred.

One feature of the two different types of interval is that the percentile method does not necessarily result in a symmetric interval whereas the normal based ones do. It is clear that the percentile method will be more suitable over a wider

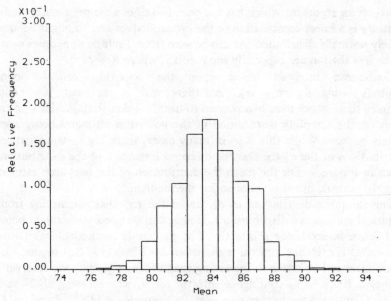

**Figure 4a.** Histogram of the Bootstrap Means.

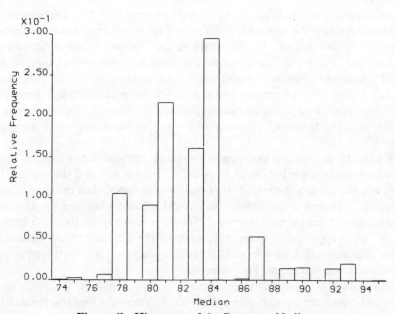

**Figure 4b.** Histogram of the Bootstrap Medians.

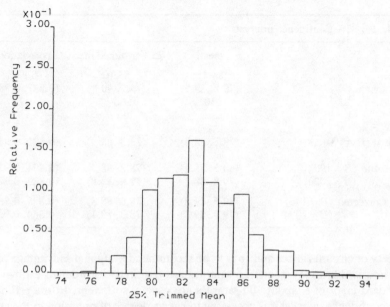

**Figure 4c.** Histogram of the Bootstrap Trimmed Means.

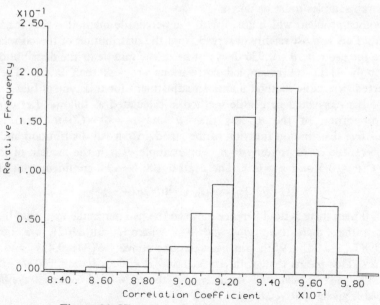

**Figure 4d.** Histogram of the Bootstrap Correlations.

**Table 10.** 95% Confidence intervals

|  | mean | 25% trimmed mean | correlation |
|---|---|---|---|
| $\hat{\theta}$ | 84.15 | 83.10 | 0.936 |
| JACKKNIFE | (78.8, 89.5) | (75.7, 90.5) | (0.887, 0.985) |
| $n_J$ | 10 | 6 | 17 |
| BOOTSTRAP | | | |
| Normal ($B = 100$) | (79.5, 88.8) | (73.3, 88.9) | (0.891, 0.981) |
| Percentile ($B = 100$) | (80.5, 88.6) | (78.2, 88.2) | (0.894, 0.970) |
| ($B = 2000$) | (79.8, 88.8) | (78.0, 88.8) | (0.885, 0.975) |
| Bias Corrected ($B = 100$) | (80.5, 88.8) | (78.6, 88.8) | (0.895, 0.961) |
| ($B = 2000$) | (79.9, 89.3) | (78.3, 89.1) | (0.864, 0.968) |

variety of circumstances and so is to be recommended. One disadvantage of this method is that many bootstrap samples are required. In order to estimate the standard error of $\hat{\theta}$ about 100 samples are usually sufficient. In the estimation of a confidence interval it is necessary to have a degree of precision in the tails of the resampled distribution. This means that 1000 samples is probably a minimum for the calculation of a confidence interval. If only 100 samples were used then a 99% confidence interval would use the minimum and maximum of the $\theta_i^*$. Generally the larger the confidence coverage required the more bootstrap samples must be taken.

Another problem which arises with the percentile method is that it may be biased. This is most readily observed from the distribution of the correlations where the estimate $\hat{\theta} = 0.936$ does not lie in the middle of the distribution. In fact, only 41.1% of resampled correlations are less than 0.936. The bias corrected percentile method makes an adjustment for this type of bias.

The bias-corrected percentile method is calculated as follows. Let $\hat{C}(\hat{\theta})$ be the proportion of the $\theta_i^*$ less than $\hat{\theta}$ and $z_0 = \Phi^{-1}(\hat{C}(\hat{\theta}))$. $\Phi(z)$ is the cumulative distribution function of the standard normal distribution and $z_0$ is the percentile corresponding to $\hat{\theta}$. For example, if $\hat{\theta}$ is the median of the $\theta_i^*$, then $\hat{C}(\hat{\theta}) = 0.5$ and $z_0 = 0.0$. The central $100(1 - \alpha)$% confidence interval is

$$(\hat{C}^{-1}[\Phi(2z_0 - z_{\alpha/2})], \, \hat{C}^{-1}[\Phi(2z_0 + z_{\alpha/2})]).$$

If $z_0 = 0$ then there is no difference between the two percentile methods. If $z_0 \neq 0$ then, rather than using $\theta_{(l)}^*$ and $\theta_{(h)}^*$ where $l = \text{int}[\alpha B/2]$, we use $l = \text{int}[B\Phi(2z_0 - z_{\alpha/2})]$. With the correlation above, $\hat{C}(\hat{\theta}) = 0.411$ and $z_0 = -0.225$. This means that, with $\alpha = 0.05$ and $B = 2000$, $l = \text{int}[2000 \, \Phi(-0.45 - 1.96)]$, with $h$ calculated similarly and the 95% bias corrected confidence interval is given by $\hat{\theta}_{(15)}^*, \, \theta_{(1869)}^*$.

Introducing the bias correction has virtually no effect in the case of the mean

(Table 10). This is to be expected in view of the symmetry of the distribution. There is a minor adjustment with the 25% trimmed mean to cater for the slight skew in the distribution. There is a major shift with the correlation coefficient and the bias corrected interval is preferred in this instance.

There is, at present, a considerable amount of research on the calculation of confidence intervals based on the bootstrap and a number of different points of view are being put forward. The percentile method is easy to use and the bias corrected version does not require a great deal more work. Efron (1987), Diciccio & Tibshirani (1987) and Diciccio & Romano (1988) have published reviews of bootstrap confidence intervals and have suggested improvements. Hall (1988) has proposed using symmetric bootstrap confidence intervals and shows that these have a better coverage probability than the percentile based methods.

Confidence intervals based on the jackknife do not appear to be as reliable as those based on the bootstrap in small sample sizes. They are, however, better than no interval at all, and can be used if necessary.

## TESTING

### Randomization tests

In this section and the subsequent one attention is focused on the testing problem as opposed to estimation. This has links with the bootstrap method which can be used to provide the critical region of a significance test. This section, like the previous ones, is motivated by consideration of an example. The data in Table 11 are taken from a study of organization in the memory of mildly retarded children attending a special school. A multi-trial free recall experiment was carried out in which 16 projected slides of line drawings were presented for 1 second each with a 1.5 second interval between exposures. The children recalled the names of the drawings orally. During the first trial the experimenter named the items as they were presented. More details of the data and the experiment are available in Todman (1982) and Todman & File (1983). The bidirectional subjective organization measure (SO2) was used to measure the amount of inter trial consistency in the recall lists. This is an indirect measure of organization in memory (see Sternberg & Tulving, 1977). SO2 is bounded above by 1 and below by 0, with high values indicating a large amount of consistency in the order of recall across trials.

The children were in two groups, one of which had received a considerable amount of training using sorting tasks where they were asked to sort out pictures of objects into groups. The hypothesis to be tested here is one of an increase in organization in the group which received training. The children were all the same age (12 years) with a mean mental age of 7.7 years, were all girls, and had all been at the special school since they were 5 years old.

| Table 11. SO2 scores for the two groups of children | | | | |
|---|---|---|---|---|
| | | *Training* | | |
| 0.35 | 0.40 | 0.41 | 0.46 | 0.49 |
| | | *No Training* | | |
| 0.33 | 0.34 | 0.36 | 0.37 | 0.39 |

The evidence of the data suggests, on inspection, that the training has had the expected effect. When performing a significance test here there are a number of problems. By assuming normality and equal variances in the two groups a $t$-test could be carried out. However, with such a small sample it is difficult to assess normality. Moreover, the spread of measures is much less in the No Training group indicating that the variabilities are not equal. One might then choose a nonparametric test and here the Mann-Whitney Test is appropriate. This test also requires equal variability and similar shapes to the underlying distribution in both groups (Sprent, 1988, p. 90).

Both of the above approaches assume that the data are a random sample from a population. The data are used to make inferences about the population. In this case the pupils are all at a special school, employing special teaching techniques and the pupils are all carefully selected by means of the pre-test of mental age. There is no clear population to which the results can be inferred.

In such an instance recourse can be made to randomization tests, or permutation tests (Edgington, 1987). In carrying out such tests a test statistic is defined and its distribution is evaluated over all possible permutations of pupils to groups. In the design of the experiment the 10 pupils were assigned at random to the two groups. Four of the Training group had scores in excess of all the Non Training group. If all of the Training group had scores in excess of those in the Non Training group then this would have constituted more evidence against the hypothesis of random allocation of scores to groups. A possible test statistic to use is $R$, the sum of the ranks of the scores of the Training group. This is the test statistic associated with the Wilcoxon-Mann-Whitney Test. Large values of $R$ indicate an effect of training.

The distribution of $R$ is evaluated by considering the possible permutations of pupils to groups; there are $\binom{10}{5} = 252$ in all. The probability distribution of $R$ under the randomization of pupils to groups is given in Table 12. This distribution is evaluated by writing down all 252 permutations, calculating $R$ for each, and combining the values of $R$ into the probability distribution in Table 12 assuming all permutations are equally likely. From Table 11 we find that $R = 37$ and from Table 12 it can be seen that $P(R \geq 37) = 7/252 = 0.028$. This constitutes evidence at the 5% level which would lead to rejection of our null hypothesis of no effect of training.

---

**Table 12.** Probability distribution of $R$ under randomization

| $R$: | 15 | 16 | 17 | 18 | 19 | 20 | 21 | 22 | 23 | 24 | 25 | 26 | 27 |
|---|---|---|---|---|---|---|---|---|---|---|---|---|---|
| 252 $P(R)$: | 1 | 1 | 2 | 3 | 5 | 7 | 9 | 11 | 14 | 16 | 18 | 19 | 20 |

| $R$: | 28 | 29 | 30 | 31 | 32 | 33 | 34 | 35 | 36 | 37 | 38 | 39 | 40 |
|---|---|---|---|---|---|---|---|---|---|---|---|---|---|
| 252 $P(R)$: | 20 | 19 | 18 | 16 | 14 | 11 | 9 | 7 | 5 | 3 | 2 | 1 | 1 |

---

Other test statistics may be used and $S$, the sum of the scores of the pupils in the Training group, is a candidate. High values of $S$ lead to rejection of the hypothesis of no effect of training. The upper tail of the distribution of $S$ is also evaluated in Table 13. In the example $S = 2.11$ and $P(S \geq 2.11) = 7/252$. Again there is evidence of an effect of the sorting task in increasing the organisation present in the recall lists.

The pooled or ungrouped two sample $t$-statistics could also be used and their distributions under the 252 possible randomizations evaluated. Both of these are closely related to $S$, as their numerators are $\bar{x}_T - \bar{x}_{NT} = S/5 - (S^* - S)/5 = 2S/5 - S^*/5$, where $S^*$ is the sum of the scores of the 10 pupils in the two groups and is constant over the randomization. Thus the distributions of the $t$-statistics will only differ from the distribution of $S$ as a result of the standard error estimates in the denominators. There is no effect in this example as the sample sizes are equal (Table 13). In general there is not likely to be much difference between the $t$-statistics and $S$.

With permutation tests there is no procedure for inferring the results from the sample to a population. They are used primarily in cases where the data are so highly selected and treated that no population exists. The only random element is the allocation of individuals to treatment groups. This is the randomization which permits the calculation of the probability distribution of the test statistic.

There is also a wide choice as to the appropriate test statistic. A statistic appropriate to the hypothesis can be used with relative ease. All that is necessary is to evaluate its distribution under the randomization. Statistics based on all the observations or the ranks are generally more appropriate. The data are most informative but test statistics based on it, such as $S$ and the $t$-statistics, may be influenced by outliers. Consequently the ranks may be used or other transformations such as the normal scores; see Sprent (1988), where many types of nonparametric tests are discussed.

One of the problems with permutation tests is that the evaluation of the distribution may be difficult. In many cases it is only necessary to work out the distribution in the tails. This was done in Table 13 and is an easier task than the evaluation of the complete distribution. There is, however, the associated problem that it is not always easy to check that all the relevant permutations have been considered. There are computer programs, for example Edgington

**Table 13.** A list of some of the 252 permutations corresponding to the large values of the test statistics

| | Ordered Data and Ranks | | | | | | | | | | R | S | t |
|---|---|---|---|---|---|---|---|---|---|---|---|---|---|
| Permutation | 0.33 | 0.34 | 0.35 | 0.36 | 0.37 | 0.39 | 0.40 | 0.41 | 0.46 | 0.49 | | | |
| | 1 | 2 | 3 | 4 | 5 | 6 | 7 | 8 | 9 | 10 | | | |
| 1 | | | | | | T | T | T | T | T | 40 | 2.15 | 3.90 |
| 2 | | | | | T | | T | T | T | T | 39 | 2.13 | 3.01 |
| 3 | | | | T | | | T | T | T | T | 38 | 2.12 | 2.68 |
| *4 | | | T | | | | T | T | T | T | 37 | 2.11 | 2.41 |
| 5 | | T | | | | | T | T | T | T | 36 | 2.10 | 2.16 |
| 6 | T | | | | | | T | T | T | T | 35 | 2.09 | 1.95 |
| 7 | | | | | T | T | | T | T | T | 38 | 2.12 | 2.68 |
| 8 | | | | | T | T | T | | T | T | 37 | 2.11 | 2.41 |
| 9 | | | | | T | T | T | T | | T | 36 | 2.06 | 1.41 |
| 10 | | | | | T | T | T | T | T | | 35 | 2.03 | 0.97 |
| 11 | | | | T | | T | | T | T | T | 37 | 2.11 | 2.41 |
| 12 | | | | T | | T | T | | T | T | 36 | 2.10 | 2.16 |
| 13 | | | | T | | T | T | T | | T | 35 | 2.05 | 1.25 |
| 14 | | | | T | | T | T | T | T | | 34 | 2.02 | 0.84 |
| 15 | | | | T | T | | | T | T | T | 36 | 2.09 | 1.95 |

*This permutation corresponds to the data

| S | 2.11 | 2.12 | 2.13 | 2.14 | 2.15 |
|---|---|---|---|---|---|
| P(S) | 3/252 | 2/252 | 1/252 | 0/252 | 1/252 |

(1987), which will cycle through all possible permutations to evaluate the distribution. For large numbers of observations in many groups this can be quite a task. An alternative approach is to build up the distribution of the test statistic by simulation, and use random permutation tests (Still & White, 1981).

With a particular test statistic samples are selected without replacement and the scores assigned to the groups. If this is carried out a large number of times then the distribution can be approximated. As the tails of the distribution are used in the calculation of a critical region a large number of simulations will have to be carried out. The results for the test statistics $R$ and $S$ are shown in Table 14. Comparing these results to Tables 12 and 13 it can be seen that simulation is an adequate way of estimating the randomization distribution of the test statistic. A large number of simulations is clearly necessary to build up an accurate estimate. A problem with this approximate randomization procedure is that different researchers using exactly the same data can arrive at different $p$-values as a result of the random selection of some of the permutations. This problem is reduced by selecting a large number of random permutations, see Table 14. In the small example discussed here the simulation is not necessary as the exact distribution can be evaluated. In more elaborate experiments such as randomized block designs then there is more scope for this method (see, for example, Mead,1988, chapter 9; Edgington, 1987; Still & White, 1981; Rasmussen, 1989).

**Table 14.** Simulated distributions of the test statistics

| R | | 36 | 37 | 38 | 39 | 40 | |
|---|---|---|---|---|---|---|---|
| 500 | : $\hat{P}(R)$ | 0.018 | 0.018 | 0.006 | 0.002 | 0.000 | |
| 2000 | : $\hat{P}(R)$ | 0.021 | 0.012 | 0.007 | 0.002 | 0.004 | |
| S | | 2.10 | 2.11 | 2.12 | 2.13 | 2.14 | 2.15 |
| 500 | : $\hat{P}(S)$ | 0.016 | 0.014 | 0.006 | 0.002 | – | 0.000 |
| 2000 | : $\hat{P}(S)$ | 0.013 | 0.012 | 0.007 | 0.003 | – | 0.003 |

## Monte Carlo tests

In a permutation test the exact distribution of the test statistic is evaluated under the randomization procedure. The data are treated as fixed and the individuals are allocated to the observations. The null hypothesis is one of no difference between the groups and the significance level associated with the hypothesis is obtained by evaluating the randomized distribution.

Monte Carlo tests are based on parametric models and can be used to test more general hypotheses. In such tests, data are simulated assuming that the null hypothesis is true. In this way the distribution of the test statistic under the null hypothesis is estimated and the test statistic calculated from the experimental data is compared to the simulated distribution.

Data from a free recall experiment are presented in Table 15. Twelve subjects were presented with a list of 36 photographs of famous personalities. These personalities were arranged in 6 clusters based on the occupation of the personalities though the presentation order was random. Data from a similar experiment are discussed in more detail in Robertson & Ellis (1987).

Cowan (1966) proposed a model of recall order which has been extended by Robertson (1982). If the association strength between two personalities is denoted $S(i,j)$ then the model postulates that the probability of a recall list conditional on the first item is

$$P(x_2, \ldots, x_m | x_1) = \prod_{i=1}^{m-1} \frac{S(x_i, x_{i+1})}{\sum_{j=1}^{n} \delta_{ij} S(x_i, j)},$$

where $x_i$ is the item recalled in position $i$, $m$ items are recalled and $n$ presented, and $\delta_{ij} = 1$ if item $j$ has yet to be recalled at position $i$, otherwise $\delta_{ij} = 0$. In this model the recall probabilities are ratios of association strengths. To take into account the effect of the six occupational categories of the personalities, it is postulated that $\ln S(i,j)) = 1 + \alpha$ if personalities $i$ and $j$ are in the same category,

**Table 15.** Recall lists for 12 subjects recalling names of personalities

| 25 | 27 | 26 | 18 | 8  | 11 | 29 | 10 | 2  | 19 | 9  | 35 | 34 |    |    |    |    |    |    |    |
| 28 | 21 | 30 | 3  | 35 | 1  | 6  | 33 | 7  | 8  | 4  | 11 |    |    |    |    |    |    | 11 | 29 |
| 31 | 4  | 24 | 33 | 5  | 12 | 26 | 16 | 15 | 9  | 21 | 20 | 28 | 10 | 25 | 27 | 30 | 35 | 2  |    |
| 35 | 5  | 10 | 11 | 28 | 30 | 22 | 16 | 14 | 33 | 6  | 7  | 20 | 26 | 19 | 27 | 25 |    |    |    |
| 13 | 18 | 15 | 16 | 29 | 6  | 5  | 28 | 35 | 32 | 33 | 4  | 13 | 26 | 36 | 2  |    |    |    |    |
| 12 | 11 | 27 | 25 | 28 | 30 | 7  | 6  | 1  | 36 | 10 | 13 | 25 | 22 | 31 | 22 | 13 |    | 30 |    |
| 7  | 12 | 28 | 30 | 5  | 6  | 4  | 11 | 14 | 26 | 27 | 25 | 33 | 20 | 30 | 20 | 27 | 28 |    |    |
| 6  | 11 | 9  | 28 | 30 | 15 | 29 | 2  | 10 | 13 | 16 | 24 | 21 | 13 | 25 | 27 |    |    |    |    |
| 11 | 30 | 28 | 1  | 16 | 32 | 27 | 25 | 26 | 6  | 4  | 36 | 9  |    |    |    |    |    |    |    |
| 16 | 22 | 33 | 15 | 20 | 19 | 4  | 36 | 21 | 10 | 11 | 25 | 15 |    |    |    |    |    |    |    |
| 35 | 33 | 2  | 18 | 17 | 34 | 11 | 6  | 7  | 23 | 21 | 3  | 32 |    |    |    |    |    |    |    |
| 28 | 30 | 4  | 5  | 6  | 1  | 11 | 9  | 13 | 25 | 27 | 15 | 31 | 31 |    |    |    |    |    |    |

Occupation Categories

| | | |
|---|---|---|
| (A) | 1–6   | Politicians |
| (B) | 7–12  | Pop singers |
| (C) | 13–18 | Film stars |
| (D) | 19–24 | TV personalities |
| (E) | 25–30 | Comedians |
| (F) | 31–36 | Sporting personalities |

otherwise $\ln(S(i,j)) = 1$. The parameter $\alpha$ is a measure of the clustering of personalities from the same category in the recall lists. The log link function is used to ensure that the association strengths will always be positive and the mean is set equal to 1 to ensure identifiability of the parameters. Details are in Robertson & Ellis (1987).

When this model is fitted to the data in Table 15 using maximum likelihood estimation, the estimate of the clustering parameter is $\hat{\alpha} = 1.34$ with an estimated (asymptotic) standard error of 0.204. The log-likelihood at the maximum is $-298.29$. If $\alpha$ is constrained to be zero then the model $\ln(S(i,j)) = 1$ is fitted. This model is completely specified and has a log-likelihood of $-318.52$. Comparing the two log-likelihoods yields a log-likelihood ratio test statistic of 40.46 on 1 degree of freedom.

In this example there are only 12 independent lists and, although there are many more transitions, these are not independent (see Robertson, 1990). Consequently it is not clear that the asymptotic properties of the maximum likelihood estimates are valid in this instance. A Monte Carlo test of the clustering model, $\ln(S(i,j)) = 1 + \alpha$, against the no clustering model, $\ln(S(i,j)) = 1$, is accomplished as follows. Generate $t$ sets of data based on the no clustering model. For each simulated set of data calculate the log-likelihood under both models and hence build up a set of $t$ values of the test statistic. Under the hypothesis that $\alpha = 0$ the $t$ simulated test statistics together with the observed value form a random sample of $(t+1)$ observations from the null distribution of the test statistic. If the observed value comes in the middle of this distribution then there is no evidence against the null hypothesis; if the observed value is in the tail of the distribution then there is such evidence. Suppose the observed value is the $k$th largest of the $t+1$ values then the significance level of this test is $k/(t+1)$. In practice, usually $t = 99$ is taken, though smaller values are occasionally used (Atkinson, 1985, p. 35).

In Figure 5, the stem and leaf plot of 99 simulated test statistics is presented. It is clear that the observed value of 40.5 is much larger than all of them and there is evidence at the 1% level that the clustering parameter is necessary. The goodness of fit of the clustering model can also be assessed by simulating data under the model with $\alpha = 1.34$. If the observed log-likelihood is consistent with the simulated values then the model can be considered adequate. Simulation tests can also be used to check the adequacy of the residuals from this and other models (see Atkinson, 1985, and Robertson, 1990).

The variability and bias of the estimate $\alpha$ can be assessed by using the bootstrap or jackknife approaches. Such checks are useful here as the maximum likelihood estimate may be biased in small samples. The results are presented in Table 16. These suggest that there is little bias and that the asymptotic standard error based on the information is valid. A 90% confidence interval for $\alpha$ using the percentile method is (0.99, 1.66), which compares favourably with the asymptotic interval (0.94, 1.74).

Leaf Unit = 0.10

```
(52)  0 000000000000000000000000011111111122222222233333333344
 47   0 555666678888999
 32   1 00111123
 24   1 9
 23   2 122233
 17   2 89
 15   3 012
 12   3 567899
  6   4 234
  3   4 7
  2   5 23
```

**Figure 5.** Stem and leaf plot of the 99 simulated values of the log likelihood ratio test statistic

**Table 16.** Bootstrap and Jackknife estimates of the clustering parameter

| JACKKNIFE | $\hat{\alpha}$ | $\hat{\alpha}_J$ | $\hat{b}_J$ | $\hat{\sigma}_J$ |
|---|---|---|---|---|
| | 1.338 | 1.336 | 0.002 | 0.228 |
| BOOTSTRAP ($B = 100$) | $\hat{\alpha}$ 1.338 | $\hat{\alpha}_B$ 1.337 | $\hat{b}_B$ −0.001 | $\hat{\sigma}_B$ 0.200 |

Monte Carlo tests are not without their difficulties (see, for example, Ripley, 1987, Chapter 7.1). From a practical point of view the main drawback is that the critical region of a test is random as it is based upon simulation. Conceivably, two experimenters with exactly the same data and fitting exactly the same models could come to different conclusions as a result of this. To ensure that this problem is minimized $t$ should be large and small values of $k$ avoided. For practical purposes 99 simulations are usually sufficient.

Also, Monte Carlo tests are only defined for simple null hypotheses which are completely specified. Consequently, the goodness of fit test described above is an extension, as the null hypothesis is composite. Care should be taken in extending Monte Carlo tests to composite hypotheses, though in the absence of any theory, performing simulations to check the adequacy of a model is better than doing nothing at all. This is similar to the conclusion regarding the use of the jackknife. Despite its drawbacks it is better to have some (imprecise) knowledge of variability than no knowledge at all (Mosteller & Tukey, 1977, p. 145).

## CONCLUSIONS

The topics discussed here are all relatively recent additions to statistics. The jackknife was introduced by Quenouille in 1949, the bootstrap by Efron in the mid 1970s and Monte Carlo tests were discussed by Barnard (1963). Randomized tests have been used for a considerable time and indeed form the basis for many nonparametric tests (Sprent, 1988). The resurgence of such tests and the use of the other procedures has been heralded by the widespread availability of computers. The advantages that these techniques bring are that parametric assumptions do not have to be made unless the experimenter wishes to do so. A parametric analysis, when appropriate, will be more efficient. The nonparametric approach is relatively crude but is more trustworthy.

To an extent, all of these approaches require experimentation. While it might appear a daunting task for a person who does not deal with computers to consider such techniques the rewards are there. Also the time taken is not particularly great. Many of the simulations and resamplings can be carried out within a statistical package such as MINITAB (Ryan *et al.* 1985) by writing macros. Indeed, some versions of the package, s, (Becker & Chambers, 1984) have a special command which allows one to perform bootstrap samplings for any statistic. The simulation and statistics package, SMTBPC, (Lewis *et al.* 1986, Lewis & Orav, 1989) has jackknife and bootstrap facilities. Generally Monte Carlo tests require specially written programs.

As much of this work involves simulation using random numbers generated on computers it is important to use a good and well tested generator. All of the results may be invalid if a biased random number generator is used. Ripley (1987, Chapter 2) stresses this point and provides a number of tests (see also Morgan, 1984).

With the bootstrap and Monte Carlo methods relevant properties of a statistical procedure are simulated. In the case of the bootstrap minimal model assumptions are made. Simulations can be used with permutation tests to yield an estimate of the distribution of the test statistic. The jackknife does not use simulation but Efron & Gong (1983) discuss its similarities to the bootstrap.

One advantage of the jackknife over the bootstrap is that it is balanced. Each observation is deleted in turn whereas with the bootstrap the observations may not be resampled an equal number of times. Hinkley (1988) discusses balanced sampling in the context of the bootstrap. There is a potential here for reducing the number of bootstrap samples required at the expense of a more complicated sampling procedure. Another possible advantage of the jackknife is that it can be extended to the deletion of observations in groups (see Miller, 1974). This makes it attractive in large samples (Tukey, 1986), where the selection of many bootstrap samples may prove to be very time consuming.

Efron & Gong (1983) discuss the links between the jackknife, bootstrap and cross validation. The jackknife has more potential here as a comparison of $\hat{\theta}_{(i)}$ with $\hat{\theta}$ will provide some idea of the effect of the $i$th observation on the estimate. This technique is used extensively in diagnostic methods in regression analysis (see, for example, Chapter 5 in this volume; Cook & Weisberg, 1982; and Atkinson, 1985). The use of the bootstrap in regression analysis has also been considered. This is discussed by Hinkley (1988), Efron & Gong (1983), Efron & Tibshirani (1986), and Hall (1988). The main thrust here is in inferences about the regression parameters often within the realms of robust estimation.

Both the jackknife and bootstrap are useful methods of eliminating bias in an estimator. This is particularly useful when estimating a ratio such as a ratio of two means which is a common requirement in surveys (Cochran, 1977). Standard methods of obtaining standard errors are approximate and the jackknife and bootstrap correct the bias as well as estimating the variability. It should be noted that the jackknife and bootstrap will only eliminate bias of order $1/n$ (Miller, 1974; Efron & Gong, 1983). They do not eliminate all bias, though the jackknife can be extended (Miller, 1974; Lewis & Orav, 1989, p. 271).

It is in the area of interval estimation that the bootstrap performs better than the jackknife. The repeated resampling of the data allows the estimation of the distribution of $\hat{\theta}$ and hence confidence limits can be calculated. Jackknife confidence limits rely on a normal approximation and hence are symmetric. In small samples particularly, the distribution of $\hat{\theta}$ can be skew and asymmetric intervals are required. Consequently the bootstrap approach is likely to be more useful.

It also appears that the bootstrap is applicable over a wider range of parameters than the jackknife. The jackknife only really works well if the estimator is a linear combination of the data. It is not good with single order statistics as very few distinct pseudo-values result (Mosteller & Tukey, 1977, p. 162).

There have also been attempts to link the bootstrap to significance tests (Hinkley, 1988). This relies on resampling from the distribution of the data under a null hypothesis. In some cases this can be achieved (Young, 1986), but in general appears to be an area in which research is required. The difficulty lies in using $\hat{F}(x)$ as an estimate of $F(x)$ under the null hypothesis. In cases where a bootstrap test can be derived there are very close ties with randomization tests. The difference lies in sampling with replacement in the bootstrap and without replacement in the randomization.

Randomization tests have clear links with many of the classical nonparametric tests. Indeed, the permutation methods of deriving the distribution are exactly the same (Sprent, 1988). The main difference is in the interpretation in that the nonparametric tests are based on assumptions of sampling from a population. The randomization tests take the data as being the only population about which an inference is to be made. There is also more scope for using a more informative test statistic. Classical nonparametric methods use the ranks and signs of the data whereas permutation tests can be applied to the observed data. Thus all the information in the data can be retained which should lead to more powerful tests.

Monte Carlo tests are an intuitively appealing approach and are a practical answer in small samples especially when most of the distributional results are asymptotic. The use of such tests is likely to be greatest when specific stochastic models are used, for example, in models of memory (Murdock, 1974) and other psychological processes (Batchelder & Reifer, 1986). In many experiments it is required to check whether or not the data are adequately described by a model and also to see if any model parameters can be omitted. Monte Carlo tests have a place here, particularly if the data are limited.

## References

ATKINSON, A. C. (1985). *Plots, Transformations and Regression Diagnostics*. Oxford: Oxford University Press.

BARNARD, G. (1963). Contribution to the discussion of Bartlett's paper. *Journal of the Royal Statistical Society, Series B*, 25, 294.

BATCHELDER, W. H. & REIFER, D. M. (1986). The statistical analysis of a model for storage and retrieval processes in human memory. *British Journal of Mathematical and Statistical Psychology*, 39, 129–149.

BECKER, R. A. & CHAMBERS, J. M. (1984). *S-An Interactive Environment for Data Analysis and Graphics*. Monterey, California: Wadsworth.

COCHRAN, W. G. (1977). *Sampling Techniques*, 3rd ed. New York: Wiley.

COOK, R. D. & WEISBERG, S. (1982). *Residuals and Influence in Regression*. London: Chapman and Hall.

COWAN, T. M. (1966). A Markov model for the order of emission in free recall. *Journal of Mathematical Psychology*, 3, 470–483.

DIACONIS, P. & EFRON, B. (1983). Computer intensive methods in statistics. *Scientific American*, 248 (5), 96–108.

DICICCIO, T. J. & ROMANO, J. P. (1988). A review of bootstrap confidence intervals. *Journal of the Royal Statistical Society, Series B*, 50, 338–354.

DICICCIO, T. M. & TIBSHIRANI, R. (1987). Bootstrap confidence intervals and bootstrap approximations. *Journal of the American Statistical Association*, 82, 163–170.

EDGINGTON, E. W. (1987). *Randomization Tests*, 2nd ed. New York: Marcel Dekker.

EFRON, B. (1982). The jackknife, bootstrap and other resampling plans. In *Regional Conference Series in Applied Mathematics, No. 38*. Philadelphia: SIAM.

EFRON, B. (1987). Better bootstrap confidence intervals. *Journal of the American Statistical Association*, 82, 171–185.

EFRON, B. & GONG, G. (1983). A leisurely look at the bootstrap, jackknife and cross validation. *American Statistician*, 37, 36–48.

EFRON, B. & TIBSHIRANI, R. (1986). Bootstrap methods for standard errors, confidence intervals, and other measures. *Statistical Science*, 1, 54–77.

HALL, P. (1988). On symmetric bootstrap confidence intervals. *Journal of the Royal Statistical Society, Series B*, 50, 35–45.

HINKLEY, D. V. (1988). Bootstrap methods. *Journal of the Royal Statistical Society, Series B*, 50, 321–337.

JOHNSON, N. & KOTZ, S. (1970). *Continuous Univariate Distributions, Volume 2*. Boston: Houghton Mifflin.

LEWIS, P. A. W. & ORAV, E. J. (1989). *Simulation Methodology for Statisticians, Operations Analysts and Engineers, Volume 1*. Pacific Grove, California: Wadsworth & Brooks/Cole.

LEWIS, P. A. W., ORAV, E. J. & URIBE, L. (1986). *Advanced Simulation and Statistics Package*. Pacific Grove, California: Wadsworth and Brooks/Cole.

MEAD, R. (1988). *The Design of Experiments*. Cambridge: Cambridge University Press.

MILLER, R. G. (1974). The jackknife – a review. *Biometrika*, **61**, 1–15.

MORGAN, B. J. T. (1984). *The Elements of Simulation*. London: Chapman & Hall.

MOSTELLER, F. & TUKEY, J. W. (1977). *Data Analysis and Regression*. Reading, Mass: Addison-Wesley.

MURDOCK, B. B. (1974). *Human Memory: Theory and Data*. Potomac, M.D.: Erlbaum.

QUENOUILLE, M. H. (1949). Approximate tests of correlation in time series. *Journal of the Royal Statistical Society, Series B*, **11**, 68–84.

RASMUSSEN, J. L. (1989). Computer intensive correlation analysis: Bootstrap and approximate randomization techniques. *British Journal of Mathematical and Statistical Psychology*, **42**, 103–112.

RIPLEY, B. D. (1987). *Stochastic Simulation*. New York: Wiley.

ROBERTSON, C. (1982). Modelling recall order in free recall experiments. *British Journal of Mathematical and Statistical Psychology*, **35**, 171–182.

ROBERTSON, C. (1990). A matrix regression model for the transition probabilities in a finite state stochastic process. *Applied Statistics*, **39**, 1–19.

ROBERTSON, C. & ELLIS, H. (1987). Estimating the effects of various clustering schemes on recall order. *British Journal of Mathematical and Statistical Psychology*, **40**, 1–19.

RYAN, B. F., JOINER, B. L. & RYAN, T. A. (1985). *Minitab Handbook*, 2nd ed. Boston: PWS-Kent.

SPRENT, P. (1988). *Applied Nonparametric Statistical Methods*. London: Chapman & Hall.

STERNBERG, R. J. & TULVING, E. (1977). The measurement of subjective organisation in free recall. *Psychological Bulletin*, **84**, 539–556.

STILL, A. W. & WHITE, A. P. (1981). The approximate randomization test as an alternative to the *F* test in analysis of variance. *British Journal of Mathematical and Statistical Psychology*, **34**, 243–252.

TODMAN, J. B. (1982). Sequential consistency and subjective clustering in the multitrial free recall of children. *Acta Psychologica*, **51**, 163–180.

TODMAN, J. B. & FILE, P. E. (1983). Output organization in the free recall of mildly retarded children. Unpublished report, University of Dundee.

TUKEY, J. W. (1986). Sunset Salvo. *American Statistician*, **40**, 72–76.

VINOD, H. D. & RAJ, B. (1988). Economic issues in Bell System divestiture. *Applied Statistics*, **37**, 251–261.

YOUNG, A. (1986). Conditioned data-based simulations: some examples from geometrical statistics. *International Statistical Review*, **54**, 1–13.

# 4

# Classification Trees

## DAVID HAND

The most widespread technique for formulating classification rules using a sample of cases belonging to known classes is the Fisher-Anderson classical discriminant analysis approach. This is based on first and second order statistics and, in theory at least, is only suited to continuous interval scaled data. The ubiquity of this method is accounted for in part by its early origin (Fisher, 1936) and in part by the fact that the method often performs well on data for which theory suggests poor performance in principle. However, other techniques also exist (see Hand, 1981, for a review). For example, a completely different class of techniques is represented by nonparametric kernel and nearest neighbour methods. These are now beginning to find their way into the large statistical software packages (for example, a basic nearest neighbour routine is included in the SAS system).

Kernel and nearest neighbour methods are very much products of the computer age. Without the abilities for high speed computation and rapid search of modern computers, such methods would have been completely non feasible. Another approach, and also one whose practical development has been stimulated by the computer, is the classification tree approach.

The ideas of classification trees have a long and respectable history, and have appeared under many guises – sometimes with researchers in one field being unaware of parallel or earlier work in other fields. Prior to the development of the computer, however, the construction of classification trees used *ad hoc* methods, based on the knowledge or opinion of experts. Nowadays trees can be constructed from samples of cases of known classification, permitting optimal (in a sense described below) and objective trees to be built, and also making use of very large data sets. The development of programs for this kind of problem has also encouraged their application in an exploratory mode. In view of this, it will hardly be surprising to learn that much of the motivation for the further development of such approaches has come from social and behavioural scientists.

Examples of early computer programs along these lines are AID and THAID (Morgan & Sonquist, 1963; Morgan & Messenger, 1973; Fielding, 1977). More recently, a number of other research groups have published papers describing similar programs (e.g. Sturt, 1981*a,b*; Mabbett *et al.*, 1980; Breiman *et al.*,

1984; Loh & Vanichsetakul, 1988). In the related field of identification keys in taxonomy algorithms have been presented by several authors, including early ones by Pankhurst (1970), Hall (1970), Morse (1971), and Payne (1974). Payne & Preece (1980) give an excellent survey of work in this area.

Research in the discipline of artificial intelligence has stimulated work in similar directions. The fundamental problem there is one of automating the knowledge acquisition process for expert systems, in an attempt to overcome the difficulties inherent in getting experts to articulate the basis of their expertise. Examples of this work are Quinlan (1979), Clark & Niblett (1987), and Bratko & Kononenko (1987).

As with other techniques for discriminant analysis and classification, such as those referred to above, we should recognize that there are two potential objectives in building a classification tree. One is to produce a rule by which new cases can be classified, and the other is to gain an understanding of which variables are important in distinguishing between the various classes.

Tree methods are probably best applied if the former is the objective. Of the latter, Breiman *et al.* (1984) say: 'We have found this a hazardous and chancy business. Even though the tree structured approach generally gives better insights into the structure than most competing methods, extensive exploration and careful interpretation are necessary to arrive at sound conclusions.'

Of course, one could argue that this final sentiment is true of all exploratory statistical methods. In general, one should never throw data at a statistical algorithm without thinking carefully about what one is trying to do.

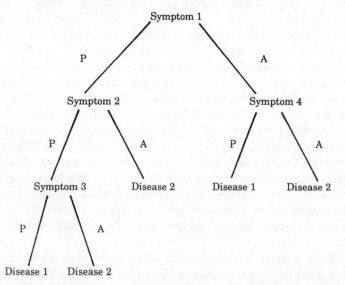

**Figure 1.** An imaginary tree for classifying patients as suffering from disease 1 or 2. (P = present; A = absent)

## THE BASIC METHOD

Figure 1 illustrates an imaginary tree constructed for classifying hospital patients into one of two disease classes. To classify a new case one first notes whether symptom 1 is present or absent. If it is absent one examines symptom 4. Its presence signifies disease type 1 and its absence disease type 2. If symptom 1 is present, however, one looks for symptom 2. And so on. Real examples are given below. This particular example is a *binary tree* because at each node (i.e., each symptom evaluation) there are only two possible outcomes. Other trees, also illustrated below, permit more than two possible outcomes.

In general, to classify a new case, one works down the tree until a *leaf* or *terminal node* is reached. Each such node is given a class label and cases ending up there are classified accordingly. Typically, of course, each class will have more than one leaf node associated with it.

Application of a classification tree, once constructed, is thus very straightforward (and very rapid – which can be important in some applications). Interest in trees, and the thrust of recent developments, lies in their construction.

The basic method is as follows. A 'learning sample' ('design set ', 'training sample') of $n$ cases of known classification is taken and all relevant variables are measured on these $n$ cases. This set of $n$ cases comprises the initial (root) node of the classification tree. The variables are then examined to identify that variable and that division of the values of the variable (most commonly into two groups) such that the resulting two subsets of cases are each 'purer' than the original set of $n$ cases. 'Purer' here means that each of the subsets is more clearly dominated by a particular class or classes than was the original set. Figure 2 illustrates this. Here the initial node has 53% cases from class 2. Node 2, however, has 64% belonging to class 1, while node 3 has 83% belonging to class 2. Thus, in moving

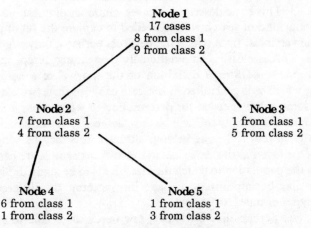

**Figure 2.** A simple tree showing how node purity increases as one works down the tree.

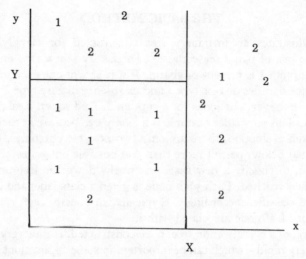

**Figure 3.** A way of viewing the effect of the sequence of partitions.

down the tree from node 1 to either of nodes 2 or 3, one increases one's chance of correctly classifying a case. This increase in accuracy is obtained by virtue of knowledge of the value of $x$, the variable used to split node 1.

More accuracy still might be obtained by splitting the nodes yet further. For example, Figure 2 shows that splitting node 2 according to whether or not $y$ is greater than $Y$ yields nodes with 86% belonging to class 1 and 75% belonging to class 2.

A useful way of conceptualizing the effect of the splits is shown in Figure 3. Each split partitions a region of the $x/y$ space into smaller subregions in such a way that each subregion is more clearly dominated by some class than was the parent region. This basic description leaves a number of questions unanswered.

First, some kind of search will be needed to explore the set of possible splits on possible variables, from which the best (or, perhaps, only a 'good') split can be chosen. This is clearly computationally demanding except in the simplest cases. Second, some formal definition of the 'purity' of a node is needed – something which will generalize to the case of more than two classes.

Third, some rule is needed for determining to which class a final leaf node will be assigned. Typically this will be the class to which the majority of learning sample cases in that leaf node belong, although this may be weighted to take account of the fact that the class sizes in the learning sample are not proportional to those in the population to which the classifier is to be applied. Similarly, some weighting may be appropriate to take into account the differential costs of different types of misclassification.

Finally, and perhaps less obviously, one needs to be able to decide when a node is a leaf node – when splitting should stop. A superficially obvious approach is to keep splitting until all leaf nodes are homogeneous; that is, all contain members of just one class. This would lead to an overall impurity measure of zero for the tree. However, recall that the aim is not to produce a tree which perfectly classifies the learning sample, but to produce a tree which is sufficiently accurate when applied to future cases. For any learning sample one can always produce a tree with zero impurity (for example, by taking the tree which has $n$ leaf nodes, one for each learning sample point.) But samples are only samples, and it is likely that new cases will differ from those in the learning samples so that 100% accuracy will not be achieved on new cases.

In fact, the situation is worse than this. By taking the tree too far we are *overfitting* the learning data and reducing the accuracy of classification which could be obtained if we stopped earlier.

Early work and some more recent work (see, for example, Loh & Vanichsetakul, 1988) attempted to define a stopping rule, so that splitting of nodes continues until no split leads to sufficient improvement in some sense (see below). Such an approach has the disadvantage that some split may in itself be poor (so the tree will not be developed past it) while it might lead to very effective splits later on (which will never be discovered).

In fact this sort of difficulty is ubiquitous in statistical problems involving search; for example, it also occurs in variable selection in regression and discriminant analysis. A stepwise approach is often adopted whereby at each step the best next variable is added. Unfortunately 'best next' does not lead to a final set which guarantees global best – and the alternative of explicitly examining every possible subset is typically too time-consuming. Attempts to tackle this have been made involving both adding and removing variables in order to arrive at a good subset. As we shall see, similar attempts have been made in classification tree construction.

## SPLITTING RULES

A splitting rule is a prescription for deciding which variable should be used to divide the cases in a node into subgroups and where the threshold(s) defining the split(s) should be. As was remarked at the end of the preceding section, recursive application of a splitting rule is effectively a stepwise procedure which it is hoped will lead to a good tree – though there is no guarantee that it will be best. (Dynamic programming techniques have been applied to produce globally optimal trees, but such methods are much more time-consuming than stepwise methods.)

Many splitting rules are based on 'impurity measures'; that is, measures of the extent to which a particular node contains learning sample cases from multiple classes: measures of node homogeneity. Such a measure should take its largest value when all classes are equally represented, its smallest value when the node contains members of a single class, and will be restricted to non-negative values. Normally one would also require the function to be symmetric in the way it treats the different classes. Thus, if $i(t)$ is the impurity measure at node $t$ and $p(j|t)$ is the proportion of cases at this node which belong to class $j$ then $i(t) = \Phi[p(1|t), \ldots, p(c|t)]$, $c$ being the number of classes, with maximum $\Phi$ at $p(1|t) = \ldots = p(c|t)$, and minimum at $(p(k|t) = 1, p(j|t) = 0$, for $j \neq k)$ for all $k = 1, \ldots, c$.

If an impurity measure is used, one will seek the split which maximizes the impurity decrease at each node. That is, one will seek to maximize

$$i(t) - p(t_R)i(t_R) - p(t_L)i(t_L)$$

(in a binary tree) where $t_R$ and $t_L$ refer to right and left descendant nodes respectively and $p(x)$ is the proportion of cases in node $x$. Following from this, an overall tree impurity can also by simply defined as

$$\sum_t p(t)i(t),$$

where the summation is over leaf nodes.

Perhaps the most obvious choice of splitting rule is based on resubstitution error rate; that is, simply count the number of learning sample points misclassified after a proposed split. This, however, has disadvantages. First, it is possible that the child nodes each have a majority from class 1 (say) for all possible splits. In this case there will be no change in resubstitution error rate when a split is made. Secondly, a good rule will tend to identify subgroups which can be accurately classified with a great degree of certainty. Consider Figure 4, for example (from Breiman *et al.*, 1984). In (a) the split leads to a resubstitution estimate of $200/800 = 0.25$. In split (b) the resubstitution estimate is also $0.25$. However, in (a) each subnode has 25% misclassified – hence requiring further partitioning. In (b) 200 of the cases are classified apparently without error. Such a high degree of confidence leads to preferring (b) over (a). Breiman *et al.* (1984), for the two class case, present a simple modification using a quadratic in the resubstitution error to overcome this problem. Finally Breiman *et al.* (1984) suggest that the single node resubstitution error rate criterion does not lead to a globally good tree and that other criteria are better.

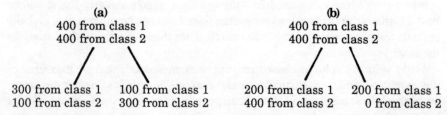

**Figure 4.** Alternative splits with the same resubstitution error rate. One is preferable to the other.

For multiclass cases Breiman *et al.* (1984) suggest the Gini index of diversity

$$i(t) = \sum_{i \neq j} p(i|t)p(j|t)$$

and the 'twoing rule'

$$\frac{p(t_L)\, p(t_R)}{4} \left[ \sum_{j} \left| p(j|t_L) - p(j|t_R) \right| \right]^2 .$$

This rule is based on the idea of grouping the classes into two sets of classes, and then finding the split which best separates the cases comprising the two sets. This apparently tends to group similar classes together near the tree's root while tending to isolate single classes near the leaves.

Loh & Vanichsetakul (1988) find the variable with the largest between to within class variance ratio and use this if it is greater than a threshold. If it is less than the threshold, the splits are based on dispersion.

There is obviously scope for creativity in choice of splitting rule and many others have been explored. We shall introduce some more below in the context of other variants of tree methods.

## STOPPING, PRUNING, AND SHRINKING

I remarked earlier that classification accuracy for future cases decreases if a tree is grown too large. Recognizing this, researchers have attempted to define stopping rules: deciding not to split a node if the best available split produces an impurity decrease of less than some threshold. Examples of stopping rules are Sturt's (1981a) $\chi^2$ based rule and the cross-validation approach of Mabbett *et al.* (1980). The former of these involves comparing the $\chi^2$ statistic of the cross-tabulation of class by proposed nodes with a threshold. A high $\chi^2$ value is indicative of different proportions being assigned to different nodes. Mabbett *et al.* (1980) calculate a loss function based on comparing each learning case's true classification with the predicted classification derived using the other cases. They illustrate this using a $\chi^2$ scoring function.

Stopping rules have the potential disadvantage that they may lead to stopping tree growth before a very powerful split has been made – a poor split being a necessary precursor of the highly effective split.

In an effort to overcome this Breiman *et al.* (1984) adopted a 'pruning' strategy, whereby the tree was grown large and then had its leaf nodes merged back to produce a smaller tree. As remarked above, there is a parallel here to stepwise addition and removal of variables in some multiple regression algorithms. Again various measures have been explored, Brieman *et al.* (1984) suggesting a 'cost-complexity' compromise which attempts to combine the number of nodes and the misclassification rate.

Pruning is a way of achieving a compromise between bias and variance. The larger the tree (the less pruning) the smaller the leaf nodes and so the greater the variance of the proportion belonging to each class – but the closer the expected proportions within that node will be to the probabilities that cases will belong to the classes. Conversely, for large leaf nodes bias may be great for some cases in the node, while the variance of the estimated proportions will be small.

This problem is ubiquitous throughout statistics, and a classical approach is to *shrink* estimates towards some value. In the case of tree classifiers Pregibon (1989, personal communication) has suggested shrinking the proportions of cases in the leaf nodes back up the tree towards the proportions in their parent nodes. That is, one takes a weighted combination of the leaf and parent proportions. Shrinking in this way decreases the variance from that in the smaller leaf node but again at the risk of increased bias.

## OTHER ASPECTS

I have already remarked that the resubstitution estimate has disadvantages as a measure of performance. In general it is optimistic, since it involves reclassifying data which the classification rule (tree, in this case) has been designed to classify optimally. Moreover, blind application leads to larger trees being favoured. Table 1, from Breiman *et al.* (1984) illustrates the effect, showing that the resubstitution rate decreases with increasing number of nodes while an estimate based on an independent test set first decreases and then increases.

**Table 1.** Resubstitution and independent test set estimates of error rates against increasing number of nodes

| Number of terminal nodes | Resubstitution estimate | Test set estimate |
|---|---|---|
| 1 | 0.86 | 0.91 |
| 5 | 0.53 | 0.61 |
| 10 | 0.29 | 0.30 |
| 40 | 0.10 | 0.32 |
| 63 | 0.00 | 0.40 |
| 71 | 0.00 | 0.42 |

If large amounts of data are available then a test set can be used. If not then cross-validation is popular, as with other discriminant rules (see Hand, 1986). With other methods the class of bootstrap techniques, due to Efron (1983), are also popular. For large trees, however, the bootstrap method can be substantially biased. In general, it seems that the performance assessment area could be further developed, especially given the rich diversity of methods that have been explored for other classification techniques.

In Figure 3 we saw that, for ordinal variables, the methods described above which split according to scores on single variables at a time produce splits orthogonal to the other variables. If the true separating surface is not orthogonal to the variables then a complex tree can result, where a very simple non-orthogonal separating surface might be possible. Thus, if one permits the use of non-orthogonal splits, considerable simplification in tree topology might result, (but at a cost of possible difficulty in terms of interpretation or explaining which variables are important).

Non-orthogonal splits compare functions of the form $\Sigma a_i x_i$ with a threshold, where the $a_i$ are weights and the $x_i$ are the scores. Classical methods of discrimination also use such linear combinations – but only one, not a sequential set. The combination of the two approaches produces a very rich and flexible tool. Such a combination is described by Loh & Vanichsetakul (1988), who use Fisher's discriminant analysis with a tree. (It seems that one potential problem with this approach is that as the tree grows so the subsamples in the nodes tend to have singular covariance matrices. Loh & Vanichsetakul sidestep this problem by using only the larger principal components at each node.)

Missing values can also cause problems with conventional discrimination techniques. If linear functions are computed, then missing values mean a case's score cannot be evaluated. Similar problems arise if cases with missing values are to be used to build a classifier.

For tree classifiers, construction will be based on scores which are present. When classifying a case with missing values, a common approach is to use surrogate variables, splitting on a variable most closely related (in some sense) to the missing one. One can also adopt procedures which have been developed for conventional classifiers such as replacing missing values by means (see, for example, Loh & Vanichsetakul, 1988).

In classical discriminant analysis and regression analysis high correlation between predictor variables leads to instability of the associated estimated coefficients, so that a small change in the learning sample can lead to a big change in the estimate. A similar phenomenon can occur in tree classifiers, where high correlation can induce instability in the tree topology – slight changes in the learning sample causing splits to be made on different variables. The importance of this depends on the objectives of building the tree. If classification of new cases is the aim then internal topology is unimportant, but if interpretation, in terms of which variables matter, is the aim, then things may be more problematic. This also parallels the classical situation.

Most of the discussion so far refers to binary trees; trees for which each node has two branches. Sometimes, however, it may be more convenient to have more than two branches. Sturt (1981*a,b*) describes one approach to such trees. She assumes categorical variables and lets each node produce as many branches as there are categories in the variable on which the split is to be made. One property of such an approach is that each variable need only be looked at once. Another property is that no splitting rule need be defined. Instead one simply needs a measure of how well each variable separates the classes at a given node.

Sturt defines such a measure as follows. For the node in question, let $N_{ij}$ be the number of elements from class $i$ scoring value $j$. Then define

$$D = \sum_j \max_i (N_{ij}).$$

For a particular category $j$ of the variable, this finds the class with the largest number of cases in the node and sums this over all the categories. $D$ is thus a measure of the discriminating power of the variable in question.

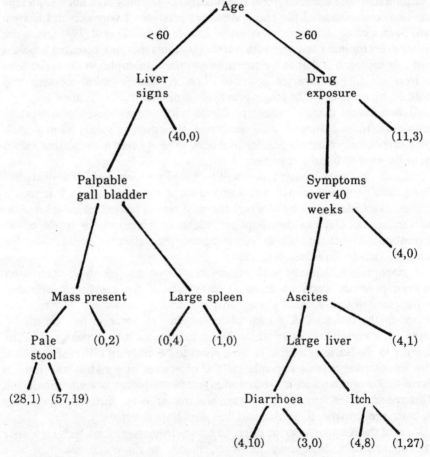

**Figure 5.** Tree for classifying jaundice patients (from Mabbett *et al.*, 1980).

## SOME EXAMPLES

Mabbett *et al.* (1980) give examples of three trees constructed using their approach. One of them involves using 28 binary variables (symptoms) to classify a patient suffering from jaundice as a medical or surgical case. The learning sample had 162 medical and 75 surgical cases. Twelve of the 28 variables were used in the tree, which is shown in Figure 5.

Sturt (1981a) classified people as psychiatric cases and non-cases using her tree method. Case definition was based on the 'index of definition' and the Present State Examination (Wing *et al.*, 1978) and the variables were also those of the Present State Examination. (This means that the aim was not to build a classifier, but to explore similarities and differences between the objective tree approach and the human diagnostic approach.) Sturt reports results of applying the method to two samples. The tree in Figure 6 is for a sample of 237 women aged 18–65 living in Camberwell.

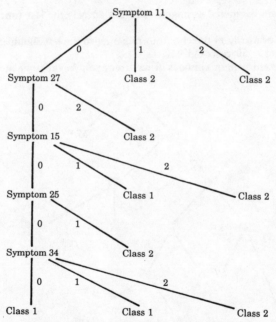

**Figure 6.** Tree for classifying subjects according to psychiatric caseness (from Sturt, 1981a). Class 1 is non-case; class 2 is case.

Goldman *et al.* (1982) applied the tree methodology to chest pain and myocardial infarction. About two-thirds of patients admitted to hospital with myocardial infarction suffer from chest pain. However, the presence of chest pain does not imply a myocardial infarction. Since it is obviously essential to try to avoid mistakenly refusing admission to infarct cases there is a natural tendency to admit all patients with chest pain. In some cases this has gone so far that only 30% of patients admitted to coronary care units turn out to be suffering from acute myocardial infarction. Considerable savings could be made if identification was more precise.

Figure 7 shows the tree produced by Goldman *et al.* (1982). The numbers correspond to symptoms as follows:

1. Does the emergency room EKG show ST-segment elevation or a Q wave that is suggestive of infarction and is not known to be old?
2. Did the present pain or episodes of recurrent pain begin 42 or more hours ago?
3. Is the pain primarily in the chest but radiating to the shoulder, neck, or arms?
4. Is the present pain (a) similar to but somehow worse than prior pain diagnosed as angina or (b) the same as pain previously diagnosed as MI?
5. Was the chest pain associated with diaphoresis?
6. Does the emergency-room EKG show ST or T wave changes that are suggestive of ischemia or strain and not known to be old?
7. Does local pressure reduce the pain?
8. Is the patient ≥ 70 years old?
9. Is the patient ≥ 40 years old?
10. Was this pain diagnosed as angina (and not an MI) the last time the patient had it?
11. Is the pain primarily in the chest but radiating to the left shoulder?
12. Is the patient ≥ 50 years old?
13. Did the present pain or episodes of recurrent pain begin 10 or more hours ago?

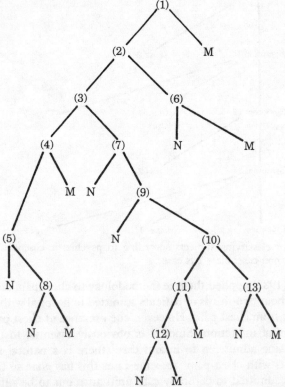

**Figure 7.** A tree classifier for patients with acute chest pain (from Goldman *et al.*, 1982). N = non-myocardial infarction. M = myocardial infarction. Left branch from each node is always 'no'.

## CONCLUSION

Tree based methods for classification have a long history but it is only with the advent of the electronic computer that it has become feasible to build such trees objectively from samples of cases of known classification. Within the last 15 or so years, however, such methods have been widely applied, with research groups working, often independently, in many disciplines, including statistics, artificial intelligence, biological taxonomy, medicine, psychology and sociology.

Tree methods have some obvious appeal. They do not make the (often gross) assumptions about the population distributions made by other methods of classification, and they will handle mixed variable types with ease. Despite this promise, however, there is as yet no very clear evidence that tree methods do substantially better than other methods. It will also be clear from the above that there are many ways in which trees can be built. Although some conclusions are emerging (that, for example, pruning is more effective than stopping) there is as yet no general consensus on best tree methods. It is an area which would benefit from further exploration. In any case, the flexibility and generality of tree methods, in addition to the ease with which one can communicate the ideas to non-statisticians, means that they are a very useful addition to the statistician's armoury.

**References**

BRATKO, I. & KONONENKO, I. (1987). Learning diagnostic rules from incomplete and noisy data. In R. Phelps (Ed.), *Interactions in Artificial Intelligence and Statistical Methods*. Aldershot: Gower Technical Press.

BREIMAN, L., FRIEDMAN, J. H., OLSHEN, R. A. & STONE, C. J. (1984). *Classification and Regression Trees*. Belmont, California: Wadsworth.

CLARK, P. & NIBLETT, T. (1987). Learning if then rules in noisy domains. In R. Phelps (Ed.), *Interactions in Artificial Intelligence and Statistical Methods*. Aldershot: Gower Technical Press.

EFRON, B. (1983). Estimating the error rate of a prediction rule: improvements on cross-validation. *Journal of the American Statistical Association*, **78**, 316–331.

FIELDING, A. (1977). Binary segmentation: The automatic interaction detector and related techniques for exploring data structure. In C. A. O'Muircheartaigh & C. Payne (Eds), *The Analysis of Survey Data, Vol. I: Exploring Data Structures*. New York: Wiley.

FISHER, R. A. (1936). The use of multiple measurements in taxonomic problems. *Annals of Eugenics*, **7**, 179–188.

GOLDMAN, L., WEINBERG, M., WEISBERG, M., OLSHEN, R., COOK, E. F., SARGENT, R. K., LAMAS, G. A., DENNIS, C., WILSON, C., DECKELBAUM, L., FINEBERG, H., STIRATELLI, R., and the MEDICAL HOUSE STAFF at Yale – New Haven and Brigham Women's Hospital (1982). A computer derived protocol to aid in the diagnosis of emergency room patients with chest pain. *New England Journal of Medicine*, **307**, 588–596.

HALL, A. V. (1970). A computer-based system for forming identification keys. *Taxon*, **19**, 12–18.

HAND, D. J. (1981). *Discrimination and Classification*. Chichester: John Wiley & Sons.

HAND, D. J. (1986). Recent advances in error rate estimation. *Pattern Recognition Letters*, **4**, 335–346.

LOH, W-Y. & VANICHSETAKUL, N. (1988). Tree-structured classification via generalized discriminant analysis. *Journal of the American Statistical Association*, **83**, 715–725.

MABBETT, A., STONE, M., & WASHBROOK, J. (1980). Cross-validatory selection of binary variables in differential diagnosis. *Applied Statistics*, **29**, 198–204.

MORGAN, J. N. & MESSENGER, R. C. (1973). THAID: A Sequential Search Program for the Analysis of Nominal Scale Dependent Variables. Ann Arbor: Institute for Social Research, University of Michigan.

MORGAN, J. N. & SONQUIST, J. A. (1963). Problems in the analysis of survey data, and a proposal. *Journal of the American Statistical Association*, **58**, 415–434.

MORSE, L. E. (1971). Specimen identification and key construction with time sharing computers. *Taxon*, **20**, 269–282.

PANKHURST, R. J. (1970). A computer program for generating diagnostic keys. *Computer Journal*, **13**, 145–151.

PAYNE, R. W. (1974). Genkey: a program for constructing diagnostic keys. In R. J. Pankhurst, (Ed.), *Biological Identification with Computers*. London: Academic Press.

PAYNE, R. W. & PREECE, D. A. (1980). Identification keys and diagnostic tables: a review. *Journal of the Royal Statistical Society, Series A*, **143**, 253–292.

QUINLAN, J. R. (1979). Discovering rules by induction from large collections of examples. In D. Michie (Ed.), *Expert Systems in the Micro-electronic Age*. Edinburgh: Edinburgh University Press.

STURT, E. (1981a). Computerized construction in Fortran of a discriminant function for categorical data. *Applied Statistics*, **30**, 213–222.

STURT, E. (1981b). An algorithm to construct a discriminant function in Fortran for categorical data. *Applied Statistics*, **30**, 313–325.

WING, J. K., MANN, S. A., LEFF, J. P., & NIXON, J. M. (1978). The concept of a 'case' in psychiatric population surveys. *Psychological Medicine*, **8**, 203–217.

# 5

# Regression Diagnostics

## A Rough Guide to Safer Regression

PAT LOVIE

For well behaved data least squares offers a simple and elegant method of fitting a linear regression model. Unfortunately, for many 'real life' situations model fitting by this method is a risky business with a multitude of tank traps for the unwary.

Difficulties will arise whenever a proposed model is deficient in some way as a vehicle for explaining the data. Such inadequacy may be in respect of the assumptions made, the variables or the observations. For example, the relationship between the response and explanatory variables may be nonlinear or too weak without additional predictors; the assumptions about the form of the errors may not be met; correlations between the explanatory variables may lead to computational problems.

The causes of such deficiencies may be endemic and thus require radical and global treatment. Sometimes, however, the culprits are revealed as one or more discrepant observations which exert an unjustified degree of influence in determining the fitted model. In either situation, we try to diagnose the problem, prescribe and apply suitable remedies to data or assumptions, and then restart the fitting process.

The explosion of cheap computing power that has taken much of the drudgery out of data analysis (not least for regression) has also encouraged a flurry of activity in developing graphical and numerical tools for uncovering skeletons in just about any regression cupboard. This is not to imply that good data analysts in the past neglected a thorough exploration of their data, but rather that the work on these *regression diagnostics* is now within a more formal framework and, consequently, should be accessible to all.

Whilst many of the tools have found their way into popular statistical packages for both mainframe and microcomputers, percolation of regression diagnostics ideas into the literature and statistical handbooks of consumer disciplines seems exceedingly slow. One consequence of this is a lack of pressure from users for agreements on conventions or strategies. Thus, the researcher intent on a thorough regression analysis faces the frustrating and somewhat bewildering experience of finding that many of the diagnostics appear to show much the same thing; terminology and notation are anything but standardized;

and guidelines for assessing the impact of some peccadillo are frequently vague and sometimes inconsistent.

With this in mind, we shall focus on a set of graphical and numerical tools for detecting the worst things that can go wrong in a regression analysis, sometimes with suggestions for remedies. As a survey of the market, it is undoubtedly partial (in both senses of the word): the choice of methods owes much to what modern statistical packages can provide either directly or with a little effort by the user.

## SETTING THE SCENE

Readers are assumed to have some familiarity with the concepts and techniques of regression analysis. However to fix ideas and notation, let us consider a multiple linear regression model in terms of its data values. This can be summarized in matrix form as

$$\mathbf{Y} = \mathbf{Xb} + \mathbf{e}$$

where

$\mathbf{Y}$ is an $n \times 1$ vector of observations on the response variable,

$\mathbf{X}$ is an $n \times p$ matrix of known values of $p$ predictors,

$\mathbf{b}$ is a $p \times 1$ vector of unknown regression coefficients,

$\mathbf{e}$ is an $n \times 1$ vector of independent random variables such that $E(\mathbf{e}) = 0$ and $\mathrm{Var}(\mathbf{e}) = \sigma^2 \mathbf{I}$.

In general, $\mathbf{X}$ is of full rank $p$, with columns consisting of data values from the $p$ predictor or explanatory variables, one of which may be a constant. If the relationship between the response and explanatory variables is thought to be other than linear, then some predictors may be functions of the explanatory variables. It is also assumed that the explanatory variables are fixed (non-random) values. Even if some are not, the random mechanism can be ignored for practical purposes provided that it is recognized that the distribution of the response variable will be conditional on the explanatory variables. This has implications for the interpretation and power of any statistical hypothesis tests. Although no assumption about distributional form is required to fit a model by the least squares procedure, normality is needed for inferences.

We shall follow the usual notation by taking $x_i$ and $y_i$ to be the $i$th rows of $\mathbf{X}$ and $\mathbf{Y}$, respectively; together these constitute the $i$th observation or case. The $j$th column of $\mathbf{X}$ is denoted by $X_j$. Note, though, that sometimes $X_j$ will be used to denote the $j$th predictor variable itself.

Fitting the model by least squares means that the vector of regression coefficients $\mathbf{b}$ is estimated by the vector

$$\hat{\mathbf{b}} = (\mathbf{X}^T \mathbf{X})^{-1} \mathbf{X}^T \mathbf{Y}. \tag{1}$$

A point to note here is that $(\mathbf{X}^T \mathbf{X})^{-1}$ will not exist unless the columns of $\mathbf{X}$ are linearly independent (orthogonal); practically, this requires that the predictors be uncorrelated.

The vector of fitted or predicted values of $\mathbf{Y}$ is then

$$\hat{\mathbf{Y}} = \mathbf{X}\hat{\mathbf{b}} = \mathbf{X}(\mathbf{X}^T\mathbf{X})^{-1}\mathbf{X}^T\mathbf{Y}. \tag{2}$$

If we write $\mathbf{H} = \mathbf{X}(\mathbf{X}^T\mathbf{X})^{-1}\mathbf{X}^T$ so that $\hat{\mathbf{Y}} = \mathbf{H}\mathbf{Y}$, it is easy to see that when $\mathbf{X}$ contains fixed values, each fitted value $\hat{y}_i$ is a linear combination of all the observed $y$ values with $\mathbf{H}$ providing the coefficients or weights for each observation. In other words, $\mathbf{H}$ is a projection matrix which maps $\mathbf{Y}$ into $\hat{\mathbf{Y}}$. $\mathbf{H}$ is more popularly known as the *hat matrix* because, as we see from (2), it 'puts the hats on the *ys*'.

In fact, the hat matrix figures prominently in regression analysis. For instance, the variance-covariance matrices of $\hat{\mathbf{Y}}$ and the residuals $\mathbf{r} = \mathbf{Y} - \hat{\mathbf{Y}} = (\mathbf{I} - \mathbf{H})\mathbf{Y}$ are respectively $\sigma^2\mathbf{H}$ and $\sigma^2(\mathbf{I} - \mathbf{H})$. As we shall see later, $\mathbf{H}$ is a vital component of our kit for diagnosing regression maladies.

| | BIRTHWT. | HEADCIRC. | GEST. |
|---|---|---|---|
| Case # | (gms) | (cms) | (weeks) |
| 1 | 3680 | 35.5 | 42 |
| 2 | 3240 | 35.5 | 40 |
| 3 | 3180 | 33.0 | 38 |
| 4 | 3530 | 35.0 | 41 |
| 5 | 3100 | 33.5 | 39 |
| 6 | 3690 | 37.0 | 39 |
| 7 | 3550 | 34.5 | 41 |
| 8 | 4160 | 39.5 | 41 |
| 9 | 3410 | 33.5 | 38 |
| 10 | 3600 | 36.0 | 39 |
| 11 | 3010 | 35.0 | 37 |
| 12 | 3250 | 34.5 | 41 |
| 13 | 2820 | 33.0 | 35 |
| 14 | 3390 | 34.0 | 38 |
| 15 | 3870 | 36.0 | 37 |
| 16 | 3560 | 34.0 | 40 |
| 17 | 3890 | 37.0 | 40 |
| 18 | 3020 | 34.0 | 37 |
| 19 | 3400 | 35.5 | 37 |
| 20 | 2860 | 34.0 | 34 |
| 21 | 3400 | 35.5 | 39 |
| 22 | 3130 | 34.5 | 39 |
| 23 | 3300 | 36.0 | 38 |
| 24 | 3370 | 36.5 | 36 |
| 25 | 4080 | 35.0 | 42 |

**Table 1.** The BIRTHWEIGHT data

*Source:* North Staffordshire/ Wigan assisted delivery trial

## OUTLIERS, LEVERAGE AND INFLUENTIAL OBSERVATIONS

For the moment we shall concentrate on how a fitted least squares regression model responds to the presence of observations which are isolated, or outlying, in the spaces of **X** or **Y**, or are not in accord with the hoped-for relationship. Bearing in mind that least squares tries to accommodate all observations, however discrepant, we are looking for answers to two related questions – are there *outliers* in our data and, if so, how will the fitted model be affected?

In the univariate case outliers occur at the extremes of a sample, so candidates are relatively easy to identify (see Lovie, 1986, for an introduction to this topic; or Barnett & Lewis, 1984, for a comprehensive coverage). With multivariate data, however, our search is for observations that are jointly discordant in the sense that they deviate from the pattern followed by the rest of the data. Since multivariate outliers do not necessarily lie at the extremes with respect to any of the individual variables, winkling them out can be difficult.

To avoid confusion in the following discussion I shall refer to observations isolated in the **X** space or the **Y** space as *extremes*, even though they may be outliers in their own right. Only observations which are jointly discrepant, that is, with respect to our fitted regression model, are called *outliers* (or, sometimes, *regression outliers*).

Table 1 contains data from 25 mothers and babies on three variables collected as part of a study to assess two methods of assisted delivery. This is a small subset of data from over 250 cases on 110 variables ranging from physical and

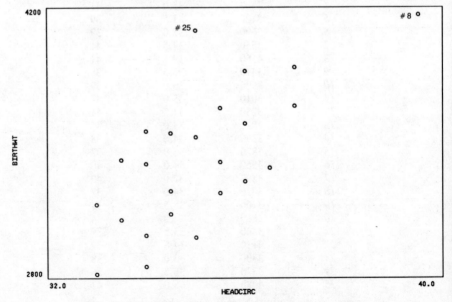

**Figure 1.** Scatterplot of birthweight against head circumference.

biochemical measures to subjective pain scores. As these cases were chosen to illustrate particular points, they cannot be considered as a representative sample.

Suppose that we wish to fit a regression model to predict birthweight (BIRTHWT) from a baby's head circumference (HEADCIRC). From the scatterplot (Figure 1), we see a moderately strong overall association between the variables, but two observations are somewhat distant from the point cloud. Case #8 in the upper right corner is an extreme in both the $x$ and $y$ directions. In contrast, #25 lies well within the range of the $x$ values and not too far outside the $y$s, but because jointly these disagree (with respect to the relationship between the variables), it is likely to be an outlier.

One obvious way to assess the effects of such discrepant cases is to fit a model using all the data and then with any offending observation omitted. As we see from the summary information in Table 2, estimates of the regression coefficients are less affected than their standard errors or the mean square error MSE. (Note that MSE estimates $\sigma^2$ and is denoted by $s^2$.) In the next sections, however, we shall discover that there are more reliable ways of picking up potentially troublesome observations than eyeballing the scatterplot and more efficient methods than refitting for gauging their impact on our regression results.

**Table 2.** Regression summaries for the BIRTHWEIGHT data with all cases and selected cases excluded (rounded to two decimal places)

| Cases | $\hat{b}_j$ | | SE($\hat{b}_j$) | | $t$ | | $F$ | MSE | $R^2$ |
|---|---|---|---|---|---|---|---|---|---|
| | Const | HEAD | Const | HEAD | Const | HEAD | | | |
| All (n = 25) | −2343.62 | 164.19 | 1277.10 | 36.35 | −1.84 (NS) | 4.52 (***) | 20.40 (***) | 68063.91 | 0.47 |
| Excl #8 | −2252.71 | 161.57 | 1664.55 | 47.65 | −1.35 (NS) | 3.39 (**) | 11.50 (**) | 71132.66 | 0.34 |
| Excl #25 | −2419.88 | 165.56 | 1088.98 | 30.99 | −2.22 (*) | 5.34 (***) | 28.53 (***) | 49463.73 | 0.56 |
| Excl #8 & #25 | −2216.49 | 159.69 | 1418.96 | 40.62 | −1.56 (NS) | 3.93 (***) | 15.45 (***) | 51687.64 | 0.42 |

| *Note* | NS: not significant at 5% level |
|---|---|
| | *: significant at 5% level |
| | **: significant at 1% level |
| | ***: significant at 0.1% level |

## Leverage

An observation which is an extreme value in the **X** space, such as *#8*, is known as a *leverage point* (or a *high-leverage point*) because it has the potential to drag the least squares line towards itself. In fact, *#8* merely follows the trend set already by the rest of the data, but a leverage point with a less consistent *y* value can have a marked effect on regression coefficient estimates. In other words, unless a leverage point is also an outlier its influence on estimation and prediction is unlikely to be great.

Since the diagonal elements $h_{ii}$ of the hat matrix (known as the *hat values*) are indicators of the remoteness of a particular point in the **X** space from the remainder of the observations, $h_{ii}$ will be large for an extreme point in the **X** space. Moreover, because $h_{ii}$ determines the contribution that $y_i$ will make to predicting itself, the hat value measures the degree of leverage exerted by the *i*th case and, thereby, its effect on prediction through the coefficient estimates and their variances and the mean square error.

Two properties of the hat values give us a framework for assessing leverage. Firstly, $h_{ii}$ lies between $1/n$ and 1 for any regression model which includes a constant term (the lower limit is zero for regression through the origin). Also, since the sum of the hat values is $p$, the average value of $h_{ii}$ is $p/n$. Thus a natural reference point for this task (analogous to the '2 standard errors either side of the mean' rule of thumb) is to say that observations with hat values greater than $2p/n$ deserve special attention (Belsley *et al.*, 1980; Hoaglin & Welsch, 1978).

Although this $2p/n$ cutoff, or 'calibration point', for $h_{ii}$ is perhaps the most commonly used, there are other contenders. Chatterjee & Hadi (1988) discuss several alternatives: one takes no account of sample size or number of predictors (Huber, 1981) whilst the others are appropriate over different ranges of *n* and *p* (Velleman & Welsch, 1981). In any case, cutoffs should never be regarded as sacrosanct: any hat values which stand apart in, say, a stem and leaf display, an index plot or a boxplot (see Chapter 2), warrant examination.

## Outliers

It is customary to plot the residuals against an explanatory variable or the fitted *y* values to check assumptions about the errors and the appropriateness of the model. If the model is correctly specified, the plot should have zero slope with all the points scattered freely about the line $y = 0$. An outlier may show up on this plot as a large residual, but this is not an infallible test because residuals for high leverage points tend to be small. The reason is that the variance of the residuals depends on both $\sigma^2$ and $h_{ii}$, so residuals for high leverage points will have smaller variances and, thus, be smaller, on average, than for cases closer to the centre. We should bear in mind too that variations in the residual variances might well explain an apparent pattern of nonconstant variances over the range of a predictor.

To avoid this problem, always assuming that the regression model is correct, the residuals $r_i$ $(i = 1, \ldots, n)$ can be standardized to have constant variance by scaling them with respect to their estimated standard errors. The $i$th *standardized residual* is

$$r_i' = r_i/s\sqrt{1 - h_{ii}}.$$

An alternative scaling uses what Atkinson (1985) calls a deletion estimate of $\sigma^2$, denoted by $s^2(i)$, which is $s^2$ calculated with the $i$th case omitted. This generates the $i$th *studentized residual*

$$r_i^* = r_i/s(i)\sqrt{1 - h_{ii}}.$$

If the linear model holds and the errors are normally distributed, $r_i^*$ follows a $t$ distribution with $(n - p - 1)$ degrees of freedom, whilst $r_i'^2/(n - p)$ is Beta(1/2, $(n - p)/2$).

We can now say that a regression outlier is an observation which has a large positive or negative standardized or studentized residual. Unfortunately, because our interest centres on a specific observation with a large absolute residual rather than on a randomly selected point, 'largeness' cannot be assessed against a value of Beta or $t$ in the conventional way. Tests for detecting the presence of such outliers are discussed in, for example, Chatterjee & Hadi (1988), Cook & Weisberg (1982) and Weisberg (1985); a more general coverage of the outlier problem in linear models can be found in Barnett & Lewis (1984). However, as a rough guide, flagging points for which $|r_i^*|$ is significant at the 10% level (under such an outlier test) corresponds to a cutoff value of about 2 (Hoaglin & Welsch, 1978; Weisberg, 1985).

In fact, the studentized residual $r_i^*$ has certain advantages over its standardized cousin in exploratory work. The deletion estimate $s^2(i)$ is free of contamination by any gross discrepancy in the $i$th case and, therefore, is less likely to mask any failings in that observation. Moreover, because $r_i^*$ is infinite when $r_i'^2$ reaches its maximum value of $(n - p)$, studentized residuals reflect large deviations more dramatically than their standardized counterparts.

A warning about nomenclature is in order here. Some authors refer to both the standardized and studentized residuals defined above as 'studentized', sometimes qualified as being internally or externally studentized, respectively (for example, Cook & Weisberg, 1982; Montgomery & Peck, 1982; Weisberg, 1985). Nor is there consistency in what standardization means; 'standardized' to Montgomery & Peck (1982), for instance, is what is 'normalized' to Chatterjee and Hadi (1986, 1988), but 'scaled to unit length' to Belsley *et al.* (1980). Particular care is needed to determine which scaling method is used in statistical packages.

Many of the features of the leverage values and the residuals for a data set can be extracted by plotting, for instance, residuals and leverage values against predicted values or an explanatory variable. Stem and leaf displays or index plots over cases will highlight individual candidates for examination. In addition, the combined effect of leverage and outliers can be gauged rather effectively from a *leverage* plot of $r_i^*$ versus $h_{ii}$ (Hoaglin & Kempthorne in Chatterjee & Hadi, 1986; see also Chatterjee & Hadi, 1988, for similar plots using differently scaled residuals). Points appearing in the upper and lower right corners suggest influential observations, but clearly judgements must be made in relation to the actual sizes of the residuals and hat values.

### Influence

As was hinted earlier, neither $h_{ii}$ nor $r_i^*$ alone is sufficient to locate an observation which exerts undue influence on the results of a regression analysis. Neither outliers nor high leverage points are necessarily influential. Conversely, influential observations are not invariably outliers or high leverage points. Thus, whilst the plots mentioned above may suggest influential observations, we shall require other (numerical) criteria for establishing what aspect of our analysis is affected and to what degree. For instance, the influence might be on estimates of all the regression coefficients or just some of them, on the variability of the estimates, on predicted values or on the goodness of fit of the model.

Of course, the global $F$, $t$ or $R^2$ measures can provide some insight into the robustness of results when the data are altered by some small amount (or 'perturbed' as the jargon has it). However, a more direct approach assesses these effects in relation to changes in confidence regions about parameters, or on influence curves or on likelihood functions when potentially offending observations are deleted (see, for example, Cook & Weisberg, 1982, or Chatterjee & Hadi, 1988, for accounts of the theoretical background to these influence measures).

**Changes in $\hat{b}$ and fitted values.** Suppose that we are interested in how the coefficient estimates change when the $i$th observation is omitted. We can easily obtain $\hat{b} - \hat{b}(i)$ (in our deletion notation) either by recalculating or by using one of the computational formulae (see, for instance, Atkinson, 1985; Velleman & Welsch, 1981) and then assess the size of these changes relative to some suitable measure of scale. Since changes in fitted values are of interest too, a measure which allows us to assess both simultaneously would be convenient. And, of course, we shall want a calibration point.

Cook's distance measure is defined as

$$D_i = \frac{(\hat{b} - \hat{b}(i))^T \mathbf{X}^T \mathbf{X} \, (\hat{b} - \hat{b}(i))}{ps^2}.$$

Equivalent forms for $D_i$ are

$$D_i = \frac{(\hat{\mathbf{Y}} - \hat{\mathbf{Y}}(i))^T (\hat{\mathbf{Y}} - \hat{\mathbf{Y}}(i))}{ps^2}$$

and

$$D_i = \frac{r_i^2 h_{ii}}{ps^2 (1 - h_{ii})^2} = \frac{r_i'^2 h_{ii}}{p(1 - h_{ii})} .$$

The first of these alternatives shows that we can interpret $D_i$ as the change in the vector of predicted values, that is, in the fit. From the second we see that a large value of $D_i$ may be due to a large hat value, a large (standardized) residual or indeed both. Values of $D_i > 1$ suggests points for attention (Cook & Weisberg, 1982).

A closely related measure excludes the effect of case $i$ on the estimate of $\sigma^2$ by using the deletion estimate $MSE(i) = s^2(i)$. This quantity, known as DFFITS (difference in fit scaled), can be written as

$$DFFITS_i = \frac{r_i \sqrt{h_{ii}}}{s(i) (1 - h_{ii})} = \frac{r_i^* \sqrt{h_{ii}}}{\sqrt{1 - h_{ii}}} .$$

Although $DFFITS_i$ is little different from $D_i$, it is interpreted in a slightly different way because it measures the change in coefficient estimates and MSE simultaneously; it also tells us about the direction of change.

Clearly, $|DFFITS_i|$ will be large if $h_{ii}$ or $r_i^*$ or both are large. Observations for which $|DFFITS_i|$ is greater than $2\sqrt{p/n}$ are thought worth examination (Belsley *et al.*, 1980). (Chatterjee & Hadi (1988) prefer a cutoff of $2\sqrt{p/(n-p)}$ whilst Velleman & Welsch (1981) recommend for special attention points with values greater than 1 or 2.)

Note that $D_i$ and $DFFITS_i$ are ultimately concerned with changes in the fit of the model and measure the influence on all the $\hat{b}_j$s simultaneously. Thus a large value of either of these, even for a model with only a constant and a single explanatory variable, leaves us in the dark about how the individual coefficient estimates are affected.

**Changes in $\hat{b}_j$.** The influence of the $i$th observation on the $j$th coefficient estimate, scaled by the standard error of $\hat{b}_j$, is measured by

$$DFBETAS_{ij} = \frac{\hat{b}_j - \hat{b}_j(i)}{s(i) \sqrt{(\mathbf{X}^T\mathbf{X})_{jj}^{-1}}}$$

where $(\mathbf{X}^T\mathbf{X})_{jj}^{-1}$ denotes the $j$th diagonal element of $(\mathbf{X}^T\mathbf{X})^{-1}$.

An equivalent expression in terms of residuals and hat values is

$$DFBETAS_{ij} = \frac{w_{ji}}{\sqrt{\sum_{k=1}^{n} w_{jk}^2}} \frac{r_i}{s(i) (1 - h_{ii})} = \frac{w_{ji}}{\sqrt{\sum_{k=1}^{n} w_{jk}^2}} \frac{r_i^*}{\sqrt{1 - h_{ii}}}$$

where $w_{ij}$ are the elements of $\mathbf{W} = (\mathbf{X}^T\mathbf{X})^{-1}\mathbf{X}^T$, which is sometimes called the catcher matrix.

Cutoff values for $|\text{DFBETAS}_{ij}|$ are 2 or $2/\sqrt{n}$ (Belsley *et al.*, 1980). There is, of course, little point in calculating these unless $\text{DFFITS}_i$ is large.

A further aspect to explore is the impact of the $i$th observation on the precision of the coefficient estimates whose variance-covariance matrix is $\text{Var}(\hat{\mathbf{b}}) = \sigma^2(\mathbf{X}^T\mathbf{X})^{-1}$. To do this we compare their estimated variance-covariance matrices with and without the $i$th case. In order to come out with a single number, we take the ratio of their determinants defined as

$$\text{CVR}_i = \frac{\det\ [s^2(i)\ (\mathbf{X}^T(i)\ \mathbf{X}(i))^{-1}]}{\det\ [s^2(\mathbf{X}^T\mathbf{X})^{-1}]}\ .$$

An alternative form which again emphasizes our basic building blocks of residuals, MSE and hat values is

$$\text{CVR}_i = \frac{1}{\left[\dfrac{n-p-1}{n-p} + \dfrac{r_i^{*2}}{n-p}\right]^p (1 - h_{ii})}\ .$$

Belsley *et al.* (1980), who call this measure COVRATIO, suggest flagging points with $|\text{CVR}_i - 1| > 3p/n$.

### Influential subsets

Several methods for detecting jointly influential observations, some of which are natural extensions of the single case diagnostics outlined above, are discussed by Belsley *et al.* (1980), Cook & Weisberg (1982), Gray & Ling (1984) and Chatterjee & Hadi (1988).

A simpler approach to detecting such observations is to apply the single case methods by deleting observations sequentially. Unfortunately, this is not entirely foolproof because, for instance, an influential point can sometimes be masked by the presence of another observation; moreover, observations may be jointly but not individually influential. Nevertheless, the disadvantages of this single observation approach seem to be far outweighed by the amount of computation required by multiple case methods as well as the difficulties of interpreting the results without adequate plotting or summarization routines. Some examples using multiple case methods are discussed in the references given above.

### Back to the BIRTHWEIGHT data

We noted earlier from the scatterplot of birthweight against head circumference (Figure 1) that two observations in the upper right quadrant seem somewhat isolated from the rest. Point #8 is an extreme with respect to both the response and explanatory variable but it does not look out of line with the pattern of the data. On the other hand, #25 is a potential outlier although it may not be particularly influential. Indeed, these two cases show up very differently on a plot

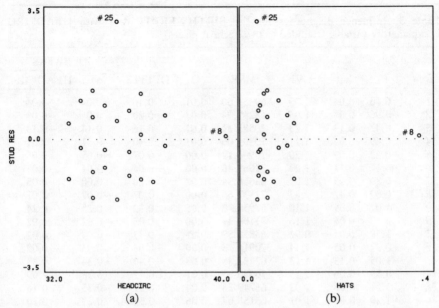

**Figure 2.** Studentized residuals from regressing birthweight on head circumference against (a) head circumference; (b) hat values (leverage plot).

of the studentized residuals of birthweight against head circumference (Figure 2a) where we find a large residual associated with #25 and an exceptionally small one for #8. A plot of studentized residuals versus hat values in Figure 2b shows these points in the top left corner and on the extreme right near $y = 0$, respectively.

Our task now is to ascertain whether the least squares routine has been too accommodating to our mavericks. Note that to conserve space many diagnostic plots and details of the influence analyses have been omitted from the following discussion.

From the lists of regression diagnostics and their cutoff values in Table 3 (to save space, no graphical displays of these diagnostics are included here), we see that observation #8, with a hat value of 0.42 and CVR of 1.87, is a high leverage point whose exclusion would *increase* the variance of the coefficient estimates. Furthermore, as we suspected, #25 is a regression outlier ($r_{25}^* = 3.11$), but because its leverage is low, it is not especially influential. In particular, whereas both DFFITS and CVR fall beyond their cutoff values, Cook's D and DFBETAS are very small. We conclude, therefore, that #25 mainly affects MSE and the coefficient estimate variances rather than the estimates themselves; excluding #25 reduces these variances.

This is, of course, essentially the same message that came through from the summary regression results in Table 2. Furthermore, since applying these

**Table 3.** Influence diagnostics for the BIRTHWEIGHT data with HEADCIRC as explanatory variable (rounded to two decimal places)

| Case# | $r^*$ | hat | CVR | MSE | D | DFFITS | DFBETAS Const | HEADCIRC |
|-------|-------|-----|-----|-----|---|--------|-------|----------|
| 1 | 0.76 | 0.04 | 1.09 | 69356.60 | 0.01 | 0.16 | −0.04 | 0.04 |
| 2 | −0.96 | 0.04 | 1.05 | 68299.94 | 0.02 | −0.20 | 0.05 | −0.05 |
| 3 | 0.42 | 0.13 | 1.23 | 70582.31 | 0.01 | 0.16 | 0.14 | −0.13 |
| 4 | 0.49 | 0.04 | 1.11 | 70396.06 | 0.01 | 0.10 | 0.01 | −0.01 |
| 5 | −0.22 | 0.09 | 1.20 | 70996.12 | 0.00 | −0.07 | −0.05 | 0.05 |
| 6 | −0.17 | 0.11 | 1.23 | 71069.46 | 0.00 | −0.06 | 0.04 | −0.05 |
| 7 | 0.89 | 0.05 | 1.07 | 68658.34 | 0.02 | 0.20 | 0.08 | −0.08 |
| 8 | 0.09 | 0.42 | 1.87 | 71132.66 | 0.00 | 0.07 | −0.07 | 0.07 |
| 9 | 1.02 | 0.09 | 1.10 | 67958.70 | 0.05 | 0.32 | 0.25 | −0.24 |
| 10 | 0.13 | 0.06 | 1.16 | 71106.49 | 0.00 | 0.03 | −0.02 | 0.02 |
| 11 | −1.59 | 0.04 | 0.92 | 63836.59 | 0.05 | −0.33 | −0.04 | 0.02 |
| 12 | −0.27 | 0.05 | 1.14 | 70916.73 | 0.00 | −0.06 | −0.03 | 0.02 |
| 13 | −1.05 | 0.13 | 1.13 | 67782.88 | 0.08 | −0.40 | −0.34 | 0.33 |
| 14 | 0.59 | 0.06 | 1.13 | 70050.85 | 0.01 | 0.15 | 0.10 | −0.09 |
| 15 | 1.21 | 0.06 | 1.02 | 66749.23 | 0.04 | 0.29 | −0.15 | 0.16 |
| 16 | 1.29 | 0.06 | 1.01 | 66156.07 | 0.06 | 0.34 | 0.22 | −0.20 |
| 17 | 0.64 | 0.11 | 1.18 | 69875.65 | 0.03 | 0.22 | −0.17 | 0.18 |
| 18 | −0.86 | 0.06 | 1.09 | 68830.16 | 0.03 | −0.22 | −0.14 | 0.14 |
| 19 | −0.33 | 0.04 | 1.13 | 70812.27 | 0.00 | −0.07 | 0.02 | −0.02 |
| 20 | −1.55 | 0.06 | 0.95 | 64186.41 | 0.08 | −0.40 | −0.26 | 0.24 |
| 21 | −0.33 | 0.04 | 1.13 | 70812.27 | 0.00 | −0.07 | 0.02 | −0.02 |
| 22 | −0.74 | 0.05 | 1.09 | 69416.22 | 0.01 | −0.17 | −0.07 | 0.06 |
| 23 | −1.06 | 0.06 | 1.05 | 67716.44 | 0.03 | −0.26 | 0.13 | −0.14 |
| 24 | −1.12 | 0.08 | 1.06 | 67306.93 | 0.05 | −0.33 | 0.22 | −0.23 |
| 25 | 3.11 | 0.04 | 0.55 | 49463.73 | 0.15 | 0.64 | 0.07 | −0.04 |
| Cut-offs | 2 | 0.4 | 1±0.24 | — | 1 | ±0.57 | ±0.4 | |

*Note:* Cutoff values calculated for $p=2$ and $n=25$ from: $2p/n$ for hat, $1 \pm 3p/n$ for CVR, $\pm 2\sqrt{p/n}$ for DFFITS, $\pm 2/\sqrt{n}$ for DFBETAS.

measures has allowed us to audit all cases without massive computational effort, we are spared the uncertainties involved in choosing suitable candidates. A point to remember, though, is that we are not in a position to say much about the joint influence of #8 and #25 or, for that matter, any other subset of cases. Indeed, as readers who run influence analyses on the reduced data discover, deleting #8 (either alone or with #25) unmasks additional problems.

Suppose now that the birthweight for point #8 had been 3160 instead of 4160 as in Figure 3a. Since the leverage plot (Figure 3b) shows up #8 in the bottom right corner as an outlier with high leverage, it is no surprise to find

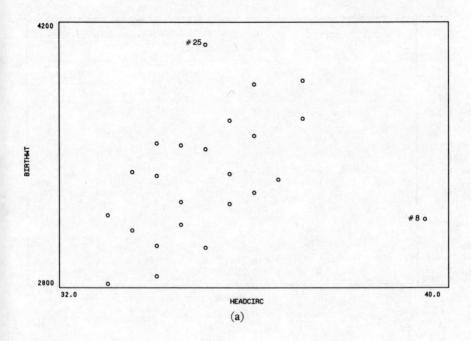

(a)

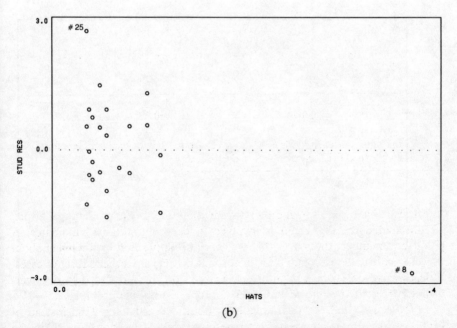

(b)

**Figure 3.** (a) Scatterplot of birthweight against head circumference; #8 = {3160, 39.5};
(b) Leverage plot.

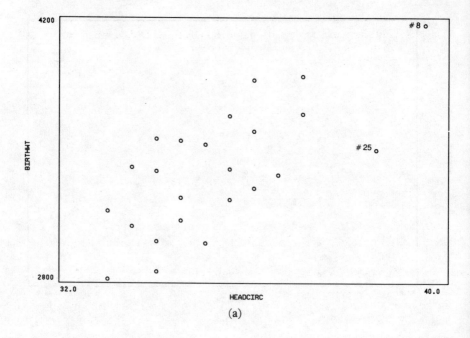

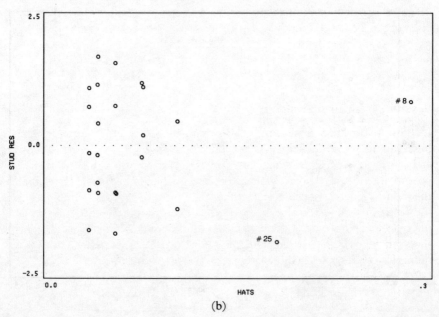

**Figure 4.** (a) Scatterplot of birthweight against head circumference; #25 = {3500, 38.5};
(b) Leverage plot.

**Table 4.** Influence diagnostics for the BIRTHWEIGHT data when #8 = {3160, 39.5} or #25 = {3500, 38.5}, (rounded to two decimal places)

| Case# | | $r^*$ | hat | CVR | MSE | D | DFFITS | DFBETAS Const | HEADCIRC |
|-------|----|-------|------|------|----------|------|--------|-------|----------|
| #8 | 8 | −2.78 | 0.42 | 1.03 | 71132.66 | 2.13 | −2.34 | 2.20 | −2.23 |
| | 25 | 2.69 | 0.04 | 0.65 | 72317.91 | 0.12 | 0.55 | 0.06 | −0.04 |
| #25 | 8 | 0.83 | 0.33 | 1.53 | 55157.79 | 0.17 | 0.58 | −0.54 | 0.55 |
| | 25 | −1.82 | 0.21 | 1.05 | 49463.73 | 0.40 | −0.94 | 0.82 | −0.84 |

*Note:* Cutoff values as in Table 3

from Table 4 that this observation is highly influential on every front except the coefficient estimate variances. Point #25's status as an influential outlier remains about the same.

Finally, suppose that we restore the original values of #8 but make the birth-weight and head circumference for case #25 3500 and 38.5, respectively. This makes #25 look a little out of kilter even though all values are kept within the ranges of each variable (Figure 4a). Although #25 is neither an outlier nor exceptionally high on leverage (Figure 4b and Table 4), it influences both the coefficient estimates and, to some extent, the MSE. From the DFBETAS and MSE we see that including it produces a flatter regression line with a larger intercept value, and also reduces MSE. Case #8, on the other hand, is partially counterbalancing #25 by pulling the line in the opposite direction. Note that in neither case is the effect on the coefficient estimates picked up by Cook's distance measure, which uses all observations to estimate $\sigma^2$.

### Several explanatory variables

I admit to making something of a drama out of a crisis for a couple of observations which looked suspect even on the original scatterplot. Unfortunately, simple scatterplots are not always an effective way of showing up potentially influential points when there is more than one explanatory variable in the model. Indeed, since we are restricted to plots of pairwise combinations of the response and explanatory variables, an observation which is influential in the space of all or some of the variables, but unremarkable in respect of pairs of them, may not be picked up at all. It is in these situations particularly that the numerical regression diagnostics come into their own.

As an illustration, suppose that we add a second explanatory variable, gestation period (GEST), to our BIRTHWEIGHT model. This variable correlates reasonably well with birthweight and the usual global measures suggest some improvement in the fit when it is added to the model. The data are in column 4 of Table 1.

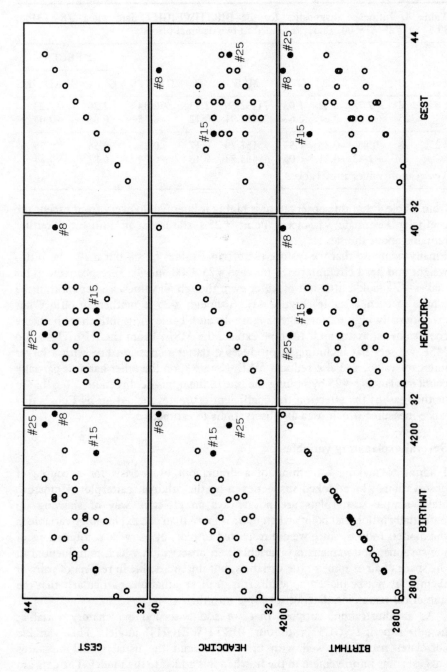

(a)

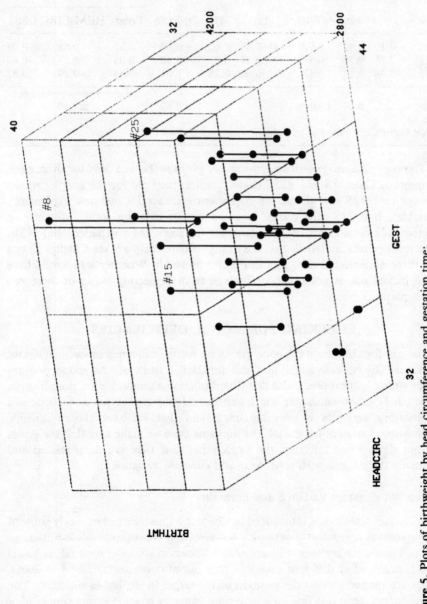

(b)

**Figure 5.** Plots of birthweight by head circumference and gestation time;
(a) Draughtsman's display (labelled points are solid circles); (b) Cube plot.

**Table 5.** Influence diagnostics for the BIRTHWEIGHT data with HEADCIRC and GEST as explanatory variables (rounded to two decimal places)

| Case# | $r^*$ | hat | CVR | MSE | D | DFFITS | Const | DFBETAS HEADCIRC | GEST |
|---|---|---|---|---|---|---|---|---|---|
| 8 | −0.10 | 0.42 | 1.97 | 44666.63 | 0.00 | −0.09 | 0.08 | −0.08 | −0.01 |
| 15 | 2.75 | 0.10 | 0.51 | 32860.89 | 0.02 | 0.92 | −0.03 | 0.53 | −0.62 |
| 25 | 2.36 | 0.15 | 0.67 | 35296.06 | 0.28 | 1.01 | −0.34 | −0.29 | 0.87 |
| Cut-offs | 2 | 0.24 | 1±0.36 | – | 1 | ±0.69 | | ±0.40 | |

*Note:* Cutoffs calculated as in Table 3 with $p=3$ and $n=25$.

To save space, diagnostics quantities are given in Table 5 only for three cases of interest. Cases #8 and #25 behave much as they did for the simpler model (except that #25 also affects the coefficient estimate for our new explanatory variable), but #15 now comes in as an outlier exerting some influence on coefficient estimates for both explanatory variables, their variances and MSE. The three points are labelled on the draughtsman's display (see Chapter 2) and the three dimensional cube plot in Figures 5a and b. Whether #15 would have been picked out as potentially influential from inspecting either of these is a moot point.

## CHECKING FOR MODEL DEFICIENCIES

To be comfortable about the conclusions we reach from a regression analysis we also need to be convinced that the functional form of the model we are entertaining is appropriate and that distributional assumptions are not seriously violated. In other words, we check that the relationship between response and explanatory variables is tolerably linear and that we have chosen sensible explanatory variables for the job. At the same time we make sure that the errors do not deviate too far from the expectation that they are uncorrelated and normally distributed with zero mean and constant variance.

### Linearity, constant variance and normality

The Neisser search data introduced in Chapter 2 illustrate rather nicely some of the graphical regression diagnostics for assessing the validity of our assumptions. These data are four subjects' search times (in seconds) for a target vowel which occurred at different positions in a list of consonants. The 160 search times are plotted against the position of the target in the list in Figure 6. The least squares regression line for search time on target position is superimposed on the plot.

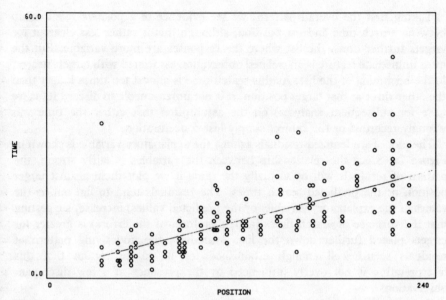

**Figure 6.** Scatterplot of search time against target position with LS line superimposed.

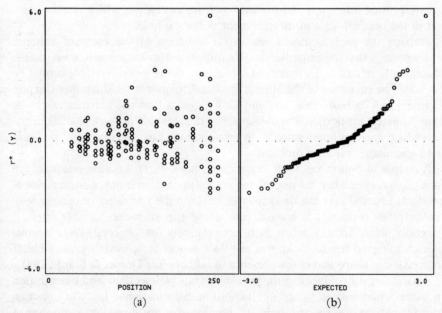

**Figure 7.** (a) Studentized residuals versus target position; (b) Normal probability plot of studentized residuals.

Taking first the overall pattern, we see evidence of a positive relationship between search time and list position, although this is rather less clearcut for targets further down the list where the responses are more variable. But the most immediate feature is an isolated observation associated with targets nearest to the beginning of the list. As this search time is almost ten times longer than the other three at that target position, it is not unreasonable to discard it (as we have for subsequent analyses) on the assumption that either the time was wrongly recorded or the subject simply lost concentration.

The plot of studentized residuals against the explanatory variable is shown in Figure 7a. Since the relationship between the variables is fairly strong, the pattern of residuals will be virtually the same if we plot them against target position or the predicted search times. The residuals tend to fan out as the values of the explanatory variable (or the predicted values) increase, suggesting that the variance of search times (and, therefore, of the errors) is greater for targets placed further down the list. Moreover, the underlying pattern of residuals seems well enough established for us to be certain that this interpretation is not overly influenced by the presence of a few discrepant observations.

Our next step is to consider transforming or re-expressing our responses to try to stabilize the variances. If we leave them as they are, the regression coefficients will have larger standard errors than necessary and this will affect any subsequent inferences. However, we have to balance this against the difficulties of interpreting inferences and predictions from an analysis which is not carried out in the original scale of measurement of the variable.

Perhaps the most common reason for violation of the constant variance assumption is that the response variable follows a distribution whose variance is functionally related to its mean. In this event, the response variable cannot be normal. The curvature of the normal (probability) plot of residuals (see Chapter 2) in Figure 7b bears this out, and also suggests that the variance might be approximately proportional to the square of the mean. With luck, a transformation which corrects nonnormality, by straightening out the curve, will also cure the nonconstant variance problem.

A couple of points are worth mentioning here. First, because residuals can look normal even when the underlying error distribution is not, a normal plot of residuals is not always the most reliable guide to the normality or otherwise of the response variable; a normal plot using the response variable itself is generally safer. Second, when there are relatively few observations, a normal plot of unsigned residuals, known as a *half normal* plot, usually gives a better impression of shape and of the presence of outliers (see Draper & Smith, 1981).

A hands-on way of tackling the problem of our Neisser data (and linearization in other situations) is to try out various transformations. Lists of common transformations for specific types of nonlinearity are given by a number of authors (for example, Weisberg, 1985; Daniel & Wood, 1980; but see also

Mosteller & Tukey's 'ladder of re-expressions', 1977; Emerson & Stoto, 1983). Essentially, these are simple rules of thumb derived from the formal analytical methods based on power transformations (see Atkinson, 1985; Emerson, 1983). Each step up (or down) the ladder of powers from a neutral point offers a stronger flattening transformation; the direction one travels depends upon whether the curve is convex or concave.

For the type of curvature we need to overcome here, either a square root or log transform of the response variable would be a reasonable starting point. However, as response time distributions are usually best described by exponential models, $\log_e$ was the obvious choice. As can be seen in the residual and normal plots of the logged search times in Figures 8a and b, give or take a few maverick points, the residuals are now contained rather more satisfactorily within a band across the range of target positions and the normal plot has straightened out. In other words, we have managed simultaneously to stabilize the variance of the errors and make them fairly normal.

The less welcome news is that we have now uncovered, or (more likely) made for ourselves, another problem. The residuals plot (Figure 8a) is unmistakedly bowed which suggests that the relationship between logged search time and target position is nonlinear.

One possible solution is adding a quadratic term to the model. Unfortunately, a quadratic model starts to bend downwards not far beyond the upper extreme

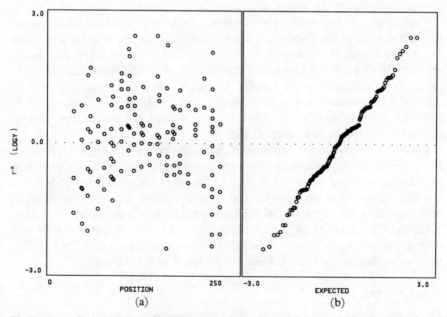

**Figure 8.** (a) Studentized residuals for logged search time versus target position; (b) Normal probability plot of studentized residuals.

of the target position, which is obviously inconsistent with a response time task and, hence, would make even a cautious amount of extrapolation risky.

An alternative tack is to find a transformation that will linearize the relationship between log search time and target position. This time our assault is on the explanatory variable. Consulting the oracle (Daniel & Wood, 1980) suggests that target position might respond reasonably well to a logarithmic transformation. This it does, as the residuals plot (Figure 9a) shows, although somewhat at the expense of normality in the tails (Figure 9b).

### Correlated errors

A further assumption is that the errors are independent; that is, the value of the error for one case does not depend on that of any other. Violations of this assumption are most likely to occur if adjacent observations can influence each other, as, for instance, when the data are ordered in time or in space. For example, each subject in the Neisser search task made responses for every value of the explanatory variable. As the observations were collected over time, it would be surprising if the errors were free of effects due to carryover, boredom, practice, and so on. If we know the order of trials for each value of the explanatory variable, then a plot of residuals over time will show if we have correlated errors. Similarly, a trend in a plot of the residuals for each time point against the residuals for, say, the previous time point, indicates pairwise correlation between the errors of adjacent observations.

Unfortunately, the presentation orders, which were randomized separately for each subject in the Neisser experiment, are lost elsewhere in time or space! So, as an alternative example, Figures 10a and b show index and lagged residuals plots for the regression of the number of deaths registered on smoke levels, both measured in the London County Council area during the first 15 days of a 'pea-souper' fog in December, 1952 (from data in Osborn, 1979). Although the number of observations is small, we can still discern clear positive correlation on the lagged residuals plot.

Finding solutions to the problem of correlated errors is not straightforward. For some situations, adding another predictor variable which reflects some relevant aspect of changes over time may do the trick; for others, methods which can take into account the correlational structure of the data, such as weighted least squares or one of the special time series methods, are indicated. Useful discussions of the problems of correlated errors and how to detect and cope with them are contained in Draper & Smith (1981) and Montgomery & Peck (1982); time series methods are the subject of Chapter 8 in this volume.

### Some residual points

Of course, we have by no means given our regression analysis of the Neisser search data a clean bill of health. For example, even though we discarded one

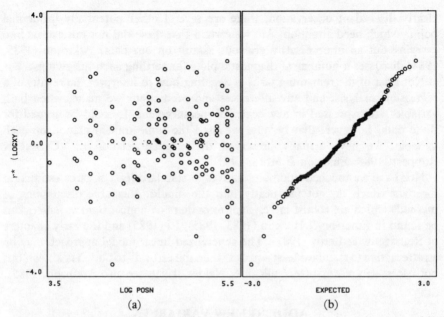

**Figure 9.** (a) Studentized residuals for logged search time versus logged target position; (b) Normal probability plot of studentized residuals.

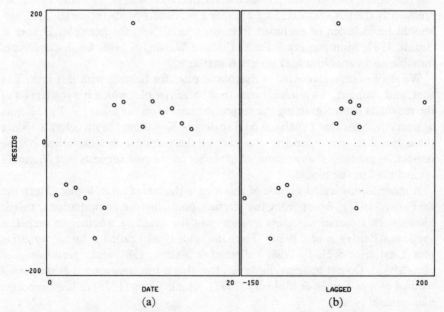

**Figure 10.** (a) Index plot of residuals from number of deaths regressed on mean atmospheric smoke (in mg/m³); (b) Residuals versus residuals lagged 1.

clearly discordant observation, there are several other potentially influential points which need attention. Are we certain that these did not mislead us into carrying out an unnecessarily grievous assault on our data? Atkinson (1985, 1988) discusses a number of diagnostic plots for settling such misgivings.

Not least of the remaining tasks is deciding how to interpret the results of a regression analysis, and any inferences and predictions we make, when both variables are expressed in new scales of measurement. It could be argued for these data, however, that because we used the same transformation on each variable, we have actually preserved the original relationship (Carroll & Ruppert, 1988; Emerson & Stoto, 1983).

Nor have we touched upon alternatives to standard least squares estimation for data which do not fall neatly into the mould. Readable discussions of methods which are robust or resistant to outliers or nonconstant variances can be found in Emerson & Hoaglin (1983, 1985), Li (1985) and the early chapters of Rousseeuw & Leroy (1987). The generalized linear model approach may be an alternative to standard least squares when the error distribution is known but not necessarily normal (McCullagh & Nelder, 1989; see also Atkinson, 1985).

## ADDING NEW VARIABLES

We now turn the spotlight on how well our chosen explanatory variables explain the responses. Global statistics, such as the overall $F$ test, $R^2$ or Mallows' $C_p$, are frequently the basis for deciding whether a particular predictor variable, $X_j$ say, should be included or excluded from the model (see, for example, Draper & Smith, 1981; Montgomery & Peck, 1982; or Weisberg, 1985, for discussions of variable and variable subset selection methods).

We shall examine a couple of diagnostic plots for helping with this task. The first, and simplest, is a *residual versus (new) predictor* plot which is a scatterplot of the residuals from regressing the response variable on the other $j - 1$ predictors against $X_j$. (Note that I shall use $\mathbf{X}[j]$ to denote $\mathbf{X}$ without the $j$th column.) Since these residuals correspond to the part of the response not explained by the remaining predictors, any relationship visible on the plot suggests that $X_j$ should be included in the model.

A more sophisticated version of this idea is the *added variable* plot (Mosteller & Tukey, 1977). Apart from the starting point for the computations, this is identical to a *partial regression leverage* plot for deciding whether to *exclude* a variable, (Belsley *et al.*, 1980). The same plot is also called a *partial regression* plot (Chatterjee & Hadi, 1988; Velleman & Welsch, 1981) and a *partial residual* plot (SPSS). Do not imagine, however, that this is the same animal as the *partial residual* plot of Larsen & McLeary (1972), which Wood (1973) calls a *component plus residual* plot!

An added variable plot sets the residuals from regressing $\mathbf{Y}$ on $\mathbf{X}[j]$ (as in the residual versus predictor plot above) against those from the regression of $X_j$ on

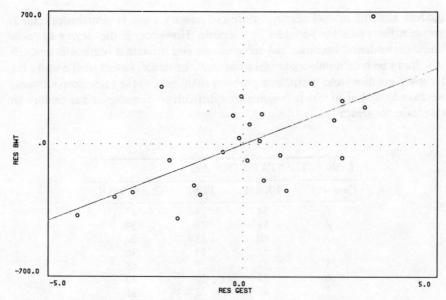

**Figure 11.** Added variable plot to decide whether gestation time be included in the model.

$X[j]$. The latter residuals are the part of $X_j$ not explained by $X[j]$. As the relationship between $Y$ and $X_j$, adjusted with respect to the remaining explanatory variables, is also the relationship between these two sets of residuals, the points will be scattered about a line passing through the origin whose slope is the estimated coefficient of $X_j$ in the regression model with $X_j$ included.

To save space, only the added variable plot is included here (Figure 11), but both plots suggest that adding gestation time to our BIRTHWEIGHT model is worthwhile, as a highly significant $t$ value for the coefficient of GEST in the regression on both predictors confirms. Both plots tend to point up the stray observations that we identified earlier. Moreover, either type of plot should show up any serious violations of nonlinearity or nonconstant variances that might arise from including the new variable.

## COLLINEARITY

In an ideal world all explanatory variables would be linearly independent of each other; that is, none of them could be predicted by a linear combination of any of the other explanatory variables. In other words, they should be uncorrelated. Fortunately, because in practice this situation is scarcely ever achievable, a modest amount of collinearity (multi-collinearity as it is sometimes called) between the predictor variables is tolerable. However, if the degree of 'near linear dependence' becomes just too great we end up with a regression analysis which can be both numerically and statistically unstable. In fact, collinearity is a far more insidious and pernicious problem than most of the regression ailments we have looked at so far. It is sometimes difficult to diagnose and is seldom an easy case for treatment.

**Table 6.** The STATISTICS data

| Case # | EXAM | TEST | CLASSWRK |
|--------|------|------|----------|
| 1 | 74 | 29 | 47 |
| 2 | 58 | 24 | 39 |
| 3 | 60 | 25 | 39 |
| 4 | 53 | 25 | 36 |
| 5 | 81 | 29 | 48 |
| 6 | 57 | 20 | 30 |
| 7 | 47 | 22 | 31 |
| 8 | 67 | 23 | 36 |
| 9 | 73 | 27 | 42 |
| 10 | 41 | 14 | 23 |
| 11 | 35 | 15 | 22 |
| 12 | 42 | 19 | 28 |
| 13 | 51 | 16 | 26 |
| 14 | 63 | 27 | 39 |
| 15 | 33 | 11 | 16 |
| 16 | 69 | 28 | 41 |
| 17 | 66 | 22 | 37 |
| 18 | 71 | 27 | 43 |
| 19 | 43 | 17 | 28 |
| 20 | 54 | 19 | 31 |

Let us take first the mathematical and computational side of the curse of collinearity. Looking back to equation (1) for finding least squares estimates of the coefficients of our regression line, we see that it involves inverting the matrix $\mathbf{X}^T\mathbf{X}$. This operation is not possible if the columns of $\mathbf{X}$ are linearly dependent (exactly collinear), in which case $\mathbf{X}^T\mathbf{X}$ is said to be singular and that is the end of the matter if we want a unique least squares solution.

It could be argued that the problems really arise when there is near collinearity between two or more of the columns but $\mathbf{X}^T\mathbf{X}$, however badly behaved (ill-conditioned, in the jargon), actually allows the regression coefficients to be estimated. The pickle we are in is illustrated in the three dimensional cube plot (Figure 12) of the data from Table 6, in which the points have been projected down onto the $X_1X_2$ plane. Notice from the scatterplot thus

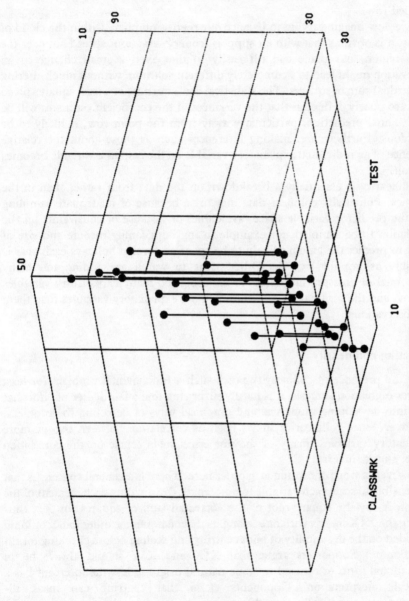

Figure 12. Cube plot of examination mark versus classwork and test scores.

formed that the two explanatory variables (TEST and CLASSWRK) are so highly correlated that the responses (EXAM) appear to lie along a somewhat lopsided row.

If we now imagine trying to balance our regression plane within the cloud of points, it is obvious that without support from observations spread out over the $X_1X_2$ region, our plane can tilt easily so that even a small change in an observation might lead to a completely different solution, without much altering the residual sum of squares. The statistical consequences of a least squares plane that is so poorly defined is that the variances of the coefficient estimates will be large. Thus, prediction, particularly away from the point row, is likely to be hazardous. Furthermore, making inferences such as those about the relative influence of an individual explanatory variable on the response variable becomes difficult.

Collinearity is essentially a breakdown on the data front rather than in the statistics. Potentially collinear data may arise because of inadequate sampling over the predictor variable space (avoidable) or because of constraints on the population to be sampled; for example, using both family income and size of house to predict the amount likely to be spent on foreign holidays each year is probably asking for trouble. Other areas to watch are adding too many polynomial or crossproduct terms or choosing too many explanatory variables anyway, and the cardinal sin of including more explanatory variables than there are observations.

## Detecting collinearity

Since the presence of collinearity poses such a fundamental problem for least squares regression analysis, it is hardly surprising that a fair degree of effort has gone into developing numerical and graphical ways of detecting the problem. Moreover, since collinearity shows itself as correlation between two or more explanatory variables, many of the numerical tools centre on the correlation matrix and its inverse.

However, a word of caution is in order here. There is a general consensus that it is sensible to scale each variable to unit length (by dividing each element of the column $X_j$ by the square root of the corrected sum of squares for $X_j$), thus leaving the $\mathbf{X^TX}$ matrix with ones along its diagonal. On the other hand, opinion is divided on the desirability of both centring and scaling before checking for ill-conditioning. Supporters argue that $\mathbf{X^TX}$ and $\mathbf{X^TY}$ should always be in correlational form or centred to some natural origin unless the intercept has a physical interpretation. Opponents claim that centring can mask ill-conditioning, specifically that due to any linear dependencies between the constant term and predictor variables. (See Belsley, 1984, Stewart, 1987, and the comments on these papers for a discussion of the arguments for and against.)

The data in Table 6 and in the cube plot in Figure 12 are observations on 20 out of 70 or so undergraduate students who attended a one year introductory statistics course in Keele in recent years. The second column (EXAM) shows final examination marks (out of 100); in the third are the scores obtained on a preliminary mathematics test (out of 30) which attempted to assess numeracy and graphical interpretation (TEST); those in column four are marks (out of 50) for the first term's class assignments (CLASSWRK). The idea is to predict final examination performance from work during the early part of the course.

Both explanatory variables correlate well with the response variable and show no serious vices (thanks to very careful screening of cases!). The expectation is that a linear regression model with both predictor variables should be a better fit to the data than a model with a single variable.

Running now through a regression analysis, we find (from the results summarized in Table 7) that the regression is almost entirely explained by just one of the two predictor variables, at least according to the $t$ tests on the individual coefficients. The overall $F$ test, on the other hand, suggests that a model with both coefficients is worth entertaining. We know also that both variables correlate highly and positively with the response variable and yet one of the coefficients is negative. In addition, added variable plots (not shown) would tell us to forget about including TEST. Inconsistencies have arisen because the correlation between the explanatory variables is just too high.

**Table 7.** Regression summary for the STATISTICS data (rounded to two decimal places)

| Variable | $\hat{b}_j$ | SE($\hat{b}_j$) | $t$ | $R^2$ |
|---|---|---|---|---|
| Constant | 7.14 | 4.47 | 1.60 (NS) | |
| TEST | −1.19 | 0.88 | −1.36 (NS) | 0.08 |
| CLASSWRK | 2.23 | 0.55 | 4.06 (***) | 0.89 |

MSE = 21.56                           $n$=20
$F$ = 74.66 (***)
*Note*    NS: not significant at 5% level
        *: significant at 5% level
      **: significant at 1% level
   ***: significant at 0.1% level

One way to track down the source of the collinearity is to look at scatterplots, influence diagnostics and so on, to see if there is perhaps a small cluster of outlying values causing the collinearity. Such collinearity influential points are sometimes, but not invariably, high leverage points. For these data. the scatterplot of classwork mark against preliminary test score (formed by the projected points) in Figure 12 is sufficient to show us that the relationship is strong, even if we were to exclude the odd straggly point.

However, homing in on the source may not be quite so straightforward when there are more than two explanatory variables to deal with because pairwise scatterplots will not necessarily help in picking up variables involved in collinearities in three or more dimensions or in distinguishing between, say, a dependency involving four variables or two separate pairwise ones. The same limitations apply to cube plots once we have at least four explanatory variables. Nor, of course, will examination of the correlation matrix of the explanatory variables reveal such higher order dependencies. This is not to argue that graphical methods are no help at all but additional information in the shape of numerical measures is needed to piece together the whole story.

**Collinearity diagnostics and the correlational structure of X.** In view of the criticism made above about the shortcomings of the correlation matrix as a source of collinearity information, it might seem a little perverse to start our discussion with measures derived from it. However, these statistics will detect overall collinearity, as well as showing how the precision of the coefficient estimates is affected. Also, from a practical viewpoint, we cannot overlook the fact that the correlation matrix and its inverse are accessible within most statistical packages.

The first measure is $R_j^2$, the squared multiple correlation coefficient for the $j$th explanatory variable $X_j$ regressed on the other $p-1$ predictors. This is defined as

$$R_j^2 = 1 - 1/c_{jj},$$

where $c_{jj}$ is the $j$th diagonal element of $\mathbf{C}$, the inverse of the correlation matrix. (Note that $\mathbf{C} = (\mathbf{X}^T\mathbf{X})^{-1}$ when the data have been centred with respect to their means and scaled as mentioned earlier.) The value of $R_j^2$ will be close to 1 if strong collinearity exists between $X_j$ and any other subset of the remaining $p-1$ explanatory variables. Large values, say, $R_j^2 > 0.9$, are worrying.

The diagonal elements of $\mathbf{C}$ also provide valuable information about the effect of collinearity on the precision of the $\hat{b}_j$s. Recalling that $\mathrm{Var}(\hat{\mathbf{b}}) = \sigma^2(\mathbf{X}^T\mathbf{X})^{-1}$, the variance of the estimate of the $j$th coefficient for centred and scaled data is clearly proportional to $c_{jj}$. Now, for orthogonal (uncorrelated) variables each diagonal element of $\mathbf{C}$ is unity, so the estimated variance of any $\hat{b}_j$ would be equal to MSE. From the expression for $R_j^2$ we see that $c_{jj}$ is greater than unity whenever $X_j$ is involved in a collinearity, resulting in a larger variance for the coefficient estimate. For this reason, the $c_{jj}$ are often referred to as *variance inflation factors*, VIFs. $\mathrm{VIF}_j = c_{jj} > 10$ is generally considered high.

However, when there is a large number of predictors, we shall have to dig deeper into the structure of $\mathbf{X}$ for a more comprehensive picture of which other variables are implicated in the particular collinearity.

**Collinearity diagnostics based on the eigenstructure of $\mathbf{X}$.** Briefly, ill-conditioning in $\mathbf{X}$ induces the ill-conditioning in $\mathbf{X}^T\mathbf{X}$ that causes our computational problems. An indication that all is not well in $\mathbf{X}$ is that at least one of the $p$ singular values of $\mathbf{X}$ is close to zero. What is relevant here is that the singular values of $\mathbf{X}$ are the square roots of the eigenvalues of the matrix $\mathbf{X}^T\mathbf{X}$. Thus, one or more small eigenvalues in $\mathbf{X}^T\mathbf{X}$ provide evidence of collinearity in $\mathbf{X}$.

'Smallness' of eigenvalues must be gauged rather carefully, though, since their absolute values depend on the units in which each explanatory variable is measured. This is a nuisance because it means that, for instance, re-expressing measurements in inches as centimetres on one predictor variable also changes the ratios of, say, the largest to the smallest of the eigenvalues and thereby appears to alter the degree of ill-conditioning, even though the regression models are otherwise equivalent. In fact, one of the advantages of scaling each column of $\mathbf{X}$ (excluding the constant) to unit length is that it allows us to set up some general guidelines about the relative sizes of the eigenvalues whatever the original scale of the data.

The question of whether or not collinearity exists and, if so, how many separate dependencies there are, is answered by looking at the *condition indices $k_j$* ($j = 1, 2, \ldots , p$) for $\mathbf{X}$. In terms of the eigenvalues of $\mathbf{X}^T\mathbf{X}$, denoted by $l_j$, these can be written as

$$k_j = \sqrt{l_{max}/l_j}.$$

The largest condition index, which is known as the condition number, is unity for a scaled matrix with linearly independent columns. The number of large condition indices indicates the number of collinearities in $\mathbf{X}$. According to Belsley *et al.* (1980) a value of $k_j$ around 5 to 10 indicates weak dependency whilst over 30 is strong.

Locating the collinearities brings in the VIFs and their counterparts for the uncentred $\mathbf{X}$ matrix. Without going into details, the inverse of the crossproducts matrix can be rewritten as

$$(\mathbf{X}^T\mathbf{X})^{-1} = \mathbf{V}\mathbf{L}^{-1}\mathbf{V}^T$$

where $\mathbf{V}$ is a $p \times p$ matrix whose columns are the eigenvectors of $\mathbf{X}^T\mathbf{X}$ and $\mathbf{L}$ is a $p \times p$ diagonal matrix of the eigenvalues of $\mathbf{X}^T\mathbf{X}$.

Thus, the variances of the estimated regression coefficients are the diagonal elements of $\sigma^2\mathbf{V}\mathbf{L}^{-1}\mathbf{V}^T$, that is

$$\mathrm{Var}(\hat{b}_j) = \sigma^2 \sum_{k=1}^{p} v_{jk}^2/l_k.$$

The individual components in this sum show the extent to which any collinearity (associated with a small $l$ term) inflates the variance of the coefficient estimate for a particular explanatory variable. Note, of course, that this sum is $\mathrm{VIF}_j$ for centred and scaled data.

In order to compare over coefficients, it is convenient to express these elements as proportions of the whole, when they become *variance decomposition proportions* (VDPs) defined as

$$\text{VDP}_{kj} = \frac{v_{kj}^2/l_k}{\sum_{i=1}^{p} v_{ik}^2/l_i}.$$

An unusually large proportion of the variance of two or more coefficient estimates concentrated in the VDPs linked with the same small eigenvalue is a warning of near dependency between the associated variables. 'Unusually large' here is taken to be $\text{VDP}_{kj} > 0.5$ (Belsley *et al.*, 1980).

Unfortunately, interpretation is more complicated when there are competing dependencies (that is, when several condition indices are roughly the same) because the proportions tend to be distributed somewhat arbitrarily amongst the variables. Belsley *et al.* (1980) offer advice on how to proceed in such circumstances.

To summarize: for most applications, we see if any collinearities exist and if so how many there are, using the condition indices; the VIFs and VDPs are then scrutinized to determine which coefficients are affected and which variables are involved.

Table 8 shows the VIFs, eigenvalues, condition indices and VDPs for the STATISTICS data set (with the **X** matrix scaled as recommended). We note two smallish eigenvalues giving two condition indices which suggest two collinearities, one of which is weak. Reading across the row associated with eigenvalue number two, we see that only for the intercept is there a VDP beyond our cut off of 0.5. On the other hand, the pair of large VDPs in row 3 lead us to conclude that the collinearity is only between TEST and CLASSWRK.

**Table 8.** Collinearity diagnostics for the STATISTICS data (rounded to three decimal places)

|  | No. | Eigen-value | Condition Index | VDP | | |
|---|---|---|---|---|---|---|
|  |  |  |  | Constant | TEST | CLASSWORK |
| UNCENTRED | 1 | 2.962 | 1.000 | 0.006 | 0.000 | 0.000 |
|  | 2 | 0.037 | 8.942 | 0.975 | 0.011 | 0.014 |
|  | 3 | 0.001 | 45.574 | 0.019 | 0.989 | 0.986 |
| CENTRED | 1 | 1.974 | 1.000 | — | 0.013 | 0.013 |
|  | 2 | 0.026 | 8.762 | — | 0.987 | 0.987 |
|  |  |  | VIF = |  | 19.698 | 19.689 |

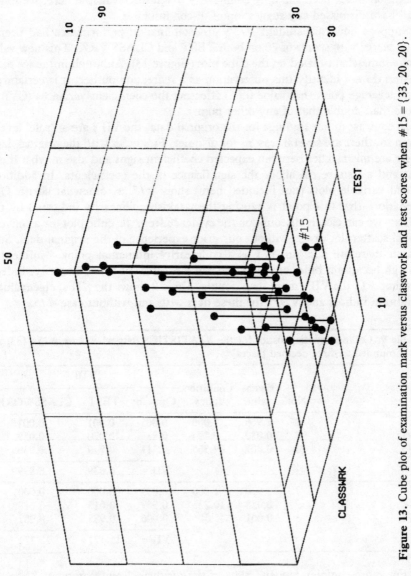

**Figure 13.** Cube plot of examination mark versus classwork and test scores when #15 = (33, 20, 20).

The values of the above diagnostics for the centred and scaled data are included in Table 8 for comparison purposes. It is worth noting that had the condition index been the only collinearity diagnostic available here, we might well have dismissed any suggestion of ill-conditioning.

Suppose now that student #15's pre-examination performance had been a little better with scores of 20 on both TEST and CLASSWRK. This new value looks somewhat isolated on the cube plot (Figure 13). Although influence diagnostics do not identify this observation as a regression outlier, it is certainly a high leverage point (hat value 0.65) affecting the coefficient variances (CVR is more than double that of any other point).

In contrast to our findings for the original data, the VIFs are at 'safe' levels. Even so, there are several reasons for disquiet. Firstly, as with the original data, there are mismatches between expected coefficient signs and also in what the $F$ test and $t$ tests reveal about the significance of the coefficients. In addition, added variable plots (not included here) show #15 as somewhat adrift. One scenario – that this point is causing the weakish collinearity indicated by the VIFs – we can clearly discount on the evidence from the cube plot (or a conventional scatterplot), even without our prior experience of the original data. Suspicion therefore falls on #15 as a collinearity influential point – influential though because it hides or masks the worst excesses of the collinearity. Indeed without #15 the VIFs more than double. Table 9 shows the VIFs, eigenvalues, condition indices and VDPs for these data with and without case #15.

**Table 9.** Collinearity diagnostics for the STATISTICS data when case #15={33, 20, 20} (rounded to three decimal places)

| | No. | Eigen-value | Condition Index | VDP Constant | TEST | CLASSWORK |
|---|---|---|---|---|---|---|
| | *1* | 2.966 | 1.000 | 0.005 | 0.001 | 0.001 |
| Incl. | *2* | 0.030 | 9.894 | 0.885 | 0.020 | 0.059 |
| #15 | *3* | 0.003 | 29.365 | 0.111 | 0.979 | 0.940 |
| | | | | VIF = | 6.839 | 6.839 |
| | *1* | 2.970 | 1.000 | 0.005 | 0.000 | 0.000 |
| Excl. | *2* | 0.028 | 10.235 | 0.989 | 0.015 | 0.018 |
| #15 | *3* | 0.001 | 45.506 | 0.006 | 0.985 | 0.982 |
| | | | | VIF = | 15.171 | 15.171 |

For more complex models, plots of the residuals from regressing $X_j$ on the remaining explanatory variables $\mathbf{X}[j]$ against each $X_j$ and also against the leverage values $h_{ii}[j]$ can help to track down potentially troublesome observations. As an illustration, the plots in Figure 14 are ordinary residuals from the regressions of TEST on CLASSWRK alone against TEST and of CLASSWRK on TEST

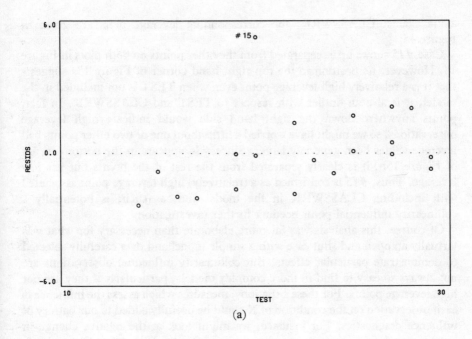

(a)

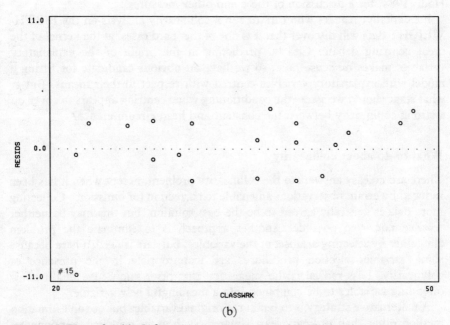

(b)

**Figure 14.** Plots of residuals from (a) test score regressed on classwork mark against test score; (b) classwork mark regressed on test score against classwork mark.

alone against CLASSWRK; the corresponding leverage plots are given in Figure 15.

Case #*15* shows up as separated from the other points on both plots in Figure 14. However, its position in the top right hand corner of Figure 15a suggests that it is a relatively high leverage point even when TEST is not included in the model; it is also an outlier with respect to TEST and CLASSWRK. In fact, points anywhere down the right hand side would indicate high leverage observations, so we might have worried a little about one or two other points had leverage values been generally larger. Since #*15* appears in the bottom corner of Figure 15b, it is clearly separated from the rest of the points but has low leverage. Thus, #*15* is confirmed as a (relatively) high leverage point associated with including CLASSWRK in the model and, as such, is potentially a collinearity influential point needing further investigation.

Of course, this analysis was far more elaborate than necessary for what was virtually an open and shut case with a simple model and data carefully selected to demonstrate particular effects. But collinearity influential observations are not always so easy to find in more complex models, particularly if they are not high leverage points. For these situations, measures which assess the influence of each observation on the condition of **X** could be usefully added to our battery of influence diagnostics. For instance, we might look at the relative change in condition indices as each observation is systematically deleted (see Chatterjee & Hadi, 1988, for a discussion of these and other measures).

Incidentally, readers who care to run a collinearity analysis on the BIRTH-WEIGHT data will discover that it is one of the 'hard cases' at the kernel of the great centring debate. Clearly, predicting at the origin of the explanatory variables makes no sense here, so we have an obvious candidate for fitting a model with explanatory variables centred with respect to their means. But at what stage should we assess the conditioning when centring appears to cover up a strong collinearity between the constant and head circumference?

**What to do about collinearity**

There are no easy answers to the collinearity problem, except when it has been induced by errant observations amenable to correction (or omission). Collecting more data is generally agreed to be the best solution, but this may be neither feasible nor even possible. Another approach is to eliminate the problem altogether by selecting a subset of the variables; but care is needed here because some variable selection procedures are inappropriate in the presence of collinearity. Less radical is the suggestion that prior knowledge might allow offending variables to be combined into a meaningful new variable.

An alternative strategy is to retain the original variables but use an estimation method other than ordinary least squares, such as in principal components, latent root and ridge regression methods (see, for example, Draper & Smith,

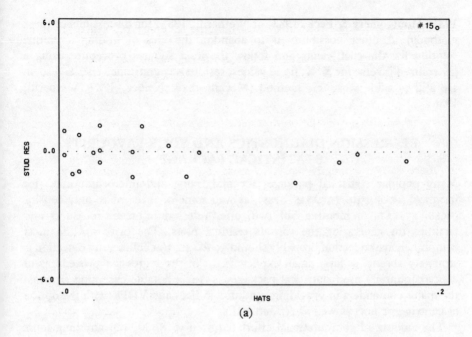

(a)

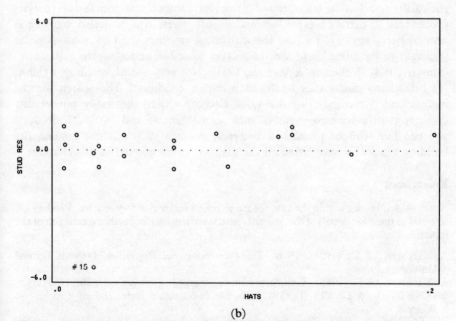

(b)

**Figure 15.** Leverage plots corresponding to (*a*) and (*b*) in Figure 14.

1981; Montgomery & Peck, 1982; or Wetherill, 1986; for discussions of these methods). Another possibility is to abandon the idea of finding a unique solution for the coefficients and follow the least squares procedure using a generalized inverse for $\mathbf{X}^T\mathbf{X}$; fitted values, residuals, significance tests and so on are still possible with this method (McCullagh & Nelder, 1989; Wetherill, 1986).

## REGRESSION DIAGNOSTICS AND YOUR FAVOURITE STATISTICAL PACKAGE

Many popular statistical packages for mainframe and microcomputers (for instance, BMDP, MINITAB, SAS, SPSS), as well some of their micro-only cousins (NCSS, SYSTAT, to mention but two) offer selected influence measures and facilities for generating the various residual plots. The prize for the most comprehensive collection probably should go to SAS. But collinearity detection is strangely absent, at least as an explicit item, in the regression procedures of many commonly used statistical packages. SAS is a notable exception amongst the major contenders in providing condition indices and VDPs (with the option of centring or not) as well as $R^2$ and VIFs.

The amount of computational effort required to winkle out anything more than $R^2$ and perhaps VIFs (or their reciprocals, the tolerances) varies considerably from package to package. For instance, in some (no names, no packdrill) one has to trail around principal components and factor analysis procedures to extract eigenvalues and eigenvectors. But, a health warning is needed here, anyway, because the numerical routines used by some popular packages to calculate these are themselves unstable under severe collinearity (Stewart, 1987; Velleman & Welsch, 1981). Not very useful, one might think, for calculating diagnostics to detect just that condition! The search for the recommended method (singular value decomposition) inevitably pushes one towards matrix-oriented systems such as GAUSS, SC and PC-ISP. Indeed, if you can live without prepacked analyses, systems such as these contain the building blocks for generating all the diagnostics mentioned in this chapter.

## References

Note: Most citations within the chapter are to books and expository articles. Readers are referred to these for details of the original journal articles and for further discussion of the topics.

ATKINSON, A.C. (1985). *Plots, Transformations and Regression*. Oxford: Oxford University Press.
ATKINSON, A.C. (1988). Transformations unmasked. *Technometrics*, **30** 311–318.
BARNETT, V. & LEWIS, T. (1984). *Outliers in Statistical Data*, 2nd ed. Chichester: Wiley.
BELSLEY, D.A. (1984). Demeaning conditioning diagnostics through centering (with Comments). *The American Statistician*, **38**, 79–93.

BELSLEY, D.A., KUH, E. & WELSCH, R.E. (1980). *Regression Diagnostics: Identifying Influential Data and Sources of Collinearity.* New York: Wiley.

CARROLL, R.J. & RUPERT, D. (1988). *Transformation and Weighting in Regression.* New York: Chapman and Hall.

CHATTERJEE, S. & HADI, A.S. (1986). Influential observations, high leverage points, and outliers in linear regression (with Comments). *Statistical Science,* **1,** 379–416.

CHATTERJEE, S. & HADI, A.S. (1988). *Sensitivity Analysis in Linear Regression.* New York: Wiley.

COOK, R.D. & WEISBERG, S. (1982). *Residuals and Influence in Regression.* New York: Chapman and Hall.

DANIEL, C. & WOOD, F.S. (1980). *Fitting Equations to Data,* 2nd ed. New York: Wiley.

DRAPER, N. & SMITH, H. (1981). *Applied Regression Analysis,* 2nd ed. New York: Wiley.

EMERSON, J.D. (1983). Mathematical aspects of transformation. In D. C. Hoaglin, F. Mosteller & J.W. Tukey (Eds) *Understanding Robust and Exploratory Data Analysis.* New York: Wiley.

EMERSON, J.D. & HOAGLIN, D.C. (1983). Resistant lines for *y* versus *x.* In D. C. Hoaglin, F. Mosteller & J.W. Tukey (Eds) *Understanding Robust and Exploratory Data Analysis.* New York: Wiley.

EMERSON, J.D. & HOAGLIN, D.C. (1985). Resistant multiple regression, one variable at a time. In D. C. Hoaglin, F. Mosteller & J.W. Tukey (Eds) *Exploring Data Tables, Trends and Shapes.* New York: Wiley.

EMERSON, J.D. & STOTO, M.A. (1983). Transforming data. In D. C. Hoaglin, F. Mosteller & J. W. Tukey (Eds) *Understanding Robust and Exploratory Data Analysis.* New York: Wiley.

GRAY, J.B. & LING, R.F. (1984). *K*–clustering as a detection tool for influential subsets in regression (with Discussion). *Technometrics,* **26,** 305–330.

HOAGLIN, D.C. & WELSCH, R.E. (1978). The hat matrix in regression and ANOVA. *The American Statistician,* **32,** 17–22.

HUBER, P. (1981). *Robust Statistics.* New York: Wiley.

LARSEN, W.A. & McCLEARY, S.A. (1972). The use of partial residual plots in regression analysis. *Technometrics,* **14,** 781–790.

LI, G. (1985). Robust regression. In D. C. Hoaglin, F. Mosteller & J. W. Tukey (Eds) *Exploring Data Tables, Trends and Shapes.* New York: Wiley.

LOVIE, P. (1986). Identifying outliers. In A. D. Lovie (Ed.) *New Developments in Statistics for Psychology and the Social Sciences, Vol. 1.* London: The British Psychological Society & Methuen.

McCULLAGH, P. & NELDER, J.A. (1989). *Generalized Linear Models,* 2nd ed. London: Chapman and Hall.

MONTGOMERY, D.C. & PECK, E.A. (1982). *Introduction to Linear Regression Analysis.* New York: Wiley.

MOSTELLER, F. & TUKEY, J.W. (1977). *Data Analysis and Regression.* Reading, Mass.: Addison Wesley.

OSBORN, J.F. (1979). *Statistical Exercises in Medical Research.* Oxford: Blackwell.

ROUSSEEUW, P.J. & LEROY, A.M. (1987). *Robust Regression and Outlier Detection.* New York: Wiley.

STEWART, G.W. (1987). Collinearity and least squares regression (with Comments). *Statistical Science,* **2,** 68–100.

VELLEMAN, P.F. & WELSCH, R.E. (1981). Efficient computing of regression diagnostics. *The American Statistician,* **35,** 234–242.

WEISBERG, S. (1985). *Applied Linear Regression*, 2nd ed. New York: Wiley.
WETHERILL, G.B. (1986). *Regression Analysis with Applications*. London: Chapman and Hall.
WOOD, F.S. (1973). The use of individual effects and residuals in fitting equations to data. *Technometrics*, 15, 677–695.

## Statistical Software

BMDP, Statistical Software Ltd, Cork, Eire.
GAUSS, Aptech Systems Inc., Kent, WA, USA.
MINITAB, Minitab Inc., State College, PA, USA.
NCSS, Kaysville, Utah, USA.
PC-ISP, Datavision AG, Klosters, Switzerland.
SAS, SAS Software Ltd, Marlow, UK.
SC, Lawrence Erlbaum Associates Ltd., Hove, Sussex, UK.
SPSS, SPSS UK Ltd., Chertsey, Surrey, UK.
SYSTAT, SYSTAT Inc., Evanston, IL. USA.

# 6

# Unbalanced Designs

RANALD MACDONALD

This chapter is about the analysis of unbalanced designs, that is, designs where there are unequal numbers of observations in each condition. Such designs can arise for a variety of reasons and may be planned or unplanned. Planned inequalities may occur where there is particular interest in certain of the conditions or where data collection is easier in some conditions than in others. If the inequalities are unplanned they could be due to missing data (because of equipment failure, non-compliance with instructions, or a host of other reasons). The problems which arise due to balance are related to the nature of the study and to the generalizations which it is wished to make from the results. Balanced designs are not necessarily best, as we shall see. The nature of studies and generalizations from them will be discussed first. A review of different possible tests in the analysis of variance framework follows, and several examples are presented and discussed. Sometimes something is known about missing data, and ways of using this information to estimate the missing values have been developed. An assessment of these is given. Finally there is an attempt to pull together the issues of generalization which are at the heart of this chapter.

Analyses of variance on balanced designs give equal weight to each of the means in each treatment. Because of this, tests of main effects have equal power against any alternative hypothesis, regardless of where the differences between treatments lie; this is not true with unbalanced designs. If an experimenter wanted to manipulate the power of an experiment so as to have more power against a specific hypothesis, then he or she could deliberately choose an unbalanced design. However, few will wish to do this and in general this argument favours the use of balanced designs. Balanced designs have also been shown to be more robust than unbalanced ones against violations of assumptions of normality and homogeneity of variance (for example Glass et al., 1972, and Milligan et al.,1987). Despite these drawbacks, the analysis of one factor unbalanced designs is uncontentious. In a one way analysis of variance, if a significant effect is found, it demonstrates significant differences between the means of the conditions involved. It is with two or more factor studies that problems of interpretation arise since in unbalanced designs the hypotheses being tested will not be independent. I discuss this in more detail below.

135

## EXPERIMENTS AND GROUP STUDIES

A distinction should be made between studies of existing groups, here referred to as group studies, and experimental studies. In experiments, subjects are randomly allocated to groups and then manipulated in different ways. Thus a group study might investigate patients diagnosed as suffering from different illnesses, whereas an experiment would involve the random allocation of subjects to groups which would then be systematically infected with an appropriate illness. Any naturally occurring groups of patients are unlikely to have equal sizes whereas the size of the experimental groups is up to the experimenter. There is a difference in the interpretation that can be put on significant differences between the conditions in the two types of study. When a difference is found between any naturally occurring groups of patients one cannot be sure that it was caused by the illness since the pre-existing groups may differ in many ways quite independently from the effects of the illness. For example it is quite common for illnesses to be differentially prevalent in different ages and sexes. However, when a difference is found in an experiment it can be said to be caused by the ways in which the experimental groups have been manipulated since the experimental groups started the experiment as equivalent.

In an experiment, balanced designs are often recommended as there is no reason for allocating different numbers of subjects to the different groups and balanced designs are the most mathematically tractable. When a population is categorized according to some natural criterion, for example, sex or blood group, the resulting groups will not be of equal size nor will they be equivalent to random samples with respect to other variables. In nonexperimental studies where the interest is in extant groups then balanced designs may not be best. Constraining groups of subjects defined with respect to one variable to have equal numbers of subjects as classified by some other variable, for example, males and females, introduces systematic and unknown biases into estimates of group means. Only where the observations are random samples from some target population can we obtain unbiased estimates of the parameters we require. We shall call these OSCAR designs since the data are Observations Sampled Completely At Random. Others designs are usually sampled Randomly Only Within Treatment and these will be referred to as ROWT designs. Designs which are neither OSCAR nor ROWT are in general unanalysable, since most statistical tests require the randomness assumption. Thus group studies which are OSCAR enable generalization to naturally occurring populations. As experimental studies are constrained to be ROWT, such inferences are restricted to hypothetical replications of the initial study rather than to naturally occurring populations.

Many psychologists suppose that experiments are better than group studies. As Huitema (1980) put it 'randomized designs' (as opposed to group studies) 'are not just a slight preference – they are SO much better'. However as we have seen, while experiments make casual inference easier, their random samples do not occur in nature, and so their results generalize directly to the potential results of hypothetical replications of the same experiment. Only group studies can generalize directly to naturally occurring populations which have not been manipulated.

## THE PARTIAL CONFOUNDING OF EFFECTS IN FACTORIAL DESIGNS

The confounding problems of unbalanced designs appear in factorial designs having two or more factors. Here the variance cannot be analysed into the same main effects and interactions that are possible in a balanced design. The main effects and interactions are confounded, that is to say, some variance is common to more than one of the components. Let us consider an example of a study in which we wish to compare the attitude to religion held by male and female students in the arts, science and social science faculties in a particular university. If the science faculty is predominantly male, the social science faculty has roughly equal proportions of males and females and the arts faculty is predominantly female, differences between the faculties will be confounded with sex differences and vice versa. To make matters worse, the main effects will also be confounded with the interaction. In this example we can imagine two types of study. The first would be a balanced design where equal numbers from each of the six sex by faculty combinations were randomly sampled from the target population. Here, although the observations in each condition constitute a random sample, when they are aggregated they cease to be random. Thus no faculty sample is random since all are constrained to have equal numbers of males and females. Here, calculation of unbiased estimates of the main effects of faculty and sex as they appear in the population is not possible. In the second approach a random sample of students ignoring sex and faculty is drawn. Here, one would expect an unbalanced design, but aggregated conditions are still random samples and unbiased estimates of main effects as they appear in the population can be calculated. This emphasizes the point that 'balanced' is not always best; to enable generalizations to naturally occurring populations unbalanced OSCAR designs are better.

The position in two way and higher order factorial designs can be summarized in the following way. The effects of factors in OSCAR designs will in general not be independent, while in ROWT designs, if any factor is ignored, the design is no longer ROWT since the sample within treatment is stratified with respect to the ignored factor. Returning to the study of student attitudes, if the design was balanced with respect to sex and faculty, then when either factor was ignored the samples would no longer be random. If sex was ignored the science faculty sample would have too many women and the arts sample too many men. Thus generalizations from ROWT designs cannot ignore any of the factors in the design. Bearing these distinctions in mind we shall proceed to examine the possible tests within an analysis of variance.

**Table 1.** Linear models underlying the ANOVA tests.

$$Y_{ijk} = \qquad\qquad\qquad\qquad\qquad e_{ijk} \quad (1)$$
$$Y_{ijk} = A_j + \qquad\qquad\qquad\qquad e_{ijk} \quad (2)$$
$$Y_{ijk} = \qquad B_k + \qquad\qquad\qquad e_{ijk} \quad (3)$$
$$Y_{ijk} = \qquad\qquad\qquad A^*B_{jk} + \quad e_{ijk} \quad (4)$$
$$Y_{ijk} = A_j + B_k + \qquad\qquad e_{ijk} \quad (5)$$
$$Y_{ijk} = A_j + \qquad A^*B_{jk} + \quad e_{ijk} \quad (6)$$
$$Y_{ijk} = \qquad B_k + A^*B_{jk} + \quad e_{ijk} \quad (7)$$
$$Y_{ijk} = A_j + B_k + A^*B_{jk} + \quad e_{ijk} \quad (8)$$

## POSSIBLE STATISTICAL TESTS

Most discussions of the analyses of unbalanced designs have viewed analyses of variance as multiple regression problems. This involves fitting linear equations to the data. An effect is found to be significant if an equation incorporating that effect fits the data significantly better than the equivalent equation without that effect. Irrelevant differences between conditions should not affect the relative fit of the pair of equations being tested. It is therefore assumed that differences between conditions independent of the treatment effects in a pair of equations under consideration have been removed from the data before the fits are computed. In a two factor design there are eight linear equations which could be fitted to the data. These are given in Table 1. With eight equations there are 28 possible comparisons of the goodness of fit between two equations. Such a multiplicity of tests gives rise to many different suggestions as to what tests are appropriate. Some consensus does however exist in that only one comparison has been suggested for testing the significance of the interaction effect while three comparisons have been suggested for each main effect. Surprisingly no one has suggested reporting the results of all the recommended tests. This is probably because, in cases where the results were conflicting, interpretation would be difficult.

The only test which has seriously been considered for the interaction is equation 8 vs. equation 5. The interaction is defined as those differences between conditions which are independent of the main effects. If equation 4 were tested against equation 1 in an unbalanced design the interaction effect would be confounded by some main effects. It would also result in using an error term which pooled the main effects and the usual error term thereby reducing the power of the test in the presence of the main effects. The usual recommendation is therefore that the interaction is tested by seeing if equation 8 fits the data better than equation 5. This test will be denoted by *AB* c *A, B*; meaning the test of the *AB* interaction controlling for *A* and *B* effects. I shall suggest some complications and alternatives to this procedure later when discussing higher order factorial designs.

The three possible tests of the *A* effect are equation 8 vs. equation 7, equation 5 vs. equation 3 and equation 2 vs. equation 1. Using the same notation as used for the interaction these tests will be denoted by (1) *A* c *B, AB*, (2) *A* c *B*, and (3) *A*, respectively. The first of these tests (*A* c *B, AB*) is usually the most frequently recommended. It tests whether there is an *A* effect present independent of the *B* effect and the *AB* interaction. That is to say, it tests the hypothesis that, if the means of each *AB* condition are computed, the means of these means at each level of *A* will be equal. Thus the means of each *AB* condition are equally weighted and not weighted according to the number of observations on which they are based. The literature confusingly refers to this analysis as an analysis of unweighted means. As Howell (1987) remarks, a better name would be an analysis of equally weighted means. We shall take up his suggestion and refer to this as a test of equally weighted means (EWM). The second test (*A* c *B*) tests the hypothesis that the *A* effect is significant after removing the *B* effect but not the interaction effects. This hypothesis is not easily expressible in terms of differences between the condition means, though Carlson & Timm (1974) have produced the appropriate formula. It is extremely complicated and has no meaningful interpretation in words (Howell & McConaughy, 1982). The third test (*A*) tests the existence of the *A* effect regardless of the possibility that it may be due to other effects present in the study. Because this tests the hypothesis that the means of the observations in each of the levels of *A* are the same it corresponds to testing the means of the means in each level of *A* weighted by the number of observations contributing to them. Thus it is referred to in the literature as the 'weighted means' analysis. To avoid the pejorative connotations of the standard nomenclature I shall refer to this test as the test of Equally Weighted Observations (EWO). After more discussion of possible procedures, I have included an example of both EWO and EWM analyses (see Tables 3, 4, 5 and 6).

## A REVIEW OF THE TEST PROCEDURES IN THE LITERATURE

Different authors have advised using different strategies for applying these tests. Since all advised testing *AB* c *A, B* for the interaction I shall only review how they have approached testing the main effects. However, I shall return to the interaction tests later. Overall & Spiegel (1969) suggested three possible approaches : the EWM analysis *A* c *B, AB* and *B* c *A, AB*, the same analysis when the interaction is ignored, *A* c *B* and *B* c *A*, and a hierarchical analysis *A* and $B$ c $A$. The authors favoured the second method as they were in general happy to ignore interaction effects. In a subsequent paper (Overall, 1975) they revised their preference in favour of the first method since most texts on analysis of variance choose not to ignore interactions. Use of the third analysis is advised only in the special case where one wishes to test first if the $A$ effect is significant as it stands and then test if the $B$ factor has an effect independent of the $A$ factor. In the example they quote, the first test is whether a father's social class affects the psychopathology of his children, and the second is whether the children's social class affects the psychopathology independently from their father's social class. Using this analysis it was hoped to test the different effects of ascribed and achieved social class.

Applebaum & Cramer (1974) suggested a radically different stepwise approach. If the interaction is significant they claim that no tests of main effects are appropriate. If the interaction is not significant, test $A$ c $B$ and $B$ c $A$. In the event of one or both of these tests being significant, conclude that the significant effects exist and stop testing. If none of these tests is significant, test $A$ and $B$. If either one of these tests is significant, conclude that it exists. However, if both are significant, conclude that the situation is indeterminate and that one or other but not both of $A$ and $B$ is significant.

O'Brien (1976) pointed out that the $A$ c $B$ test could be significant while the $A$ test was not. The logic of such a result is that both $A$ and $B$ are contributing to a significant effect; the $B$ effect is suppressing the $A$ effect. He therefore recommended that the Applebaum and Cramer procedure should be modified to check for such a situation.

Cramer & Applebaum (1980) claimed that their procedure was more powerful than the EWM analyses with either no or small interactions. Overall *et al.* (1981) disputed this and performed a simulation which showed that the two methods had similar power but Cramer & Applebaum's resulted in biased estimates of the main effects in the presence of a small interaction. Further they disliked letting the data determine which statistical test is to be applied.

Howell & McConaughy (1982) and Howell (1987) emphasized the importance of simplicity. In particular they recommended that the 'peculiarly weighted means' test ($A$ c $B$) be abandoned on the grounds that it has no simple interpretation in terms of differences between treatment means. They disliked the sequential model-fitting approach of Cramer & Applebaum in which the hypotheses to be tested are determined by the results of the previous test. Such procedures must change the overall probability of getting a significant effect when no effects are present. In Cramer & Applebaum's case the probability of a significant $A$ effect must be the probability of getting no significant interaction and either a significant $A$ c $B$ effect or no significant $A$ c $B$ effect but a significant $A$ effect together with no significant $B$ effect. Howell & McConaughy (1982) and Howell (1987) recommended the EWM analysis ($A$ c $B$, $AB$ and $B$ c $A$, $AB$) as standard and using only the EWO analyses ($A$ and $B$)

where the frequencies are representative of those in the population and the experimenter wishes to generalize to differences in this population.

## CLARIFICATIONS AND RECOMMENDATIONS

Cramer & Applebaum (1980) claim that main effects cannot be tested in the presence of interactions. Other authors, for example, Scheffé (1959), hold the opposite view. As MacRae (1988), following Lord (1953), pointed out, it is the interpretation which can be put on the results of a statistical analysis that is important. We have to ask the question, can the results of our tests enable us to make the generalizations we would wish?

A problem arises in two or more factor ROWT designs for tests of interactions lower than the highest order interaction or for tests of main effects when the aim is to generalize the main effects to a real population. Here, as in every higher order ROWT design, there is no way of estimating the mean score when the data have been collapsed over one or more factors. This depends on how the scores in each condition are distributed over the collapsed factor. One has to estimate a weighted mean where the weights are unknown. In this situation there can be no test of the main effects.

It seems to me that the crux of the problem is the population to which one wishes to generalize. In ROWT designs the only possible aim is to generalize to hypothetical populations of subjects in balanced replications of the study. Here if an EWM analysis is used it is assumed that equal numbers of subjects have been allocated to each condition. It is important to note that these hypothetical replications must include all the factors in the original study. Thus in a three way factor design with factors $A$, $B$ and $C$, a significant $AB$ interaction generalizes to $AB$ interactions found in balanced factorial $ABC$ designs. The $AB$ interaction only generalizes to balanced $AB$ designs if we are prepared to assume that factor $C$ has no effects and can be ignored.

There is, however, a partial way forward for ROWT designs where one wants to generalize to a real population whose distribution across the conditions is unknown. This is to perform a simple effects analysis. To examine the main effect due to one factor, the variation due to this factor is estimated at each combination of levels of all the other factors. We cannot tell how this factor affects the population as a whole because we do not know how many subjects are in each condition. However I have provided a test for differences due to one of the factors at each combination of the other factors. Simple effects analysis effectively performs separate one way analyses of variance on one factor for each level of the other with a pooled error term. I shall denote the simple effects analysis of $A$ at each level of $B$ as $A @ B1$, $A @ B2$, etc. Similar analyses of lower order interactions are possible, for example testing two way interactions at every combination of factors not included in the analyses. However, referring to such analyses as simple seems inappropriate.

Analyses of OSCAR designs are more straightforward. As I remarked, when the data in such designs have been collapsed over some of the factors, the data still remain a random sample. Here not only do EWO analyses generalize to the target population but also EWM analyses can be applied to only the cells involved in an interaction. In this way these analyses can generalize to the results of balanced designs including only the factors involved in the effect. Thus, a significant $AB$ interaction can generalize to a balanced design involving $A$ and $B$ irrespective of how many factors were in the original study. In this respect OSCAR designs contrast favourably with ROWT designs.

So, to conclude this section, here are my recommendations, which depend on whether the design of the study was OSCAR or ROWT. With OSCAR designs, EWO analyses of main effects and EWM analyses (of just the cells involved) of lower order interactions are possible. The EWO analyses generalize to the target population while these EWM analyses generalize to balanced designs using only the factors in the interactions. If it is wanted to generalize to full replications of the overall study an EWM analysis weighting ALL the cells equally is also possible. There is no problem about testing for a main effect whether or not an interaction is present, as its interpretation remains valid.

With a ROWT design, we can only generalize to the results of hypothetical replications. Simplicity suggests that these should be balanced so that the appropriate tests are EWM tests of interactions and main effects (weighting all the cells equally). Here a problem arises where, despite the nature of the design, you wish to say something about the target population when a higher order interaction is present. The interaction implies that each main effect depends on the associated level of the other main effects and similar problems arise for lower order interactions. Where the distribution of the observations across the levels is unknown we cannot tell what the effects in the population would be. If the design is two factor a simple effects analysis, $A @ B1$, etc., is useful; however, if one were to allow for the possibility of a three way interaction the analysis would be $A @ B1C1$, etc. In a three way design one might also wish to test the two way interactions at each level of the third factor. This may be seen as approaching the limits of usefulness owing to the numbers and complexity of the tests involved. The recommendations are summarized in Table 2. The next section applies these ideas to specific examples.

## EXAMPLES OF POSSIBLE DESIGNS

We shall now look at a number of specific instances of empirical studies. For simplicity we shall restrict ourselves to two way studies. Here $AB$ c $A, B$ is used to test the interaction and we focus on the tests of main effects. It should be remembered in higher order designs the same problems that arise in testing main effects in two way designs also arise in testing interactions lower than the highest possible. The cases looked at consist of the true experiment, an experiment generalizing to pre-existing groups, the group study, and two hybrid cases.

**Table 2.** Possible analyses and generalizations recommended in the text. (EWO is equally weighted observations. EWM is equally weighted means. SE hold *B* is a simple effects analysis holding *B* constant.).

| Generalization DESIGN | Target Population | Main Effect *A* balanced AB Design | Main Effect *A* balanced ABC Design | Interaction *AB* balanced AB Design | Interaction *AB* balanced ABC Design |
|---|---|---|---|---|---|
| *AB* OSCAR | EWO or SE hold *B* | EWM | | EWM | |
| *A* OSCAR *B* ROWT | SE hold *B* | EWM | | EWM | |
| *A* ROWT *B* OSCAR | EWO or SE hold *B* | EWM | | EWM | |
| *AB* ROWT | SE hold *B* | EWM | | EWM | |
| *ABC* OSCAR | EWO or SE hold *BC* | EWM *AB* Cells or SE hold *C* | EWM *ABC* cells | EWM *AB* cells or SE hold *C* | EWM *ABC* cells |
| *ABC* ROWT | SE hold *BC* | SE hold *C* | EWM | SE hold *C* | EWM |

### Case a. The true experiment

■ We are interested in the effects of noise level and lighting conditions on subjects' susceptibility to headaches. Noise levels and lighting levels are decided upon and subjects are randomly assigned to one of all possible noise/lighting combinations resulting. This design is ROWT, not OSCAR, since there is no clearly defined population from which to sample.

This is a paradigmatic example of a case in which a balanced design is most appropriate. Any inequality in the numbers of observations made will be unrelated to the hypothetical target population since there is no reason for postulating any inequalities in it. It is therefore entirely appropriate to apply an EWM analysis in this case. Any significant main effect implies that if we were to repeat the experiment with a balanced design we should expect to replicate this effect.

### Case b. The experiment generalizing to pre-existing groups

■ Here again we are interested in the effects of noise and lighting levels on susceptibility to headaches in office workers. This time we wish to find random samples of people and subject them to different noise/lighting conditions matching the naturally occurring conditions. However in the absence of knowing what these are we run the same experiment as in case *a*.

This may be an impossible generalization anyway. Problems of differences between the selection of experimental and real groups may invalidate it. The unknown numbers in each category in the target population make it impossible to estimate the main effects when an interaction is present. If the effect of one of the variables depends on the level of the other then the overall effect of the first variable could be any weighted average of its effects at each level on the second variable. Indeed it should be the weighted average of its effects over all naturally occurring levels of the second variable including those not used in the experiment. Since this design is not OSCAR, the numbers of observations in the experimental conditions do not correspond to population frequencies. Thus an EWO analysis is inappropriate. For the main effects we shall have to confine ourselves to a simple effects analysis. The alternative is to give up attempting to generalize to existing groups and analyse the data as for case *a*.

## Case *c*. The group study

■ We are interested in the effects of age and sex on memory loss in head injured patients. Samples of male and female head injured patients in each of a number of age groups are obtained.

Here the design could be regarded as OSCAR. If, because of sampling bias, we were not prepared to make the assumption that the design was OSCAR, it would be difficult to justify the assumption that the design was ROWT. It is hard to imagine that there is a bias in the sample which affects only the age and sex of the sampled subjects and not any other related characteristics. The numbers in the different groups reflect differences in that real population. The EWM analysis of main effects depends arbitrarily on the other factors in the study. We wish to test whether the mean of male patients differs from the female mean and whether the means in the different age groups differ. Here an EWO analysis is appropriate for both main effects. An EWM analysis would only be of interest if one wished to generalize to the hypothetical results of a study on this population which used a balanced design.

## Case *d*. The first hybrid case

■ We are interested in differences in reading between a dyslexic group (assumed to be a random sample from a population of dyslexics) and a control group, together with the effects of social class on the two groups. The control group is assumed to be a random sample of children from the same age cohorts.

Here we assume we have a design which is OSCAR with respect to the social class factor but is ROWT with respect to the other factor. The unequal numbers in each social class would therefore reflect the true population differences. In this case the EWM main effect of dyslexics versus controls would be arbitrarily related to the categories of social class we had defined. Only an EWO analysis of the differences between the dyslexics and normals generalizes to the population of dyslexics. An EWM analysis refers to a population of dyslexics equally distributed across the social classes. As the relative sizes of the dyslexic and control groups are arbitrary, a simple effects analysis of social class effects in dyslexics and normals seems appropriate, or perhaps an EWM analysis of the differences between classes generalizing to the results of balanced design replications of this study.

*Case e.* **A hybrid study with a matched design**

■ We are again interested in differences in reading between a dyslexic group (assumed to be a random sample from a population of dyslexics) and a control group, together with the effects of social class on the two groups. Here the control group is a sample of children from the same age cohorts matched for social class.

Here the design is OSCAR for the dyslexic group with respect to social class but in other respects it is ROWT. An EWO analysis of dyslexics versus controls tells us whether dyslexics differ from a sample of matched normals, whereas an EWM analysis tells us whether we could expect this difference in a balanced replication. Again a simple effects analysis or an EWM analysis should be used to investigate social class.

To sum up, in two factor designs EWO tests of main effects are recommended for OSCAR designs generalizing to natural populations. In two factor balanced designs or where the interaction is assumed to be negligible, EWM tests of main effects can be used. Here one is generalizing to hypothetical results from balanced replications of the experiment. In all other cases no overall test of the main effects is possible and one should resort to simple effects analyses.

## A WORKED EXAMPLE

Suppose we obtained a random sample of students at a particular university and classified them by sex and whether they were studying predominantly arts or science subjects. The attitude of these students to proposed changes at their university was then measured on a twenty point scale; the results are in Table 3.

**Table 3.** Data used in example

| Arts | Male | 10 | 14 | 11 | 12 | 12 | 15 | 14 | 12 | | | | | | | | |
|------|------|----|----|----|----|----|----|----|----|----|----|----|----|----|----|----|----|
| | Female | 10 | 12 | 11 | 11 | 12 | 9 | 13 | 8 | 13 | 9 | 10 | 8 | 9 | 10 | 12 | 9 |
| Science | Male | 13 | 15 | 13 | 13 | 15 | 13 | 13 | 15 | | | | | | | | |
| | Female | 14 | 10 | 10 | 8 | | | | | | | | | | | | |

**Table 4.** Equally weighted observations analysis of variance for main effects on data in Table 3

| Source | SS | df | MS | F | P |
|--------|-----|----|-----|------|-------|
| Science vs. Arts | 20.26 | 1 | 20.26 | 7.34 | <0.05 |
| Sex | 66.01 | 1 | 66.01 | 23.93 | <0.01 |
| Science × Sex | 2.25 | 1 | 2.25 | 0.82 | n.s. |
| Error | 88.25 | 32 | 2.76 | | |

This is an OSCAR design and an EWO analysis of main effects and an EWM analysis of the interaction is appropriate. The results of the analysis appear in Table 4.

It can be seen that both the main effects are significant; sex at the 0.01 level and faculty at the 0.05 level. This means that we can conclude that in this university population males have greater attitude scores than females and science students have greater attitude scores than arts students. Since the imbalance in the study implies that the hypotheses being tested are related one could ask the question: 'Suppose we performed a balanced replication could we still expect the differences to be present?' This question could be answered by applying an EWM analysis to the main effects. The results of the analysis appear in Table 5. It now appears that the main effect of the subject area is no longer significant. The $F(1, 32)$ testing for an effect of faculty has changed from 7.34 in the EWO analysis to 1.22 in the EWM analysis, from an effect almost significant at the 0.01 level to barely a trace of an effect. The conclusions of the analyses are that sex differences have been established in both OSCAR designs and ROWT designs balanced with respect to sex and subject area; whereas the subject area difference has only been established with respect to OSCAR designs. It has not been demonstrated that we could expect to find a subject area difference in samples balanced with respect to sex.

Now suppose the same data had been obtained but this time the arts and science groups were random samples of arbitrary size from the two faculties. This time the design is OSCAR with respect to sex but ROWT with respect to subject area. Using the ROWT analysis in Table 5 to generalize to the results of balanced designs is still legitimate. If we want to generalize to the population of arts and science students the tests applied to the subject area effect and the

**Table 5.** Equally weighted means analysis of variance applied on data in Table 3

| Source | SS | df | MS | F | P |
|--------|-----|----|-----|------|-------|
| Science vs. Arts | 3.36 | 1 | 3.36 | 1.22 | n.s. |
| Sex | 51.36 | 1 | 51.36 | 18.62 | <0.01 |
| Science × Sex | 2.25 | 1 | 2.25 | 0.82 | n.s. |
| Error | 88.25 | 32 | 2.76 | | |

**Table 6.** Simple effects analysis of sex on data in Table 3

| Source | SS | df | MS | F | P |
|---|---|---|---|---|---|
| Sex in Arts | 24.08 | 1 | 24.08 | 8.73 | <0.01 |
| Sex in Science | 28.17 | 1 | 28.17 | 10.21 | <0.01 |
| Error | 88.25 | 32 | 2.76 | | |

interaction in Table 4 still stand. However the main effect of sex cannot be tested without assuming the interaction is zero. Instead, separate simple effects analyses of sex in the arts and in the science groups should be performed. These appear in Table 6. From the analysis we can conclude that there is a difference in sexes in both the science and the arts groups at the 0.01 level. From this we can be sure that there will be an overall effect of sex regardless of the distribution of arts and science students. If the sex effect had not been significant in both the groups we could not have concluded that there would be an overall effect of sex unless we assumed that the interaction between sex and faculty was zero.

The above analyses were performed using BMDP4V which has facilities for all the tests discussed so far. SPSSX also performs such analyses. If you do not have a big statistical package to hand, the EWO analysis of main effects can be performed by treating the analysis as one way and ignoring the other factors. Several methods exist for approximating to the EWM analysis when the design is unbalanced. For example, Bartlett (1937) used a procedure involving a multiple covariance analysis, and Winer (1971) gives a harmonic means analysis. These procedures may be useful where one does not have access to a modern computing environment but the EWM analysis is available on SPSSX, BMDP and SAS and is to be preferred.

## FILLING IN FOR MISSING DATA

So far we have assumed that the only results we have are the observed data. Sometimes we know in addition that it was intended to make more observations in a particular condition but because of such factors as experimenter error, equipment failure, subject refusal, or failure to understand instructions, a known amount of data was lost. Missing data can only be handled by knowing the nature of the mechanism giving rise to it. The simplest case is where the data are Missing Completely At Random (MCAR). Here each observed value is equally likely to go missing. A more complex case occurs when some conditions are more likely to produce missing data than others but within each condition each observation is equally likely to be missing. This we have called Missing At Random Only Within Treatment (MROWT). Yet more complex cases arise when the missing data depend on the observed score (for example, high values are more likely to go missing). This changes the nature of the distribution of scores and one must either use nonparametric analyses or specify the distribution of the missing data. The case where missing data depend on the combination of the treatment and the value of the score makes the concept of average differences, in both observed and missing data, between conditions, exceedingly hypothetical. The more complex the assumptions necessary for the analysis the better it is to restrict oneself to inferences about observable data. Little & Rubin (1987) describe some such models which make complex assumptions about missing data. These will be discussed below.

All the analyses we have considered assume that the data are MCAR or MROWT. This being so the missing data are ignorable, so why not just analyse the data using the procedures suggested earlier? There are three answers. The analyses of unbalanced designs are less robust against violations in the underlying assumptions (Milligan *et al.*, 1987) and imputing new data to restore the balance would also restore the robustness. Secondly, in the analysis of OSCAR designs, we may have tried to obtain data from a known number of subjects in each condition but have been unsuccessful in certain cases. Here it may be preferable to use the known number of subjects in each condition rather than the number of observations for which data exist, since this is a more accurate estimate of the relative sizes of the conditions in the target population. Finally, in appropriate circumstances, knowledge of a covariate can tell us something about the likely values of missing data. This information can be used to increase the precision of the analysis.

The simplest way of handling missing data is to replace them with something else. Perhaps the most obvious way is to collect more data. Less desirable *ad hoc* methods include selecting data at random from previous studies or randomly sampling the current data and duplicating the selected points. An alternative procedure is to substitute the mean of the condition where the missing data occurred. This method reduces the error variance but this can be corrected using the actual numbers of observed data points. When this is done the analysis is equivalent to weighting the sample means with the frequencies of missing and observed rather than just the frequency of the observed data.

In designs with covariates it is possible to use the covariate to estimate what the missing score might be. Buck (1960) suggested performing a linear regression analysis predicting the score from the covariates on the complete cases, using it to predict the missing scores, and then substituting the predicted scores for the missing ones. An improvement in this procedure is the Expectation-Maximization (EM) algorithm which repeats the regression analysis including the substituted data and then resubstitutes the missing data from the new regression equation. The process iterates until stability is reached. The process is a very general algorithm for maximum likelihood estimation in incomplete data problems. It can be used where the relation between the covariate and the dependent variables can be specified by other than a linear equation. Other algorithms designed to find maximum likelihood estimates, for example Newton-Raphson iteration, could be used to solve the same problem. Both algorithms are currently available in BMDP5V (see Schluchter, 1988).

There is a problem with the application of analysis of covariance to test for differences between pre-existing groups. Lord (1967) and (1969) have shown dramatically that the analysis of variance and the analysis of covariance are testing quite distinct hypotheses. Interpretation of analysis of covariance is often misunderstood in what Huitema (1980) refers to as nonequivalent group designs. If subjects have been randomly assigned to the groups, or if the subjects have been assigned to their groups on the basis of their scores on the covariate, then interpretation is not a problem. If the groups are pre-existing, for example, male vs female or sufferers from different diseases, then there are problems in interpreting the results of a covariance analysis. In such cases similar problems arise where missing data have been imputed using information from covariates. What does it mean to say that the differences between the means of the different groups are zero when they have been adjusted for the covariate? It does not mean there is no difference in a target population in the unadjusted means. Thus there is little justification in employing covariance analyses on data from OSCAR designs, especially where EWO analyses are used. Covariance analyses and imputing missing values with covariance techniques are only justified in experiments where subjects have been allocated randomly to groups or subjects have been allocated to groups on the basis of their covariate scores. This means that if we did an experiment ensuring that the mean values of the groups on the covariate were the same then we would observe no differences in the scores. It means that if we were to obtain a random sample of matched pairs from each of the groups on the covariate we would not expect their means to differ on the dependent variable. It does not mean that if we took a random sample from the two groups their means would be the same. Natural groups differ on most possible covariates.

The case of the repeated measures design is similar to that of a factorial design with covariates. Here the other dependent variables as well as any covariates can be entered into the regression equation used to predict the missing values. Again iterative maximum likelihood procedures are used to estimated the missing values in such cases. Such procedures should be used with care. Essentially they are guessing the most likely missing values assuming that they come from the same population as the observed ones. The analysis then proceeds as if the guessed data had been observed. If the use of the covariate makes a big difference to the imputed values this implies that the subjects with missing data differ from those without missing data with respect to the covariate. If the difference on the covariate is not due to sampling error the MROWT assumption has been violated and the analysis is inappropriate. Tabachnick and Fidell (1983) when discussing this problem recommend this method 'only when the sample size is substantial and there is not much missing data'.

For complex cases where the missing data are not MROWT to make any progress one must be able to model the distribution of the observed and missing scores. Again the Expectation-Maximization (EM) algorithm can be used for estimating parameters. Little & Rubin (1987) have made some progress with certain specific cases. One such case is where data are censored, that is, where observations less than some value, known or unknown, cannot be observed. Another case is where data go missing when a normally distributed variable correlated with the covariates exceeds some threshold. However, Lilliard *et al.* (1986) applied these techniques to reported earnings. The estimates of non reported earnings were found to be extremely sensitive to transformations applied to reported earnings. Depending on the nature of the transformation the missing earnings were variously estimated to be substantially less or more than the reported earnings. This does not inspire confidence in the approach.

Little & Rubin also propose a Bayesian approach in which *a priori* specifications of population parameters are updated in the light of non-missing observations. These methods seem over complex for the average user as they fail to get round the basic problem that if the data are missing you do not know what they would have been. Mathematical sophistication only enables you to develop the consequences of supposing certain things about the missing data.

Little & Rubin (1987) suggest you try several different models in an attempt to find out what the data might have been like. The problem with this is that in any application you could be looking at the wrong class of models. It is better in my view to stick to analysing only the observed data rather than proposing complicated models of what might have been.

To sum up, if we can assume that the missing data are a random sample of the observed data then all is well and we can use the mathematical hardware to estimate what they would have been like. If however the missing data differ on some dependent variable or covariate we can only answer the question: 'What would the observed data look like if we took a random sample of observed data and discarded data haphazardly until the distribution of the observed data on the variable on which the difference was detected was the same as that for the missing data?' It should be noted that this is not the same as the question, 'What would the missing data have been like?' If the missing data are unlike the observed in one respect they are almost inevitably unlike them in some others. We can have little confidence in predictions of what the data would have been in such cases. Similarly where we cannot be confident that the missing data are MROWT we would have to specify the exact distribution of the missing data. If we cannot do this we should confine the analysis to the observed data.

## THE ROBUSTNESS PROBLEM

Unbalanced designs are much more sensitive to departures from the underlying assumptions than balanced designs (Milligan *et al.*, 1987). This means that when the variances vary across conditions or the data depart from normal or both, the significances produced by the analyses discussed above may be incorrect.

When the degree of imbalance is small unbalanced designs may be little different from balanced designs. Johnson & Herr (1984) suggest a criterion based on the degree of imbalance. However, whether the robustness of the tests is an important consideration in any application is a complex question depending on the size and nature of the violations of the assumptions as well as the degree of imbalance. One would also expect to be more worried about marginally significant results than those which were highly significant.

For researchers seriously worried about the nature of their data, simulations could be undertaken. These could either be on the basis of population parameters estimated from the data (Milligan *et al.*, 1985) or by performing randomization tests (Still & White, 1981; Siegel & Castellan, 1988). Both approaches are too demanding on computer time to be suitable for routine analysis.

An obvious alternative is to use nonparametric procedures. With OSCAR designs nonparametric one way analysis of variances could be applied on each factor ignoring the other. This corresponds to the weighted means analysis. As I have argued, this is not suitable for the ROWT designs where simple effects analyses are more appropriate. Here again, nonparametric equivalents could be used. The situation with testing interactions is more difficult since they assume interval measurement. Conover & Iman (1981) suggested that ranked data could be entered directly into analyses of variance programs. It is easy to produce data with main effects and no interactions which would appear to have interactions in such analyses. Other data could have large interactions which would not be picked up. A better analysis would be to first remove the main effects by subtraction and then rank the data before using a parametric test of an interaction. Such an analysis has been suggested by Hettmansperger (1984).

## WHAT WOULD THE WORLD BE LIKE IF IT WERE NOT AS IT IS?

This question lies behind many of the problems that have been raised in this chapter. If we want to know what an extant population is like we sample randomly from it and apply inferential statistics to our data. If the members of this population can be classified in a number of different ways then these classifications will rarely be independent. If these classifications are treated as factors in an analysis of variance the design will be ROWT if the data are not one random sample. When the data are collapsed over one of the factors it ceases to be ROWT; instead the samples in each condition are biased by the numbers of observations at each level of the ignored factor. Unless we can estimate the extent of this bias we cannot usefully analyse the data. An EWM analysis can be applied to data without ignoring any factors but it only tells us what main effects and lower order interactions we could expect in a balanced replication of the full design without ignoring any factors. This is not equivalent to asking the question what would the world be like if there were equal numbers in each condition, since these changes in category size do not normally occur by random sampling. Returning to the attitudes example, we are asking the question what would the mean attitude of the science students be if the science students were equally distributed across sexes? If the balance were achieved by randomly discarding excessive arts females or science males and this operation had no effect on the remaining students' attitudes this test provides an answer. If the balance were achieved by nonrandom sampling we have no idea what the attitudes of the science students would be. The problem is that balanced designs and random samples are artefacts required by mathematics and rarely if ever found in nature.

Experiments are attempts to manipulate an independent variable or variables and observe the consequences of this on a dependent variable. In psychology the dependent variable is some measure or score relating to individuals. In a between subjects design subjects are randomly allocated to groups which are then manipulated as specified by the levels of the independent variables. Such a design is ROWT and any differences between the groups are attributed to the experimental manipulations. An EWM analysis of these differences generalizes to effects to be expected in balanced replications of the experiment involving all of the original factors.

There are strong advantages to designs for group studies involving more than one factor being OSCAR. Here all conditions are random even after collapsing over any number of factors. EWO analyses generalize directly to the population sampled and EWM analyses generalize directly to the results of balanced studies involving only these factors specified in the effects. Effects due to other factors in the original study are irrelevant since they have been randomized out. ROWT group studies involving more than one factor answer only conditional questions of the sort: 'What is the effect of one factor at particular levels of the others?' If balanced designs are to be used, such considerations favour limiting the number of factors in the design to as few as possible. Who can understand a main effect or an interaction that depends on the design being balanced with respect to another, say, two factors?

## References

APPLEBAUM, M.I. & CRAMER, E.M. (1974). Some problems in the nonorthogonal analysis of variance. *Psychological Bulletin*, 81, 335–343.
BARTLETT, M.S. (1937). Some examples of statistical methods of research in agriculture and applied botany. *Journal of the Royal Statistical Society*, B4, 137–170.
BLAIR, R.C. & HIGGINS, J.J. (1978). Tests of hypotheses for unbalanced factorial designs under various regression/coding method combinations. *Educational and Psychological Measurement*, 38, 621–631.
BUCK, S.F. (1960). A method of estimation of missing values in multivariate data suitable for use with an electronic computer. *Journal of the Royal Statistical Society*, Series B, 22, 302–306.

CARLSON, J.E. & TIMM, N.H. (1974). Analysis of nonorthogonal fixed effects designs. *Psychological Bulletin*, 81, 563–570.

CONOVER, W.J. & IMAN, R.L. (1981). Rank transformation as a bridge between parametric and nonparametric statistics. *American Statistician*, 35, 124–129.

CRAMER, E.M. & APPLEBAUM, M.I. (1980). Nonorthogonal analysis of variance – once again. *Psychological Bulletin*, 87, 51–57.

GLASS, G.V., PECKHAM, P.D., & SANDERS, J.R. (1972). Consequences of failure to meet assumptions underlying the fixed effects analysis of variance and covariance. *Review of Educational Research*, 42, 237–287.

HETTMANSPERGER, T.P. (1984). *Statistical Inference Based on Ranks*. New York: Wiley.

HOWELL, D.C. (1987). *Statistical Methods for Psychologists*, 2nd ed. Duxbury Press: Boston.

HOWELL, D.C. & McCONAUGHY, S.H. (1982). Nonorthogonal analysis of variance: Putting the question before the answer. *Educational and Psychological Measurement*, 42, 9–24.

HUITEMA, B.E. (1980). *The Analysis of Covariance and Its Alternatives*. New York: Wiley.

JOHNSON, R.E. & HERR, D.G. (1984). The effect of nonorthogonality on the dependence of *F* ratios sharing a common denominator. *Journal of the American Statistical Association*, 79, 702–708.

LILLIARD, L., SMITH, J.P. & WELCH, F. (1986). What do we really know about wages? The importance of nonreporting and census imputation. *Journal of Political Economy*, 94, 489–506.

LITTLE, R.J.A. & RUBIN, D.B. (1987). *Statistical Analysis with Missing Data*. New York : Wiley.

LORD, F.M. (1953). On the statistical treatment of football numbers. *American Psychologist*, 8, 750–751.

LORD, F.M. (1967). A paradox in the interpretation of group comparisons. *Psychological Bulletin*, 68, 304–305.

LORD, F.M. (1969). Statistical adjustments when comparing pre–existing groups. *Psychological Bulletin*, 72, 336–337.

MACRAE, A.W. (1988). Measurement scales and statistics: what can significance tests tell us about the world? *British Journal of Psychology*, 79, 161–172.

MILLIGAN, G.W., WONG, D.S. & THOMPSON, P.A. (1987). Robustness properties of non orthogonal analysis of variance. *Psychological Bulletin*, 101, 464–470.

O'BRIEN, R.G. (1976). Comment on 'Some problems in the nonorthogonal analysis of variance.' *Psychological Bulletin*, 83, 72–74.

OVERALL, J.E., LEE, D.M. & HORNICK C.W. (1981). Comparison of two strategies for analysis of variance in nonorthogonal designs. *Psychological Bulletin*, 90, 367–375.

OVERALL, J.E. & SPIEGEL, D.K. (1969). Concerning the least squares analysis of experimental data. *Psychological Bulletin*, 72, 311–322.

OVERALL, J.E., SPIEGEL, D.K. & COHEN, J. (1975). Equivalence of orthogonal and nonorthogonal analysis of variance. *Psychological Bulletin*, 82, 182–186.

SCHEFFÉ, H. (1959). *The Analysis of Variance*. New York: Wiley.

SCHLUCHTER, M.D. (1988). BMDP 5V – Unbalanced repeated measures models with structured covariance matrices. *Technical Report*, 86, BMDP Statistical Software Inc.

SIEGEL S. & CASTELLAN N.J. (1988). *Nonparametric Statistics for the Behavioral Sciences*, 2nd ed. McGraw Hill: New York.

STILL, A.W. & WHITE, A.P. (1981). The approximate randomization test as an alternative to the *F* test in analysis of variance. *British Journal of Mathematical and Statistical Psychology*, **34**, 243–253.

TABACHNICK, B.G. & FIDELL, L.S. (1983). *Using Multivariate Statistics*. New York: Harper & Row.

WINER, B.J. (1971). *Statistical Principles in Experimental Design*, 2nd ed. Tokyo: McGraw Hill/Kogakusha.

# 7

# Repeated Measures: Groups × Occasions Designs

ALAN ANDERSON

In the broad sense, the term 'repeated measures' has come to be applied to investigations in which responses are observed for the same study units on more than one occasion. Undoubtedly this nebulous usage contributes to the confusion surrounding the topic; one has only to scan the indexes of statistical textbooks to discover the variety of interpretations that are covered by such an entry.

I shall argue that the designation 'repeated measures' should be reserved for studies in which time effects are intrinsically of interest and I shall restrict attention to these. I shall also exclude from discussion lengthy investigations usually described as 'longitudinal' that are to be found mainly in sociology and related disciplines and which have already been reviewed by Plewis (1986) in the previous volume of this series. This presentation is therefore intended to cover experiments in fields such as psychology and education where human subjects or animals are repeatedly observed at (usually fixed and equal) intervals of time. In the biological sciences, developmental changes through time are most often expressed in a growth model though the same principles would apply to degeneration. In engineering, repeated measurements are often made to determine patterns of wear or corrosion. For psychology, the analogous time effects relate to curves of learning, acclimatization, forgetting and so on. In the design of all such studies, some care must be taken to eliminate factors confounded with time and these problems will be briefly touched on in what follows. However, the main difficulty arises from the presence of correlation among observations due to the serial nature of the study and the consequent possible invalidation of straightforward methods of analysis.

At first glance, the most elementary presentation of the data as a two-way array in which the $N$ rows (subjects) could be taken as blocks and the $T$ columns (occasions) as treatments might suggest use of an analysis appropriate to the randomized block design. (Indeed, in an early exposition of two-way analysis of variance, Fisher (1925) exemplified the method using data subject to serial correlation and admitted the probable deficiencies resulting from such an inadequate analysis.) Those whose knowledge of statistical method extends a little beyond the basic have suggested that the appropriate analysis is that

155

applicable to the split-plot design, failing to recognize that the impossibility of randomizing the levels of the time factor renders this approach equally invalid.

In what follows some questions will be answered either at length or in passing:

- What is the nature of serial correlation?

- When and why can it cause problems? Are there other difficulties inherent in experiments over time? What is the experimenter trying to achieve?

- Are there any circumstances in which a standard elementary method of univariate analysis would be valid? Could amendments to such a method provide reasonably valid tests in all cases?

- Do multivariate methods resolve the difficulties?

- What is the 'best' approach? Of what value are the popular computer packages?

Above all, readers should not become so petrified or enthralled by the intricacies of analytic methods that they omit to define their goals with sufficient care, allow those goals to be subverted by what is available in computer packages, or fail to apply common sense in the application of basic principles.

## SERIAL CORRELATION

For some response, $y$, consider a sequence of observations, $y_1, y_2, y_3, \ldots, y_t,$ $\ldots, y_T$, made on a single individual. To start with, let us assume that, over the period of study, the average value of $y$ for this individual is stable in the sense that it does not systematically vary over the time periods, although unknown factors will superimpose random fluctuations ('residuals'), $e_t$, to give the observed $y_t$. Thus

$$y_t = \text{average } y + e_t.$$

To make this concrete, let us suppose that the $y_t$ are daily measurements (at a particular time of day) of the time to complete a well-practised task. All manner of 'environmental insults' will conspire to vary performance from day to day and most of these influences will be relatively fleeting in comparison with the inter-observation gap. But if, for example, our subject contracts influenza on day $t$ so that completion time is elevated by an amount $e_t$ above average, it is likely that $e_{t+1}$ will also be a positive quantity. This linkage between residuals is the unavoidable consequence of repeated measurement and is known as serial correlation. It is true that extension of the period between measurements will diminish serial correlation by reducing the set of insults capable of maintaining an influence. But the problem does not disappear: even monthly determinations of completion time could show correlation arising from factors as upsetting as, say, a death in the family. Of course, allowance might be made for such known perturbing influences as illness and bereavement but nothing can be done about those that go unrecognized.

It must also be emphasized that the phenomenon of serial correlation attaches to the residual discrepancies of observations from their mean. That is to say, everything that has been said above remains true even when the mean response is not constant but allowed to vary with time according to some rule such as a proposed learning curve. However, the manifestation of serial correlation can be distorted if some component of variation in $y$ is ignored or mis-specified by the model that defines its mean.

Suppose, for instance, that the variance of the $e_t$ as defined above is $\sigma_e^2$ and that the within-subject correlation between residuals at times $i$ and $j$ is $\rho_{ij}$; let us suppose also that we consider a population of subjects whose mean performances vary about their overall mean with variance $\sigma_s^2$ but that we overlook this by failing to allow mean response to be partly determined by subject. In that event, the apparent correlation between responses at times $i$ and $j$ will be

$$\rho_{ij}^* = \frac{\sigma_s^2 + \rho_{ij}\sigma_e^2}{\sigma_s^2 + \sigma_e^2}$$

and, even if $\rho_{ij}$ were zero, $\rho_{ij}^*$ would not be.

## QUESTIONS AND DESIGNS

Having accepted the likely presence of serial correlation in the simplest possible case let us now see what happens as factors are introduced into the design of the experiment with the aim of exploring their influence on mean response.

First let us suppose that the passage of time does not itself influence the mean; this is the scenario we have already considered. We could now associate with each of the $T$ occasions of measurement a different treatment or stimulus either given at the time or at a prior time but since the last observation point. For each subject, these $T$ treatments (which may or may not have a factorial structure) are separately randomized over the $T$ occasions. The effect of this is to eradicate the basic serial correlation as applied to any pair of treatments, that is, the responses from different treatments are uncorrelated because the randomization decouples the treatments from the temporal ordering. Such a design can be analysed as a straighforward split unit (split-plot) experiment with subjects as main plots; no special difficulties should arise provided neither time itself nor treatment order have any effect.

Both of these requirements are likely to be suspect. Furthermore, if the occasions are not sufficiently far apart, carryover effects may be present so that the response at time $t$ is affected not only by the treatment randomly allocated to the $t$th occasion but residually by that allocated to the $(t-1)$th occasion. Such difficulties are usually confronted by means of a crossover design in which treatment sequences are balanced over the experiment usually by some combination of Latin squares. Neither split-plot nor crossover designs will be considered further here as they are free of the difficulties encountered in true repeated measurement studies where the focus is on the possible effect of time.

We will assume, therefore, that any treatment or stimulus given to a subject does not change during the course of the experiment, though it may either be given once and for all or it may be reinforced throughout the sequence of observations, in which case there may be an interplay between the passage of absolute time and the frequency of reinforcement. It must also be appreciated that, almost inevitably, there are influences on response that are confounded with the possible effect of time. Subjects will be affected by changes external to themselves such as seasonal or daily variation in temperature and light or by 'internal' fluctuations exemplified by increasing hunger or boredom as the experiment progresses. A special case is presented by a subject ceasing to participate after some point. Campbell & Stanley (1966) give a fairly extensive account of such problems.

If the experimental units are from the same population then the only interest centres on variation of response with time. The crudest hypothesis would be that the mean response is constant over occasions but, for most psychological variables, this is likely to be rejected and more searching questions about the pattern of change will need to be answered.

Much more common are experiments in which subjects are divided into different groups either by some characteristic such as sex or by random allocation to different treatments or stimuli. The effect of time, ignoring the grouping, can still be considered. In addition, equality of groups in respect of average response over time could be investigated. But the question that must logically precede either of these, and is often the most important of the three in its own right, is whether or not the profiles of response over time are the same for all groups. In other words, 'Is there a groups × occasions interaction?' If an interaction were demonstrated, the other two questions relating to the main effects of groups and of occasions would be largely meaningless.

An example may help to make this concrete. Figure 1 shows the observed mean profiles for four men and six women, the response being the median time (in milliseconds) to decide whether or not full face photographs had been seen before. Ten slides were used on all twenty occasions mixed with twenty 'distractor' photographs, different on each occasion; memory was therefore being reinforced. Slides were each displayed for 1500 msecs with a two-minute break between runs and an extra five-minute break between runs 10 and 11. Clearly it is hardly worth asking whether subjects' average performances changed during the experiment – it would be most surprising if they did not. But the form of the learning curve could be of interest and, in particular, whether it becomes asymptotic (that is, average change in performance is negligible beyond a certain point). Nor is an average difference between the

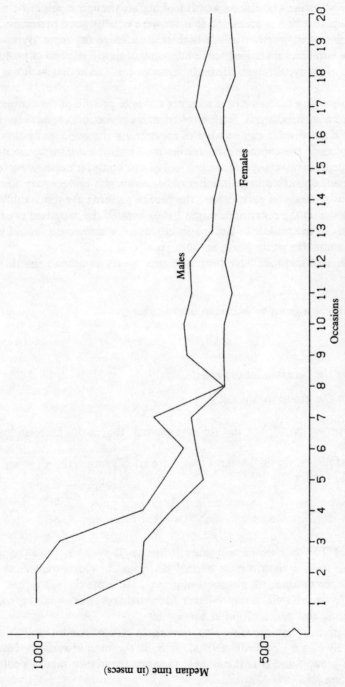

**Figure 1.** Plot of median recognition times of faces over 20 occasions

sexes over all twenty occasions worth looking at, though it might be useful to discover whether or not males and females were equally good performers on the first occasion, and whether or not both sexes achieve the same asymptote. At least these latter two questions are not dependent on parallelism of profiles over the period of study, although the figure gives no indication that such was not the case.

Note in passing the value of producing a simple picture of the group profiles as a first step in the analysis. Such an elementary procedure is not to be despised especially if the display can be used to concentrate the mind and guide further consideration of the experimental results rather than submitting the data to a standard computer package. For instance, in this study, it can now be seen that measurement on such a large number of occasions was unnecessary since, even with so few subjects in each group, the profile patterns are remarkably stable. Cutting down on the repetitions might have obviated the supposed need for the extra break in the middle of the sequence, an interruption that could possibly have had some distorting effect on later results.

A number of methods have been advanced to try to answer the three basic questions:

▶ (i) Is there a groups × occasion interaction?

If not

▶ (ii) Are the occasion means equal?

▶(iii) Are the group means equal?

These approaches all attempt to circumvent the basic problem of serial correlation.

In what follows, we shall assume that there are $G$ groups, the $j$th group having $n_j$ subjects, so that

$$N = \sum_{j=1}^{G} n_j.$$

The set of $T$ responses for subject $i$ in group $j$, $y_{ij1}, y_{ij2}, \ldots, y_{ijt}, \ldots, y_{ijT}$, come from a multivariate normal distribution with variance-covariance matrix, $\Sigma_j$, common to all members of group $j$. In some cases, we shall require that all $\Sigma_j$ (or related variance-covariance matrices) are equal, a condition referred to in this presentation as *homogeneity*.

A test of this homogeneity requirement is clearly needed and is in part provided by Box's (1949) $M$-statistic. If $S_j$ is the sample variance-covariance matrix in group $j$ and $S$ is the sample variance-covariance matrix pooled over groups, then let

$$M = N \ln|\mathbf{S}| - \sum_{j=1}^{G} n_j \ln|\mathbf{S}_j|,$$

$$A = \frac{2T^2 + 3T - 1}{6(T+1)(G-1)} \left( \sum_{j=1}^{G} \frac{1}{n_j} - \frac{1}{N} \right),$$

$$f = \tfrac{1}{2} T(T+1)(G-1).$$

Then $(1 - A)M$ has approximately the $\chi^2$ distribution with $f$ degrees of freedom under the homogeneity hypothesis. Unfortunately, the approximation is poor if any $n_j$ is not a good deal in excess of $T$ and indeed the statistic is unavailable if $n_j < T + 1$ for any group since then, $|\mathbf{S}_j| = 0$. For instance, the test cannot be applied for the full set of occasions in the case of the experiment described above. Furthermore, it is generally held that Box's test is not robust against departures from multivariate normality; see, for example, Olson (1974).

## UNIVARIATE METHODS

The first approach to be considered involves the basic univariate analysis of variance or some modification of it.

We can dispose of the test for equality of group means since this is simply provided by the one way analysis of variance of the group totals over occasions. This, of course, corresponds to the main plot analysis of a split-plot design. The usual requirement for constancy of variance over groups will be satisfied as a by-product of the more stringent assumption of homogeneity of covariance matrices over groups but could be tested in its own right by Bartlett's test.

Treating the responses as though they derived from a split-plot design gives a sub-plot analysis summarized as:

Occasions mean square

$$= MS_1 = N \sum_{t=1}^{T} (\bar{y}_{\cdot\cdot t} - \bar{y}_{\cdot\cdot\cdot})^2 / (T - 1),$$

Groups × occasions mean square

$$= MS_2 = \sum_{j=1}^{G} n_j \sum_{t=1}^{T} (\bar{y}_{\cdot jt} - \bar{y}_{\cdot j\cdot} - \bar{y}_{\cdot\cdot t} + \bar{y}_{\cdot\cdot\cdot})^2 / ((T-1)(G-1)),$$

Residual mean square

$$= MS_3 = \sum_{j=1}^{G} \sum_{i=1}^{n_j} \sum_{t=1}^{T} (y_{ijt} - \bar{y}_{\cdot jt} - \bar{y}_{ij\cdot} + \bar{y}_{\cdot j\cdot})^2 / ((T-1)(N-G)).$$

(The 'dot' notation indicates averaging over that subscript.)

Now it can be shown that, provided the inter-occasion correlations have a certain pattern, the usual variance ratios provide valid tests of the corresponding null hypotheses. Thus we first examine the hypothesis of no groups $\times$ occasions interaction by referring $MS_2/MS_3$ to $F[(T-1)(G-1),(T-1)(N-G)]$ and, if this provides no evidence that the group profiles over time are not parallel, then the hypothesis of equal occasion means can be tested by referring $MS_1/MS_3$ to $F[(T-1),(T-1)(N-G)]$.

(In passing, I deprecate the presentation of univariate repeated measures analysis in terms of so-called 'mixed models' with the attendant muddle over which mean square ratios should be used for tests. The confusion arising through treating replicates (subjects) as a factor has been clearly exposed by Yates (1965); see also the additional notes on that paper in Yates (1969). In making a simple *t*-test or estimating a regression coefficient, no one would include in the underlying model a term for each sample member. Such an approach makes no more sense in the case of repeated measures analysis.)

Originally it was believed that for such *F*-test analyses to be correct, the variance-covariance matrices must be homogeneous over groups and

(i) variability in response must be the same for all occasions, and

(ii) response correlations must be the same for all pairs of occasions.

These conditions are variously referred to as (compound) *symmetry* or uniformity.

Huynh & Feldt (1970) showed the analysis to be valid under less restrictive requirements known as the circularity or *sphericity* condition. Essentially, the variance of the difference in the responses of a subject at two occasions is the same for all subjects and all pairs of occasions, i.e.

$$\mathrm{var}(y_{ijt} - y_{ijt'}) = 2\lambda \quad \text{for all } i, j, t \neq t'.$$

(It turns out that $\lambda$ = mean variance − mean covariance.)

The practical experimenter will rightly argue that it is hard to imagine circumstances in which the sphericity condition would be met. For instance if variability in response is the same at each time point, we have to believe that the correlation between responses at different time points is the same irrespective of the separation of these time points. However, it should be noted (see Mitzel & Games, 1981) that, in the absence of sphericity, confidence intervals and tests for contrasts among the occasions cannot use the usual pooled variance estimate to provide standard errors since such contrasts are intrinsically heteroscedastic. An estimate based on the between-subject variability of the individual contrast must be used.

Nevertheless, if an appeal to sphericity is to be made, a test of the condition appears to be needed; unfortunately the available procedure is somewhat cumbersome. A $(T-1) \times T$ matrix, **C**, must be set up, the rows of which are orthonormal contrasts among the occasions, that is, orthogonal contrasts with coefficients scaled to have unit sum of squares. These might be derived from the linear, quadratic, cubic, etc., components or we could define row $u$ by

$$c_{uv} = \begin{cases} 1/\surd(u^2+u), & v = 1, 2, \ldots, u, \\ -u/\surd(u^2+u) & v = u+1, \\ 0 & \text{otherwise.} \end{cases}$$

Now let $P = (T-1)$ and apply Box's homogeneity test for equality of the $C\Sigma_j C'$ matrices, i.e., replace $T$ by $P$, $S$ by $CSC'$ and $S_j$ by $CS_j C'$.

Then, if homogeneity is not rejected, let

$$W = |CSC'|/[\text{tr}(CSC')/P]^P,$$
$$d = N-G-(2P^2+P+2)/6P,$$
$$f = \tfrac{1}{2}P(P+1)-1,$$

and compare $-d\ln(W)$ with $\chi^2$ with $f$ degrees of freedom. This is Mauchly's (1940) sphericity test and checks that

$$\text{var}(y_{ijt} - y_{ijt'}) = \text{constant for all } t \neq t'.$$

The Box test checks that the constant is the same for all groups. If the overall test of the condition is to be associated with a significance level of $\alpha$, each test should be made at the $\alpha/2$ level. As with the Box test, there are doubts about Mauchly's test in the presence of non-normality and, of course, it is not available for $N-G<T$. Despite their shortcomings, the tests are remarkably powerful; that is, they almost always reject the null hypothesis of sphericity when it is false, which it almost always is. Hence we are so frequently forced towards the following approximate approach that Rouanet & Lepine (1970) and Keselman *et al.*, (1980) suggest that testing for sphericity is not worthwhile.

In the absence of sphericity, the analysis of variance $F$-tests described above will be incorrect, giving too many significant results. One way round the problem is to reduce the degrees of freedom of the $F$-distributions until the significance levels are approximately as specified. In two classic papers, Box (1954a, b) laid down the basis of this approach by defining a multiplier, $\varepsilon$, for the degrees of freedom that would be estimated as

$$\hat{\varepsilon} = \frac{T^2(\text{tr}(S)/T - \bar{s}_{..})^2}{(T-1)\left(\sum_t \sum_{t'} s_{tt'}^2 - 2T \sum_t \bar{s}_{t.}^2 + T^2 \bar{s}_{..}^2\right)} = \frac{(MS_3)^2}{(T-1)MS},$$

where MS is the residual mean square from a formal analysis of variance of $S$ as though its elements were the responses from a single replicate of a $T \times T$ design.

The revised groups × occasions interaction test now regards $MS_2/MS_3$ as being approximately $F_{[(T-1)(G-1)\hat{\varepsilon}, (T-1)(N-G)\hat{\varepsilon}]}$ and the test of equality of occasion means regards $MS_1/MS_3$ as being approximately $F_{[(T-1)\hat{\varepsilon}, (T-1)(N-G)\hat{\varepsilon}]}$.

Readers with sufficient algebraic skill can check that, under sphericity, the true value of $\varepsilon$ is 1.0.

A number of authors (Collier *et al.*, 1967; Huynh & Feldt, 1976; Huynh, 1978; Milliken & Johnson, 1984) have presented amendments to the estimates of Box's correction factor and extensive simulation studies have been made to determine the best of these without finding a conclusive winner. Geisser & Greenhouse (1958), noting that the lower bound of $\varepsilon$ is $1/(T-1)$, suggest a conservative test in which the groups × occasions and occasions variance ratios are referred to $F[(G-1),(N-G)]$ and $F[1,(N-G)]$ respectively. They remark that these are applicable even when Box's test suggests nonhomogeneity but the group sizes are equal. (Wallenstein & Fleiss (1979) give a less stringent lower bound applicable in the often plausible situation where the responses at each occasion can be assumed equally variable and the correlation between observations $\delta$ time units apart is $\rho^{\delta}$.)

In earlier days, the computation of $\hat{\varepsilon}$ was so cumbersome that Greenhouse & Geisser (1959) introduced what became known as their 'three-step' procedure:

1. Perform the traditional $F$-test. If the result is non-significant, that is the decision.

2. Otherwise make the conservative test. If the result is significant, then that is the decision.

3. Otherwise compute $\hat{\varepsilon}$ and adjust the degrees of freedom.

Nowadays the computer renders this labour-saving process redundant and calculation of $\hat{\varepsilon}$ for all non-spherical data obviates the need to adhere slavishly to fixed significance levels. This, taken with the advice of Keselman *et al.* (1980) to omit the test for sphericity, would seem to imply that approximate analysis based on adjustment of the degrees of freedom by $\hat{\varepsilon}$ should be the standard approach for all repeated measures studies. It will be argued later that this is a somewhat unimaginative answer to the problem.

## THE MULTIVARIATE APPROACH

Many authors (e.g. Potthoff & Roy, 1964; Cole & Grizzle, 1966) have championed the multivariate approach since it requires no assumptions whatever about the variance-covariance structure of the multivariate normal response vector other than homogeneity over groups. Formally, a $P \times T$ contrast matrix, $\mathbf{C}$, is used to transform the $T$ response measurements for each subject to $P$ derived variables by setting

$$\mathbf{Z} = \mathbf{YC'}.$$

For the present, as for the Mauchly sphericity test, we are assuming $P = T - 1$. The rows of $\mathbf{C}$ could be orthonormal as in the Mauchly test, though they need not be. (Hence, most of the literature takes **C** as defining first differences so that

$$z_{ijk} = y_{ij(k+1)} - y_{ijk}, \ k = 1, 2, \ldots, P.)$$

Let **H** and **E** represent the matrices of corrected sums of squares and products for **Z** between- and within-groups respectively, i.e.,

$$h_{uv} = \sum_{j=1}^{G} n_j (\bar{z}_{.ju} - \bar{z}_{..u})(\bar{z}_{.jv} - \bar{z}_{..v})$$

and

$$e_{uv} = \sum_{j=1}^{G} \sum_{i=1}^{n_j} (z_{iju} - \bar{z}_{.ju})(z_{ijv} - \bar{z}_{.jv}).$$

All four commonly-used tests of the null hypothesis of parallelism of profiles are based on the latent roots $\phi_1, \phi_2, \ldots, \phi_P$ of $\mathbf{HE}^{-1}$. Seber (1984) gives a full but technical discussion of these tests; the tables of critical values referred to below are from his book. In the following summary, for consistency with the Seber tables, let $\nu_{\mathbf{H}} = G - 1$, $\nu_{\mathbf{E}} = N - G$ and let MAX and MIN be respectively the greater and lesser of $\nu_{\mathbf{H}}$ and $P$.

### (i) Wilks $\Lambda$

$$\text{Let} -\log \Lambda = \sum_{p=1}^{P} \log(1 + \phi_p).$$

Then, under the null hypothesis,

$$-\frac{1}{C} (\nu_{\mathbf{E}} - (P - \nu_{\mathbf{H}} + 1)/2) \log \Lambda$$

is an observation from the $\chi^2$ distribution with $P\nu_{\mathbf{H}}$ degrees of freedom. For reasonably large $N$, a satisfactory approximation is obtained by taking $C = 1$; otherwise, Seber's Table D13 gives the required values of $C$ for given levels of significance and arguments

$$d = \text{MIN},$$

$$m_{\mathbf{H}} = \text{MAX},$$

$$M = \nu_{\mathbf{E}} - P + 1.$$

### (ii) Lawley-Hotelling $T_0^2$

$$\text{Let} \qquad T_0^2 = \nu_{\mathbf{E}} \sum_{p=1}^{P} \phi_p.$$

Seber's Table D15 gives critical values for $T_0^2/\nu_{\mathbf{H}}$ with arguments

$$d = \text{MIN},$$

$$m_{\text{H}} = \text{MAX},$$

$$m_{\text{E}} = \begin{cases} \nu_{\text{E}}, & P \leqslant \nu_{\text{H}}, \\ \nu_{\text{E}} + \nu_{\text{H}} - P, & P > \nu_{\text{H}}. \end{cases}$$

For large $N$, $T_0^2$ is also approximately an observation from $\chi^2$ with $P\nu_{\text{H}}$ degrees of freedom; there are, however, better but more complicated critical value approximations.

### (iii) Roy's largest root criterion

Roy's test concerns $\phi_{\text{max}}$, the largest of the $\phi_1, \phi_2, \ldots, \phi_P$, but tables (e.g. Seber, Table D14) or charts are usually entered with

$$\theta_{\text{max}} = \frac{\phi_{\text{max}}}{1 + \phi_{\text{max}}}$$

as test statistic and arguments

$$s = \text{MIN}$$

$$v_1 = (\text{MAX} - \text{MIN} - 1)/2$$

$$v_2 = (\nu_{\text{E}} - P - 1)/2$$

### (iv) Pillai's trace

Let
$$V_s = \sum_1^P \frac{\phi_p}{1 + \phi_p} \ .$$

Seber's Table D16 gives critical values for $V_s$ with arguments as for Roy's criterion. However, for large $N$, $\nu_{\text{E}} V_s$ is approximately an observation from $\chi^2$ with $P\nu_{\text{H}}$ degrees of freedom.

Unhappily, this somewhat bewildering array of tests does not entirely solve the problem. Very little is known about their powers to reject the null hypothesis of parallelism when it is false – that is why they have been competitors for so long. They are all sensitive to departures of the data from multivariate normality. And, of course, they are often inapplicable when the number of occasions is large relative to the number of experimental units.

The null hypothesis for the multivariate test of equality of occasion means can be specified somewhat differently from that of the univariate test, so as to ask whether the *vector* of group means is constant over occasions, that is: 'Are the profiles horizontal?' This statement of the question subsumes the issue of parallelism which is therefore not a requirement for the validity of the test. The four test statistics described above are used with the matrix **H** now redefined as the uncorrected between-groups matrix for $\mathbf{Z}$, i.e.,

$$h_{uv} = \sum_{j=1}^{G} n_j \bar{z}_{.ju} \bar{z}_{.jv}$$

and $\nu_H$ set to $G$ rather than $(G-1)$. The deficiencies listed in the previous paragraph still apply.

The analogue of the univariate test for equality of occasion means (that is, assuming parallelism) involves computing

$$\bar{z}'_{..} \mathbf{E}^{-1} \bar{z}_{..} \times N(\nu_E - P + 1)/P,$$

which is distributed at $F_{P,(\nu_E - P + 1)}$ under the null hypothesis. ($\bar{z}_{..}$ is the vector of means of columns of $\mathbf{Z}$.)

The test for equality of group means is identical to the univariate test. For a fuller discussion of the application of multivariate analysis of variance to repeated measurement data, see Hand & Taylor (1987). As we have noted, the multivariate approach is totally unaffected by the nature of the between-occasions covariance structure. The disadvantages compared with the univariate approaches are the greater sensitivity of the competing tests to non-normality of the multivariate response vector, their unavailability when few subjects are measured on many occasions and, above all, their relatively low power to reject false null hypotheses.

Kenward's (1987) ante-dependence approach provides a method of analysis that includes the standard multivariate technique as an extreme case. The method postulates a correlation structure such that the response for any occasion depends on the responses for a fixed number of the most recent occasions but, given those, is independent of any earlier responses. This seems a somewhat unrealistic model.

## RESPONSE CURVE DESCRIPTORS

The third group of methods is the oldest (Fisher, 1920) and probably the most helpful, focusing on selected aspects of the response curve. By taking the trouble to think about the nature of the curve, the experimenter can sharpen up the analysis whilst at the same time avoiding most of the difficulties previously discussed.

The essence of the procedure is to transform the $T$ responses for each subject to $P$ derived scores that are useful descriptors of that subject's response curve; in general, $P$ will be quite small and, in particular, we no longer consider $P$ to be $(T-1)$. The most obvious candidates as attributes for a subject's response profile are the linear, quadratic, cubic, etc., components of the polynomial regression on time. These have the advantages of being contrasts associated with individual degrees of freedom in the occasions and groups × occasions analysis of variance. Use of within-pair differences in a paired comparison study is a special and elementary case of this.

More often in psychological studies, the polynomial curve is less sensible than one having an asymptote. For example, rather than a cubic polynomial (which has no asymptote), the exponential model

$$E(y_t) = a + br^t, \qquad 0 < r < 1,$$

might be appropriate for the facial recognition experiment or, in circumstances where there could be a delay in response change, the doubly asymptotic Gompertz law

$$E(y_t) = A + B \exp(- \exp(- C(t - \mu)))$$

might be a candidate. The chosen formulation must make sense and be supported by graphical or other examination of the shapes of the group mean profiles.

Notice that this attack on the problem circumvents two difficulties that we have so far ignored:

(a) the time points need not be the same for all subjects (though, if possible, they should be);

(b) problems associated with missing values are no longer a major headache provided observations are missing at random.

After fitting the parameters of the selected response curve for each subject, we now have $N$ vectors of length $P$; for example, for the exponential model mentioned above, these would be

$$(\hat{a}_{ij}, \hat{b}_{ij}, \hat{r}_{ij}), \qquad j = 1, \ldots, G; i = 1, \ldots, n_j.$$

In many ways, the simplest and safest procedure is now to make $P$ univariate one–way analyses of variance to examine how these aspects of the response curve vary over groups. Of course, except in the case of $P$ orthogonal contrasts such as for the $P$-order polynomial, such tests will not be independent, which calls for care in interpretation. A $P$-variable multivariate analysis, although technically more attractive than that for the direct analysis of all $T$ responses (because $P$ is now small), throws the carefully separated attributes of the response curve back into a melting pot of confusion.

When the $P$ derived values arise from orthogonal contrasts, it is possible that they will satisfy the sphericity condition and hence qualify for the standard $G \times P$ two-way analysis of variance. Such contrasts might be preselected to cover hypotheses of interest or they might be the standard polynomial contrasts; they could also be derived from the $P$ most important eigenvectors of $\mathbf{R'R}$ where $\mathbf{R}$ represents the matrix of residuals after $\mathbf{Y}$ is corrected for both row and column means (Snee, 1972) though, once again, such an 'automated' approach is unlikely to make for clear interpretation. The sphericity condition being satisfied, the interaction and residual mean squares of the two-way analysis of variance both represent pooling of homogeneous variances with the result that any contrast × group interaction can be tested, giving enhanced power over the one-way analysis of variance where a contrast is tested against its own residual mean square.

Notice that covariate observations might exist for each subject (for example, a baseline score) or for each observation on each subject. In the latter case, the covariate would be incorporated into the within-subject response model and hence would influence the estimation of the $P$ derived scores for each subject; in the former case, the covariate would simply enter into the univariate analysis of variance of each of the $P$ scores in the usual way.

## EXAMPLE

The complete data set for the facial recognition experiment introduced earlier is given in Table 1. The response was actually bivariate in the sense that decision time was measured for a group of faces classed as 'easy' to recognize and another classed as 'difficult'. One of the main questions at issue was whether or not the recognition time for the difficult faces would eventually reduce to that for the easy faces.

Figure 1 has already suggested that recognition time for the easy faces decreases for both men and women until there is virtually no further improvement; there is a similar pattern for the difficult faces. Figure 2 shows the average male response times for the easy faces fitted to cubic, exponential and Gompertz models. Although the cubic is very close to the exponential for these men, it cannot make sense in the limit since it crosses the horizontal axis. In this particular case, the Gompertz provides the best fit largely because of the anomalous near-equality for the first two occasions. However, for the women on easy faces and both sexes on difficult faces, the exponential is much more clearly the correct response profile and hence Table 1 includes for each subject the estimated values of $a$, $b$ and $r$ for the curve

$$y_t = a + br^t.$$

These triples form the descriptor scores that summarize the key features of the learning curves. The asymptote is represented by $a$, the baseline response by $(a + b)$ and the rate of improvement by $r$.

Straightfoward univariate analysis (that is, unpaired $t$–tests in this case) reveals no evidence of sex differences in any of these features for either easy or difficult faces. The descriptors can be compared for easy and difficult faces (by paired $t$-tests) and show considerable evidence of a difference in $a$ but no evidence that $b$ or $r$ differ. That is, the data are consistent with a similar improvement in performance at a similar rate for the two types of faces but that the eventual performances are no closer than at the start. A key question is thus simply answered without any recourse to the vagaries of the approximate

**Table 1.** Data from face recognition experiment. (See text for details)

Easy to recognize faces

| Occasion | Male subjects | | | | | Female subjects | | | | | |
|---|---|---|---|---|---|---|---|---|---|---|---|
| | 1 | 2 | 3 | 4 | mean | 5 | 6 | 7 | 8 | 9 | 10 | mean |
| 1 | 998 | 1034 | 637 | 1344 | 1003.3 | 1134 | 785 | 1088 | 763 | 931 | 796 | 916.2 |
| 2 | 1065 | 1331 | 584 | 1035 | 1003.8 | 876 | 633 | 988 | 639 | 755 | 727 | 769.7 |
| 3 | 748 | 1452 | 695 | 908 | 950.8 | 772 | 609 | 1019 | 665 | 855 | 667 | 764.5 |
| 4 | 666 | 980 | 590 | 831 | 766.8 | 852 | 649 | 870 | 644 | 656 | 554 | 704.2 |
| 5 | 700 | 804 | 557 | 823 | 721.0 | 761 | 528 | 727 | 666 | 625 | 498 | 634.2 |
| 6 | 687 | 778 | 517 | 730 | 678.0 | 750 | 635 | 777 | 602 | 600 | 536 | 650.0 |
| 7 | 711 | 793 | 676 | 791 | 742.8 | 837 | 587 | 764 | 596 | 633 | 548 | 660.8 |
| 8 | 604 | 602 | 473 | 681 | 590.0 | 664 | 571 | 738 | 567 | 523 | 460 | 587.2 |
| 9 | 638 | 641 | 519 | 882 | 670.0 | 774 | 571 | 570 | 563 | 536 | 521 | 589.2 |
| 10 | 654 | 634 | 609 | 810 | 676.8 | 650 | 623 | 535 | 547 | 614 | 559 | 588.0 |
| 11 | 690 | 697 | 505 | 747 | 659.8 | 729 | 610 | 560 | 517 | 514 | 495 | 570.8 |
| 12 | 686 | 682 | 586 | 699 | 663.3 | 648 | 674 | 579 | 548 | 551 | 520 | 586.7 |
| 13 | 633 | 653 | 538 | 633 | 614.3 | 660 | 586 | 549 | 536 | 560 | 556 | 574.5 |
| 14 | 574 | 598 | 557 | 714 | 610.8 | 613 | 557 | 532 | 533 | 558 | 576 | 561.5 |
| 15 | 695 | 560 | 501 | 626 | 595.5 | 660 | 537 | 532 | 511 | 617 | 543 | 566.7 |
| 16 | 657 | 675 | 513 | 652 | 624.3 | 752 | 556 | 542 | 573 | 534 | 583 | 590.0 |
| 17 | 690 | 622 | 548 | 742 | 650.5 | 688 | 618 | 535 | 522 | 592 | 581 | 589.3 |
| 18 | 664 | 635 | 563 | 698 | 640.0 | 579 | 559 | 534 | 588 | 555 | 568 | 563.8 |
| 19 | 683 | 608 | 510 | 677 | 619.5 | 692 | 617 | 550 | 533 | 470 | 555 | 569.5 |
| 20 | 682 | 602 | 547 | 634 | 616.3 | 803 | 525 | 606 | 538 | 442 | 537 | 575.2 |
| $\hat{a}$ | 655 | 564 | 530 | 705 | | 692 | 588 | 508 | 532 | 531 | 539 | |
| $\hat{b}$ | 671 | 897 | 138 | 1007 | | 642 | 655 | 744 | 258 | 527 | 517 | |
| $\hat{r}$ | 0.60 | 0.82 | 0.82 | 0.61 | | 0.62 | 0.30 | 0.83 | 0.80 | 0.74 | 0.54 | |

Difficult to recognize faces

| Occasion | | | | | | | | | | | |
|---|---|---|---|---|---|---|---|---|---|---|---|
| 1 | 1189 | 1516 | 757 | 1627 | 1272.3 | 1142 | 888 | 1698 | 835 | 1264 | 752 | 1096.5 |
| 2 | 1018 | 1373 | 747 | 1568 | 1176.5 | 1074 | 755 | 1233 | 755 | 1139 | 771 | 954.5 |
| 3 | 997 | 1445 | 807 | 1161 | 1102.5 | 1006 | 742 | 943 | 714 | 967 | 740 | 852.0 |
| 4 | 757 | 943 | 686 | 1061 | 861.8 | 1026 | 775 | 960 | 733 | 855 | 578 | 821.2 |
| 5 | 833 | 917 | 710 | 1148 | 902.0 | 1015 | 826 | 835 | 717 | 846 | 574 | 802.2 |
| 6 | 796 | 745 | 679 | 1009 | 807.3 | 814 | 820 | 861 | 617 | 723 | 672 | 751.2 |
| 7 | 777 | 659 | 678 | 1061 | 793.8 | 1090 | 749 | 841 | 658 | 703 | 614 | 775.8 |
| 8 | 707 | 741 | 724 | 910 | 770.5 | 861 | 667 | 840 | 679 | 612 | 524 | 697.2 |
| 9 | 694 | 716 | 623 | 1067 | 775.0 | 896 | 603 | 588 | 603 | 665 | 507 | 643.7 |
| 10 | 672 | 585 | 652 | 855 | 691.0 | 819 | 735 | 596 | 598 | 544 | 557 | 641.5 |
| 11 | 676 | 692 | 646 | 855 | 717.3 | 809 | 714 | 664 | 665 | 638 | 535 | 670.8 |
| 12 | 689 | 625 | 691 | 795 | 700.0 | 1013 | 705 | 604 | 578 | 578 | 515 | 665.5 |
| 13 | 810 | 710 | 618 | 753 | 722.8 | 904 | 580 | 585 | 567 | 590 | 580 | 634.3 |
| 14 | 684 | 660 | 657 | 919 | 730.0 | 804 | 677 | 605 | 568 | 566 | 680 | 650.0 |
| 15 | 785 | 635 | 720 | 877 | 754.3 | 871 | 679 | 623 | 589 | 629 | 562 | 658.8 |
| 16 | 740 | 715 | 640 | 857 | 738.0 | 777 | 589 | 565 | 691 | 535 | 632 | 631.5 |
| 17 | 754 | 708 | 662 | 861 | 746.3 | 936 | 702 | 647 | 570 | 543 | 604 | 667.0 |
| 18 | 733 | 667 | 623 | 960 | 745.8 | 901 | 735 | 571 | 712 | 540 | 522 | 663.5 |
| 19 | 756 | 673 | 665 | 849 | 735.8 | 834 | 658 | 596 | 600 | 571 | 573 | 638.7 |
| 20 | 712 | 580 | 652 | 860 | 701.0 | 780 | 689 | 704 | 600 | 521 | 525 | 636.5 |
| $\hat{a}$ | 724 | 633 | 648 | 859 | | 839 | 657 | 622 | 609 | 544 | 563 | |
| $\hat{b}$ | 746 | 1343 | 160 | 1104 | | 358 | 230 | 1473 | 292 | 957 | 327 | |
| $\hat{r}$ | 0.64 | 0.73 | 0.81 | 0.72 | | 0.82 | 0.84 | 0.68 | 0.75 | 0.77 | 0.70 | |

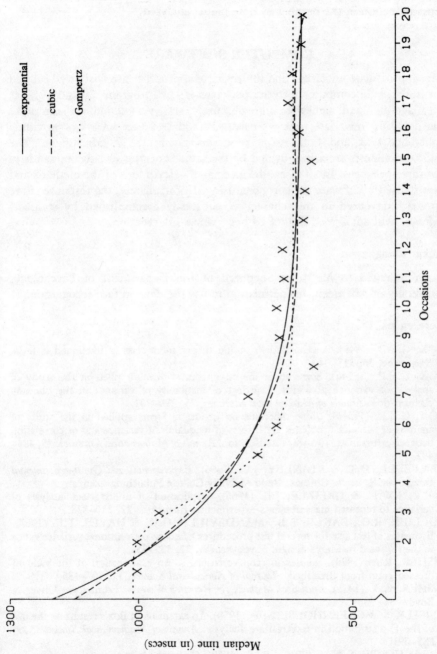

**Figure 2.** Three curves fitted to median recognition times of faces

univariate or multivariate approaches which in any case could be applied only by gross reduction in the number of time points analysed.

## COMPUTER SOFTWARE

The approximate univariate and multivariate approaches are fairly well catered for in the main computer software packages. BMDP (programs 2V and 4V), SAS (GLM and REG) and, somewhat more obscurely, SPSS (via RELIABILITY) can make the omnibus univariate tests with BMDP2V and SPSS (via MANOVA) providing sphericity tests and both BMDP programs giving the $\varepsilon$ adjustment. The multivariate tests are also provided by the same programs or subcommands in the three packages. In all cases, the associated descriptions of the methods and how to use the software are fairly confusing. Unfortunately, the response curve approach favoured in this chapter is not easily accomplished by standard software without a good deal of ad hoc manual intervention.

### Acknowledgement

I am indebted to Mr John Shepherd of the Department of Psychology, University of Aberdeen, for permission to use the data on face recognition.

### References

BOX, G.E.P. (1949). A general distribution theory for a class of likelihood criteria. *Biometrika*, **36**, 317–346.

BOX, G.E.P. (1954a). Some theorems on quadratic forms applied in the study of analysis of variance problems. I. Effect of inequality of variance in the one-way classification. *Annals of Mathematical Statistics*, **25**, 290–302.

BOX, G.E.P. (1954b). Some theorems on quadratic forms applied in the study of analysis of variance problems, II. Effects of inequality of variance and of correlation between errors in the two-way classification. *Annals of Mathematical Statistics*, **25**, 484–498.

CAMPBELL, D.T. & STANLEY, J.C. (1966). *Experimental and Quasi-experimental Designs for Research*. Chicago: Rand McNally College Publishing Company.

COLE, J.W.L. & GRIZZLE, J.E. (1966). Application of multivariate analysis of variance to repeated measurements experiments. *Biometrics*, **22**, 810–828.

COLLIER, R.O., BAKER, F.B., MANDEVILLE, G.K. & HAYES, T.F. (1967). Estimates of test size for several test procedures based on conventional variance ratios in the repeated measures design. *Psychometrika*, **32**, 339–353.

FISHER, R.A. (1920). Studies in crop variation, I. An examination of the yield of dressed grain from Broadbalk. *Journal of Agricultural Science*, **11**, 107–135.

FISHER, R.A. (1925). *Statistical Methods for Research Workers*. Edinburgh: Oliver & Boyd.

GEISSER, S. & GREENHOUSE, S.W. (1958). An extension of Box's results on the use of the *F* distribution in multivariate analysis. *Annals of Mathematical Statistics*, **29**, 885–891.

GREENHOUSE, S.W. & GEISSER, S. (1959). On methods in the analysis of profile data. *Psychometrika*, **24**, 95–112.

HAND, D.J. & TAYLOR, C.C. (1987). *Multivariate Analysis of Variance and Repeated Measures*. London: Chapman & Hall.

HUYNH, H. (1978). Some approximate tests for repeated measurement designs. *Psychometrika*, **43**, 161–175.

HUYNH, H. & FELDT, L.S. (1970). Conditions under which mean square ratios in repeated measurements designs have exact *F*-distributions. *Journal of the American Statistical Association*, **65**, 1582–1589.

HUYNH, H. & FELDT, L.S. (1976). Estimation of the Box correction for degrees of freedom from sample data in the randomized block and split-plot designs. *Journal of Educational Statistics*, **1**, 69–82.

KENWARD, M.G. (1987). A method for comparing profiles of repeated measurements. *Applied Statistics*, **36**, 296–308.

KESELMAN, H.J., ROGAN, J.C., MENDOZA, J.L. & BREEN, L.J. (1980). Testing the validity conditions of repeated measures *F* tests. *Psychological Bulletin*, **87**, 479–481.

MAUCHLY, J.W. (1940). Significance test for sphericity of a normal *n*-variate distribution. *Annals of Mathematical Statistics*, **11**, 204–209.

MILLIKEN, G.A. & JOHNSON, D.E. (1984). *Analysis of Messy Data, Vol. 1, Designed Experiments*. California: Lifetime Publications.

MITZEL, H.C. & GAMES, P.A. (1981). Circularity and multiple comparisons in repeated measures designs. *British Journal of Mathematical and Statistical Psychology*, **34**, 253–259.

OLSON, C.L. (1974). Comparative robustness of six tests in multivariate analysis of variance. *Journal of the American Statistical Association*, **69**, 894–908.

PLEWIS, I. (1986). Analysing data from comparative longitudinal studies. In A. D. Lovie (Ed.) *New Developments in Statistics for Psychology and the Social Sciences*. London and New York: The British Psychological Society & Methuen.

POTTHOFF, R.F. & ROY, S.N. (1964). A generalized multivariate analysis of variance model useful especially for growth curve problems. *Biometrika*, **51**, 313–326.

ROUANET, H. & LEPINE, D. (1970). Comparison between treatments in a repeated-measurement design: ANOVA and multivariate methods. *British Journal of Mathematical and Statistical Psychology*, **23**, 147–163.

SEBER, G.A.F. (1984). *Multivariate Observations*. New York: Wiley.

SNEE, R.D. (1972). On the analysis of response curve data. *Technometrics*, **14**, 47–62.

WALLENSTEIN, S. & FLEISS, J.L. (1979). Repeated measurements analysis of variance when the correlations have a certain pattern. *Psychometrika*, **44**, 229–233.

YATES, F. (1965). A fresh look at the basic principles of the design and analysis of experiments. *Proceedings of the Fifth Berkeley Symposium on Mathematical Statistics and Probability*, **4**, 777–790.

YATES, F. (1969). *Experimental Design – Selected Papers*. London: Griffin.

# 8

# Time Series

CHRIS SKINNER

The analysis of time series of macro-level observations such as price indices or birth rates has a long history in the social sciences, most notably in economics (for example, Granger & Newbold, 1977) but also in other areas such as demography (for example, Land, 1986). This chapter will focus instead on the analysis of time series of observations at the individual level, a topic whose development has tended to be more recent.

I begin by presenting a variety of examples of individual level time series. I then suggest a number of ways in which the nature of individual level time series might be distinguished from that of macro-level time series. One basic distinction concerns the objectives of analysis and this is dealt with separately in the third section. A second distinction concerns the fact that, whilst aggregate time series are typically unique, individual level time series are often repeated across several individuals. Two broad approaches to the analysis of such repeated time series are discussed in the fourth section. Next we survey a number of methods of analysis of time series. The description is brief since expositions of the technical details of these methods are widely available. Finally, I present an extended empirical example, where procedures which take account of the time series nature of the data produce results quite different from standard ANOVA procedures.

## EXAMPLES OF INDIVIDUAL LEVEL TIME SERIES

Time series data involve sequences of observations, usually separated by equal time intervals. The examples below are distinguished by the length of these intervals.

### (a) Intervals of seconds

(i) Figure 1 displays a time series of 360 consecutive observations. Each observation consists of the mean across 32 experimental subjects of the log electroencephalograph (EEG) activity at the Frontal ($F_z$) low alpha frequency averaged over a 3 second epoch. The log transformation was taken to achieve a better approximation to normality for the ensuing analysis. In rough terms,

174

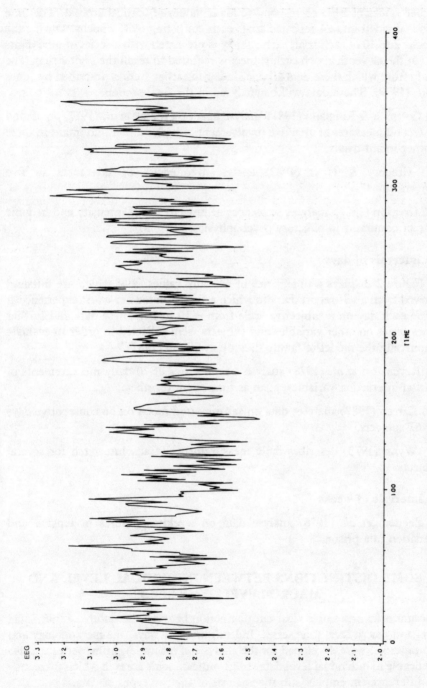

**Figure 1.** Time series of 360 consecutive values of electroencephalograph (EEG) activity.

higher values of EEG correspond to lower values of cortical arousal. The time axis is divided into 24 repeated trials each consisting of 15 epochs. During the epochs 2 to 10 of each trial, each subject is presented with a series of nine digits and at the eleventh epoch each subject is required to recall the digit string. The study from which these data arise is similar to earlier studies described by Jones *et al.* (1979). These data will be analysed in the final section.

(ii) Gottman & Ringland (1981) analyse data of Tronick *et al.* (1977) on second by second measures of affective involvement of both mother and infant in three mother-infant dyads.

(iii) Gregory & Hoyt (1982) analyse frequencies of utterances in five conversations.

(iv) Gregson (1982) analyses sequences of judgements of intensity and hedonic tone of odourants in olfactory psychophysics.

(b) **Intervals of days**

(i) Figure 2 displays a time series of 44 daily values (4 of which are missing) derived from a self-report diary in which a subject rated her worst experience at home each day on a subjective scale from −10 to 10. These data and further times series on other variables and subjects were collected in order to evaluate empirically the model of family therapy in Simon (1987).

(ii) Revenstorf *et al.* (1978) analyse a time series of 70 daily measurements of marital interaction variables, such as time spent together.

(iii) Larsen (1987) analyses data on self-reported mood on 56 consecutive days for 62 subjects.

(iv) Wynn (1973) describes daily measurements of absolute pitch for several subjects.

(c) **Intervals of weeks**

(i) Zeeman *et al.* (1976) analyse data on weekly measures of tension and alienation in a prison.

## SOME DISTINCTIONS BETWEEN INDIVIDUAL LEVEL AND MACRO-LEVEL TIME SERIES

I do not offer any single clear-cut distinction between the nature of individual level and macro-level time series. Indeed, in many ways, the methodology and computer software developed for the analysis of macro-level time series are also applicable to individual level data. I just indicate some areas in which there may be differences in emphasis in the analysis of the two types of data.

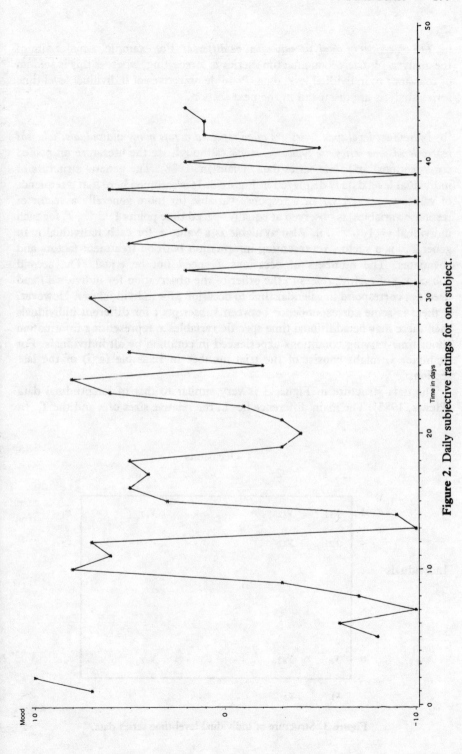

**Figure 2. Daily subjective ratings for one subject.**

(a) *The objectives of analysis may often be different.* For example, a major aim of the analysis of macroeconomic time series is forecasting, whereas this is seldom of relevance to individual level data. Possible objectives of individual level time series analysis are discussed in the next section.

(b) *Individual level time series are often repeated across many individuals, whereas macro-level time series are typically unique* (although see the literature on pooled cross-sectional and time series data, Dielman, 1988). The general structure of individual level data is displayed in Figure 3. It is assumed here that a sequence of values $y_{i1}, \ldots, y_{iT_i}$ of a response variable (or more generally a vector of response variables) is observed at equally spaced time points $1, \ldots, T_i$ for each individual $i = 1, \ldots, n$. Also available is a value $z_i$ for each individual $i$. In general $z_i$ is a vector, representing information both on treatment factors and covariates. The numbers of occasions $T_i$ need not be equal. The second subscript $t$ of each $y_{it}$ refers to the order of the observation for individual $i$ and need not correspond in calendar time to occasion $t$ for individual $j \neq i$. However, if there is some correspondence between subscripts $t$ for different individuals then there may be additional time specific variables $x_t$ representing information about time-varying conditions experienced in common by all individuals. For example, $x_t$ might consist of the trial number in Example (a)(i) of the last section.

The data structure in Figure 3 is very similar to that of longitudinal data (Plewis, 1985). The main difference lies in the relative sizes of $n$ and the $T_i$. In

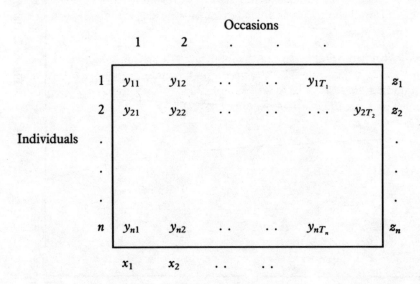

**Figure 3.** Structure of individual level time series data.

longitudinal studies the $T_i$ are usually equal and small, say between 2 and 10, whereas $n$ may be large, say several thousand, in a survey. In our context we assume that the $T_i$ are reasonably large, say greater than 50, which is necessary for many methods of time series analysis (for example, Box & Jenkins, 1976, p. 18), whereas $n$ is typically much smaller, possibly even $n = 1$.

(c) *Macro-level time series variables are often defined as a sum of values across some population and are thus more likely to be Gaussian than individual level time series because of the Central Limit Theorem.* Furthermore, even the interval-level nature of many individual level time series variables may be suspect, for example when the variable involves subjective judgement. Hence there are some reasons to suppose that individual level time series will be less well-behaved and more difficult to model than macro-level time series.

(d) *For individual level data collected under controlled experimental conditions, such as in Example (a)(i) of the previous section, the time series process may be expected to exhibit greater 'homogeneity' over time than many macro-level time series which are more susceptible to external events such as wars or stock market crashes.* Hence, there are some reasons why homogeneity assumptions such as stationarity (Gottman, 1981, Chapter 8), which underlry many methods of time series analysis, may be more plausible for individual level time series than for macro-level time series and so this effect may tend to compensate for the effect in (c). On the other hand, some individual level time series collected under less controlled conditions, such as the subjective rating series of Example (b)(i) of the previous section, will also be very susceptible to external life events such as bereavement.

(e) *Individual level time series may possess different periodicities from the usual seasonal cycles in macro-level variables.* For example, there may be cycles corresponding to trial length in Example (a)(i) or to menstrual period in Example (b)(iv) in the previous section.

## SOME OBJECTIVES FOR THE COLLECTION AND ANALYSIS OF INDIVIDUAL LEVEL TIME SERIES

I shall distinguish between objectives where time is incidental to the aim of the study and objectives which are directly concerned with dynamic questions. The reason for this distinction is that many time series applications in psychology have fallen under the former heading whereas I feel that the latter objective will often be of greater relevance to understanding psychological phenomena (*c.f.*, Gregson, 1983).

(a) **Time incidental to the objective of the study**

(i) *Repeated measurements* are often taken solely so that they may be averaged for each subject in order to increase *reliability* (Epstein, 1980).

(ii) *Repeated measures* within-subject designs are frequently used in experimental psychology to increase *efficiency* by controlling for individual differences (Keppel, 1982, p. 369). Although responses of individual subjects under different experimental conditions are recorded, the parameters of interest remain defined as averages across subjects. In principle, these parameters could also be estimated from a between-subject design, albeit less efficiently.

(iii) *Quasi-experiments* involving repeated measurements on individuals are frequently used in field settings to evaluate the effects of treatments (Campbell & Stanley, 1963; Cook & Campbell, 1979). For example, in the *interrupted time series design*, sequences of observations are recorded before and after a treatment. The parameters of interest remain the mean responses across individuals under different treatments. The reason for not using a conventional randomized between-subject design usually concerns the ethical or practical problems of controlling the allocation of treatments to subjects. The reason for using time series measurements rather than simply before and after measurements is to combat threats to validity such as maturation (Cook & Campbell, 1979).

(iv) *Single-subject or n=1 designs* involve repeated measurements on a single subject exposed to alternative experimentally controlled treatments. As an example, the daily eating behaviour of a patient with anorexia nervosa might be recorded both before and during 'reinforcement' therapy (Barlow & Herson, 1984, p. 46). The aim is to study how therapy affects eating behaviour in the given patient. Unlike quasi-experiments, the aim of single-subject research is to estimate treatment effects at the level of the individual rather than an effect averaged across individuals. These effects are generally defined as the difference between the mean responses of the individual to alternative treatments, and hence are independent of any dynamic process. The reason for the temporal design is that it is not possible to observe the response of one subject to two different treatments simultaneously. In some cases, however, such as when studying the effect of a transient intervention, for example the effect on an infant's heart-rate of an instantaneous stimulus event (Jones *et al.*, 1969), it does seem necessary to define a treatment effect dependent upon the pattern of some temporal process. As Glass *et al.* (1975, p. 5) state:

> Interventions . . . do not have merely 'an effect' but 'an effect pattern' across time. The value of an intervention is properly judged . . . by whether the effect occurs immediately or is delayed, whether it increases or decays, whether it is only temporarily or constantly superior to the effects of alternative interventions.

Hence, in such circumstances it may be more appropriate to place single-subject designs under heading (b).

(b) **Time fundamental to the objective of the study**

We make the usual distinction below between *time-domain* and *frequency domain* representations (see, for example, Gottman, 1981).

(i) Time-domain models may be fitted to univariate time series in order to assist the understanding of psychological phenomena. For example, Wing & Kristofferson (1973) and Wing (1977) propose linear models for the timing of intervals between repetitive responses which involve the combination of independent stochastic processes of timekeeping and response generation. Such applications where the parameters of linear univariate models are of psychological interest seem rare, however. In general the fitting of linear univariate models of the autoregressive integrated moving-average (ARIMA) type (Box & Jenkins, 1976) to any psychological time series is unlikely to be an objective in itself because of the lack of parameter interpretability. The use of non-linear models, such as the threshold autoregressive model of Tong & Lim (1980), seem likely to offer more interesting interpretations and Gregson (1983, p. 218) mentions possible applications to series of eating behaviour of anorexia nervosa patients or series of errors of judgement of drivers under the influence of alcohol.

(ii) The analysis of cyclical patterns of univariate time series in the frequency domain may be used to identify various phenomena of psychological interest. For example, Wade *et al.* (1973) study biorhythms and Larsen (1987) relates the magnitude of different frequency components of mood series to emotional reactivity.

(iii) Systematic change in the mean level of a univariate time series as a function of time is often of interest. For example, the effect of learning and practice on performance in repeated tasks are studied in experimental psychology (for example, Keppel, 1982, p. 370).

(iv) Models may be fitted to multivariate time series in order to understand the relationships between the variables. For example, Levenson & Gottman (1983) study the relationship between physiological and affective variables for married couples and Gregson (1982, 1984) studies the relationship between odours and their perceived intensities. Zeeman *et al.* (1976) fit a catastrophe theory model to study the relationship between tension and alienation during a period of disorder at a prison.

## TWO BROAD APPROACHES TO THE ANALYSIS OF REPEATED TIME SERIES

As displayed previously in Figure 3, individual level time series data are generally available on more than one individual. We may distinguish two broad approaches to the analysis of such repeated time series data.

*Separate* : Analyses of each individual's data $d_i = (y_{i1}, \ldots, y_{iT_i}, z_i)$ are performed separately for $i = 1, \ldots, n$. These individual analyses may then be compared in a between-subject analysis.

*Combined* : All the data $(d_1, \ldots, d_n)$ are analysed simultaneously.

In some situations a combined approach may be necessary, for example, when the $T_i$ are very small or in a complex repeated measures design, where different sequences of treatments are systematically assigned to different individuals and it is necessary to combine information from different individuals in order to separate out different effects such as carry-over effects. However, in most situations, such as in the examples given in the first section, it seems sensible to commence analysis in a separate way. This avoids assumptions about the nature of individual differences, such as the assumption, common in many combined ANOVA analyses, that all individuals' observations possess a common variance. For this reason we shall only discuss the analysis of a single time series in what follows and in particular in the empirical example of the final section. However, I do note that the question of how to combine the results of separate within-subject analyses is an important question which has received little attention. Cox (1981) mentions a number of approaches. One procedure is to fit a model for which some parameters are constant across subjects and some are completely free to vary between subjects. An intermediate empirical Bayes approach is to assume that some parameters do vary between subjects but possess a prior distribution which may be estimated from the data (e.g. Crowder & Tredger, 1981; Crowder, 1983). A final approach, which is less model-dependent and is common in practice, is to use the parameter estimates from the separate within-subject analyses as derived response variables in a between-subject analysis (Cox, 1984, p. 20).

## SOME METHODS OF ANALYSING TIME SERIES

The well-known approach of Box & Jenkins (1976) to the analysis of univariate time series involves the fitting of *autoregressive integrated moving average* (ARIMA) models. For example, the *autoregressive* model of order $p$, denoted AR($p$), for the time series $y_1, y_2 \ldots$, is represented by the equation

$$y_t = \phi_0 + \phi_1 y_{t-1} + \phi_2 y_{t-2} + \ldots \phi_p y_{t-p} + a_t, \tag{1}$$

where $a_1, a_2, \ldots$ is a sequence of independent random variables with mean 0 and constant variance. This model is analogous to the usual multiple linear regression model with coefficients $\phi_i$. However, the $\phi_i$ are less easily interpretable here than in conventional linear regression and, as suggested earlier (in (b)(i) of the section on objectives) the fitting of ARIMA models is unlikely to be an end in itself but rather may serve as some component of a more complex analysis.

Expositions of methods of fitting ARIMA models as well as other standard methods of analysis of univariate time series, such as spectral analysis, are widely available (for example, Bohrer & Porges, 1982; Gottman, 1981; Chatfield, 1984) and hence the details of such techniques are not described further here.

In addition to the values $y_1, y_2, \ldots$ of a scalar response variable, data may also be available on values $x_1, x_2, \ldots$ of a vector of variables $x$, representing external conditions at times $t = 1, 2, \ldots$. Transfer function models (Box & Jenkins, 1976, Ch. 10) provide a general class of models for investigating the impact of the $x$ series on the $y$ series. One specific example is discussed at length in the next section, where the $x$ vector represents trial number and epoch number.

An important special case of transfer function modelling arises when $x_t$ represents an intervention and consists of either a step function for a permanent intervention

$$
\begin{aligned}
x_t &= 1, & t &\geq T_1, \\
&= 0, & t &< T_1,
\end{aligned}
$$

or a pulse function for a transient intervention

$$
\begin{aligned}
x_t &= 1, & t &= T_1, \\
&= 0, & &\text{otherwise.}
\end{aligned}
$$

A common model for such data is

$$
y_t = f(x_t, x_{t-1}, \ldots) + u_t,
$$

where $f$ is a given function representing the systematic effect of the series on $y_t$, for example

$$
f_1(x_t, x_{t-1}, \ldots) = \alpha + \delta_1 x_t,
$$

or

$$
f_2(x_t, x_t, x_{t-1}, \ldots) = \alpha + \delta_1(x_t + \delta_2 x_{t-1} + \delta_2^2 x_{t-2} + \ldots),
$$

and $u_t$ is a random term, following perhaps an ARIMA process (Glass *et al.*, 1975; Box & Tiao, 1975). Thus for the step function we have

$$
\begin{aligned}
f_1 &= \alpha + \delta_1, & t &\geq T_1, \\
&= \alpha, & t &< T_1,
\end{aligned} \tag{2}
$$

representing a constant permanent effect of the intervention, or

$$
\begin{aligned}
f_2 &= \alpha + \delta_1(1 - \delta_2^{t-T_1+1})/(1 - \delta_2), & t &\geq T_1, \\
&= \alpha, & t &< T_1,
\end{aligned}
$$

representing a 'gradual permanent impact' (McDowall *et al.*, 1980, p. 75) increasing from $\delta_1$ at $t = T_1$ to $\delta_1/(1-\delta_2)$ at $t = \infty$.

For the pulse function we have

$$
\begin{aligned}
f_1 &= \alpha + \delta_1, & t &= T_1, \\
&= \alpha, & &\text{otherwise,}
\end{aligned}
$$

representing an instantaneous jump in the mean of $y_t$ at $t = T_1$, or

$$
\begin{aligned}
f_2 &= \alpha + \delta_1\delta_2^{t-T_1}, & t &\geq T_1, \\
&= \alpha, & t &< T_1,
\end{aligned}
$$

representing an 'abrupt temporary impact' (McDowall *et al.*, 1980, p. 80) decreasing from $\delta_1$ to 0 according to the rate parameter $\delta_2$. Of these models, the constant permanent effect model in (2) has been most widely used, although there is some debate about how to take account of serial correlation in the random $u_t$ term (for example, Gorsuch, 1983) and indeed to what extent such serial correlation does exist in behavioural data (Huitema, 1985). General discussions of how to fit the above models as well as models with alternative forms of $f$ are given by Box & Tiao (1975), Glass *et al.* (1975) and McDowall *et al.* (1980).

In the discussion above we have assumed that interest focuses on the dependence of $y_t$, as a response, on $x_t$, as a fixed external condition. However, often the $x_t$ variables will also be measured as responses and the *mutual* dependence between the $y_t$ series and the $x_t$ series will be of interest with $x_t$ and $y_t$ treated symmetrically. At the simplest level cross-correlations between series can be computed (for example, Revenstorf *et al.*, 1982), but such correlations are well-known to be difficult to interpret since serial correlation in individual series can induce 'spurious' patterns of cross-correlation. Brunsdon & Skinner (1987) investigate the use of alternative measures of dependence which control for serial correlation in individual series. Examples of the use of bivariate time-domain models to investigate dependence between time series are given by Gottman & Ringland (1981), Levenson & Gottman (1983) and Gregson (1984). Frequency-domain methods may also be used to study dependence (see, for example, Porges *et al.*, 1980).

When large numbers of variables are measured at each occasion, it may be of interest to model the covariance structure of such variables by assuming the existence of one or more latent time series variables. There has recently been increasing interest in the use of such dynamic factor models (Geweke, 1977; Molenaar, 1985; Molenaar & Roelofs, 1987; Otter, 1986; Pena & Box, 1987).

## ANALYSIS OF EEG DATA

We now analyse the data described in (a) (i) of the first section and displayed in Figure 1. We assume that the objective is to understand how the mean level of $y$

varies across the 24 trials and across the 15 epochs within each trial. For simplicity, we just analyse the series of subject means as a prototype for a within-subject analysis. In practice I would recommend repeating this analysis for different subjects as discussed earlier.

If their time-series nature were ignored, these data might conventionally be analysed using ANOVA. For example, in their similar study, Jones *et al.* (1979, p. 100) collapsed the EEG values across the 24 trials to obtain a data matrix of 9 epochs $\times$ 32 subjects, which they analysed by two-way ANOVA to assess the significance of EEG differences between epochs. With our data collapsed across subjects we might similarly conduct a two-way ANOVA of the matrix of 15 epochs $\times$ 24 trials. The results of this analysis, assuming no interaction, are given in Table 1, from which it appears that both differences between trials and differences between epochs are highly significant.

**Table 1.** Two-way ANOVA of EEG data ignoring serial correlation

| Source | df | SS | MS | F |
|---|---|---|---|---|
| Trials | 23 | 1.11 | 0.048 | 2.36*** |
| Epochs | 14 | 0.90 | 0.064 | 3.14*** |
| Residual | 322 | 6.56 | 0.020 | |
| Total | 359 | 8.57 | | |

Note:  NS: not significant at 5% level
        *: significant at 5% level
       **: significant at 1% level
      ***: significant at 0.1% level

To clarify the assumptions behind this analysis we may write the assumed model as

$$y_t = \alpha + \sum_{i=1}^{23} \beta_i x_{it} + \sum_{j=1}^{14} \gamma_j z_{jt} + \varepsilon_t, \tag{3}$$

where $\beta_1, \ldots, \beta_{23}$ are parameters representing the 23 df between trials, $x_{1t}, \ldots, x_{23t}$ are dummy variables representing trial effects, that is,

$$x_{it} = 1, \qquad t = 15i - 14, \ldots, 15i, \ i = 1, \ldots, 23,$$
$$= 0, \qquad \text{otherwise},$$

$\gamma_1, \ldots, \gamma_{14}$ are parameters representing the 14 df between epochs, $z_{1t}, \ldots, z_{14t}$ are dummy variables representing epochs, that is,

$$z_{jt} = 1, \quad \text{if } t - j \text{ is a multiple of 15},$$
$$= 0, \quad \text{otherwise},$$

and the $\varepsilon_t$ are normal random variables with mean 0 and constant variance. Finally, the key assumption for our purposes is that the $\varepsilon_t$ ($t=1, \ldots, 360$) are mutually independent and thus not serially correlated. A standard test of this assumption is based upon the Durbin-Watson test statistic, $d$, which in this case is computed as 1.48. Standard tables only list critical values of $d$ up to a sample size $T$ of 100. For larger sample sizes, the null distribution of $d$ under the hypothesis of no serial correlation is well approximated by the normal distribution with mean 2 and variance $4/T$ (Harvey, 1981, p. 200). Hence $d$ may be transformed into the z statistic.

$$z = \sqrt{T}(d/2 - 1).$$

A one-sided test is usually appropriate since the more negative the value of $z$, the stronger is the positive serial correlation in $\varepsilon_t$. For $d = 1.48$ and $T = 360$ we have $z = -4.93$, which is highly significant and hence we conclude that there is very strong evidence against the hypothesis of no serial correlation.

In order to allow for serial correlation, we shall assume that the $\varepsilon_t$ follow an autoregressive process of order $p$ as in (1), so that

$$\varepsilon_t = \phi_1\varepsilon_{t-1} + \phi_2\varepsilon_{t-2} + \ldots + \phi_p\varepsilon_{t-p} + a_t, \tag{4}$$

where $a_t$ is a sequence of independent normal random variables with mean 0 and constant variance. This enables us to use the procedure AUTOREG of the computer package SAS/ETS (SAS Institute, 1984) which fits models of the form

$$y_t = \mathbf{x}_t'\boldsymbol{\beta} + \varepsilon_t, \tag{5}$$

where $\mathbf{x}_t$ is a vector of known values, $\boldsymbol{\beta}$ is a vector of unknown coefficients and $\varepsilon_t$ follows the AR($p$) process in (4). There are similar procedures in other packages such as GENSTAT and BMDP.

The order $p$ of the AR($p$) process may be selected using a likelihood ratio test. Values of the likelihood ratio test statistic for model (3) and (4) with different choices of $p$ are presented in Table 2. The test statistics are calculated relative to the model with independent $\varepsilon_t$ and, using the usual large-sample approximation (Harvey, 1981, p. 163), the values of the test statistic are referred to critical values of the chi-squared distribution with degrees of freedom equal to $p$. Large

**Table 2.** Likelihood ratio tests of order $p$ of AR($p$) model for $\varepsilon_t$

| $p$ | df | $\chi^2$ | Difference in $\chi^2$ |
|-----|-----|----------|------------------------|
| 1 | 1 | 25.2*** | |
| 2 | 2 | 31.8 | 6.6** |
| 3 | 3 | 34.4 | 2.5$^{NS}$ |

values of the test statistic indicate departures from the hypothesis that $\phi_1 = \ldots = \phi_p = 0$. The difference between the $p$th and the $(p-1)$th test statistic may be used to test the hypothesis $\phi_p = 0$. Thus, the observed value of 25.2 for $p = 1$ indicates that $\phi_1$ is highly significant, in agreement with the result of the Durbin-Watson test. The increment of 6.6 from $p = 1$ to $p = 2$ also suggests that a second term in (4) is needed, whereas the next increment of 2.5 is non-significant and we select an AR(2) process as a parsimonious model for $\varepsilon_t$. The fitted model based upon maximum likelihood is

$$\varepsilon_t = 0.24 \ \varepsilon_{t-1} + 0.14 \ \varepsilon_{t-2} + a_t.$$

We now consider the choice of the systematic part $x_t'\beta$ of (5), that is, alternatives to the 38 terms in (3). In fact the choice of the systematic part of the model will itself affect the procedures discussed above for selecting an appropriate model for the random $\varepsilon_t$. For simplicity we ignore this problem here and retain an AR(2) process for the $\varepsilon_t$ throughout.

We first repeat the analysis of Table 1 for a main effects model but now allowing for serial correlation in the $\varepsilon_t$. We again employ likelihood ratio tests. In order to make the effect of the AR(2) assumption clearer we first carry out a likelihood ratio test assuming independent $\varepsilon_t$. This test can be shown theoretically to be equivalent to the $F$-test in Table 1 for large samples and indeed the chi-squared values for the trial effects and the epoch effects shown in Table 3 are both highly significant as in Table 1. It may be noted that for the likelihood-ratio test the chi-squared value for testing epochs after controlling for trials is $96.1 - 49.8 = 46.3$ which is not exactly equal to the chi-squared value of 39.9 for testing epochs without controlling for trials. This is in contrast to the $F$-test where trial and epoch effects are 'orthogonal'.

**Table 3.** Likelihood ratio tests of main effects

| Source | df | $\chi^2[\varepsilon_t \text{ independent}]$ | $\chi^2[\varepsilon_t \sim \text{AR}(2)]$ |
|---|---|---|---|
| Trials | 23 | 49.8*** | 20.5[NS] |
| Epochs | 14 | 39.9*** | 31.8** |
| Trials<br>+ Epochs | 37 | 96.1*** | 55.9* |

The important part of Table 3, however, is the last column, where we see that the effect of allowing for serial correlation is to reduce the significance of the effects substantially. Indeed the trials effect has been reduced from significant at the 0.1% level to not significant at the 5% level.

To offer a highly over-simplified explanation for this effect, suppose that $y_1$ and $y_2$ are two observations each with variance $\sigma^2$ and with mutual correlation $\rho$. Then the variance of their mean $(y_1 + y_2)/2$ is $\sigma^2(1 + \rho)/2$. Equating this to

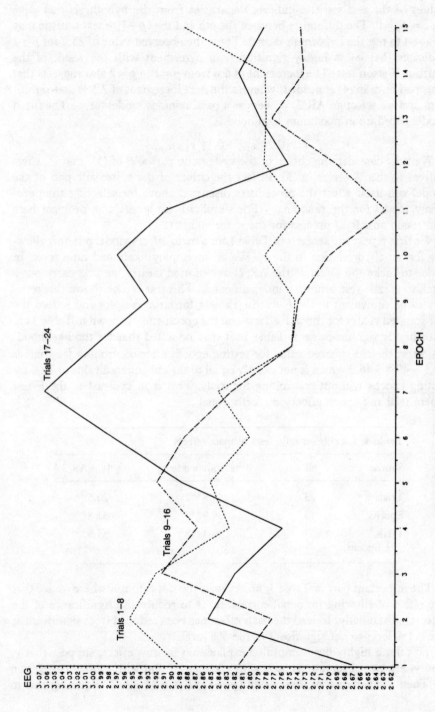

**Figure 4.** Mean EEG at each epoch across blocks of eight trials.

the usual formula for $\sigma^2/n$ we obtain $n = 2/(1+\rho)$. Hence if $\rho > 0$ then the information in $y_1$ and $y_2$ is equivalent to the information in less than 2 independent observations. Thus in Table 1 we overestimated the significance of the results because we assumed we had 360 independent observations when in fact we only had the equivalent of much less than 360 independent observations because, for example, the correlation between $\varepsilon_t$ and $\varepsilon_{t-1}$ was 0.26.

So far we have not allowed for any interaction between trials and epochs. Some indication that interactions may exist, however, is given in Figure 4 which displays the mean values for each epoch across the first, second and third block of eight trials in the experiment. Furthermore, prior psychological reasoning also suggests interaction on the grounds that subjects may be expected to learn that performance at recall improves with increased relaxation, that is, decreased arousal or increased EEG activation. In a highly schematic way, it might be expected that the EEG epoch profile might begin as in Figure 5a with arousal increasing as the subject attempts to memorize more digits and then decreasing after recall but then the profile might change to Figure 5b as the subject learns to relax to improve performance (recall that EEG is inversely related to arousal). Some evidence of such a change in profile is indeed apparent in Figure 4.

In order to fit interaction terms we first fit polynomial terms to the trial and epoch effects. The variables $TR$ and $EP$ define the number of the trial from 1 to

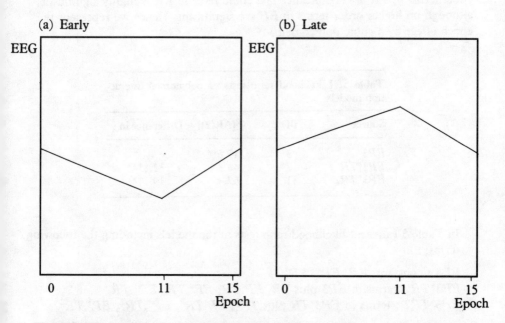

**Figure 5.** Hypothetical change in EEG profile arising from change in recall strategy.

24 and epoch from 1 to 15 respectively. Hence if $TR_t$ and $EP_t$ are the respective values of $TR$ and $EP$ at time $t = 1, \ldots, 360$ then

$$t = 15(TR_t - 1) + EP_t.$$

**Table 4.** Likelihood ratio tests of polynomial main effects

| Source | df | $\chi^2[\text{AR}(2)]$ |
|---|---|---|
| $TR$ | 1 | 1.2[NS] |
| $TR^2/TR$ | 1 | 2.1[NS] |
| $TR^3/TR, TR^2$ | 1 | 0.8[NS] |
| $EP$ | 1 | 2.6[NS] |
| $EP^2/EP$ | 1 | 1.9[NS] |
| $EP^3/EP, EP^2$ | 1 | 11.1[***] |
| $EP^4, EP^5/EP, EP^2, EP^3$ | 2 | 0.2[NS] |
| Epochs/$EP/EP^2, EP^3$ | 11 | 16.3[NS] |

Likelihood ratio tests of the order of polynomials in $TR$ and $EP$ are presented in Table 4. As with the trial effects in Table 3, none of the linear, quadratic or cubic terms in $TR$ are significant. The cubic term in $EP$ is highly significant, although no higher order terms in $EP$ are significant. Hence we represent the epoch effect by a cubic polynomial.

**Table 5.** Likelihood ratio tests of polynomial interaction models

| Source | df | $\chi^2[\text{AR}(2)]$ | Difference in $\chi^2$ |
|---|---|---|---|
| $EP3$ | 3 | 15.6[**] | |
| $EP3^*TR$ | 7 | 48.3 | 32.8[***] |
| $EP3^*TR2$ | 11 | 67.4 | 19.1[**] |

In Table 5 I present likelihood ratio tests of the models including the following terms:

$EP3$ : constant, $EP$, $EP^2$, $EP^3$,
$EP3^*TR$ : terms in $EP3$ plus $TR$, $EP.TR$, $EP^2.TR$, $EP^3.TR$,
$EP3^*TR2$ : terms in $EP3^*TR$ plus $TR^2$, $EP.TR^2$, $EP^2.TR^2$, $EP^3.TR^2$.

We see that the interactions between the cubic polynomial in $EP$ and the

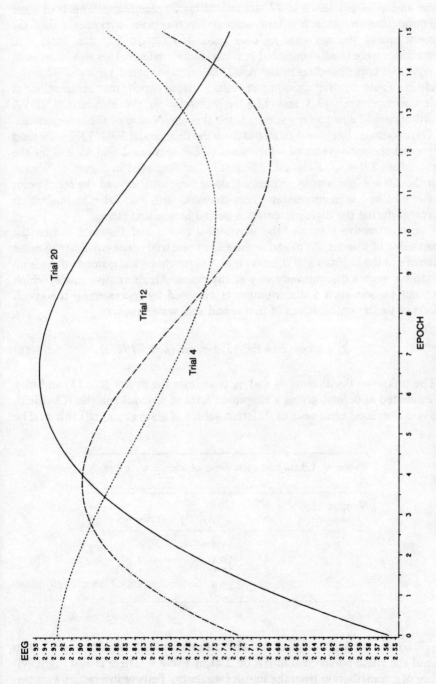

**Figure 6.** Predicted within-trial profiles based on cubic polynomial model.

linear and quadratic terms in *TR* are indeed highly significant. This is of some scientific interest since it offers support for the prior hypothesis that the subjects' recall strategy changes over time. It is interesting that these trial interactions were totally concealed in the trial main effects. It is also interesting to note that corresponding to the AR(2)-based chi-squared values of 32.8 and 19.1 in Table 5, the chi-squared values based upon the assumption of independence were 59.3 and 32.8 respectively, so the standard ANOVA approach would again have overestimated the significance of the interactions.

The maximum likelihood estimates from the final model *EP3*TR2* were used to predict the mean value of *y* for values of *EP* between 1 and 15 and for the three values *TR* = 4, 12 and 20. The results are displayed in Figure 6. We see that the *TR* = 4 line is as hypothesized, decreasing until around the recall point of *EP* = 11 and then increasing. This contrasts with the *TR* = 20 line which increases during the digit presentation period before decreasing.

One unattractive aspect of the polynomial model and Figure 6 is that the mean value of *y* under the model at the end of one trial is not equal to the mean value of *y* at the beginning of the next trial. On psychological grounds there is no reason for such a discontinuity in *y* at any point. An alternative model which does not possess such a discontinuity is obtained by representing the epoch effects as linear combinations of cosine and sine waves thus:

$$\sum_{k=1}^{q} \{\delta_k \cos(2\pi k\, EP/15) + \gamma_k \sin(2\pi k\, EP/15)\}. \tag{6}$$

The unknown coefficients $\delta_k$ and $\gamma_k$ constitute the vector $\boldsymbol{\beta}$ in (5) and may be estimated as before, giving a simplified form of spectral analysis (Chatfield, 1984). Likelihood ratio tests of different values of *q* are given in Table 6. The

**Table 6.** Likelihood ratio tests of cosine wave epoch effects

| Number of frequencies, *q* | df | $\chi^2$[AR(2)] | Difference in $\chi^2$ |
|---|---|---|---|
| 1 | 2 | 15.4*** | |
| 2 | 4 | 16.4 | 1.0[NS] |
| 3 | 6 | 17.5 | 1.0[NS] |
| 4 | 8 | 25.9 | 8.5* |

first frequency is highly significant with a similar chi-squared value on 2 df to that of the cubic polynomial in *EP* on 3 df in Table 4. There is also slight evidence of a contribution from the fourth frequency. Tests of interaction between

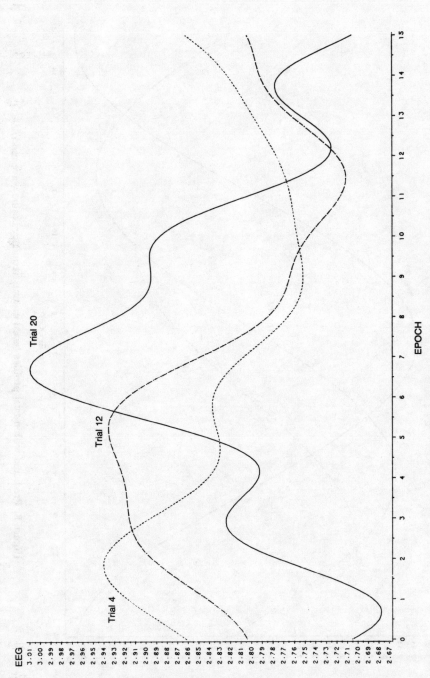

**Figure 7.** Predicted within-trial profiles based on four frequency cosine wave model.

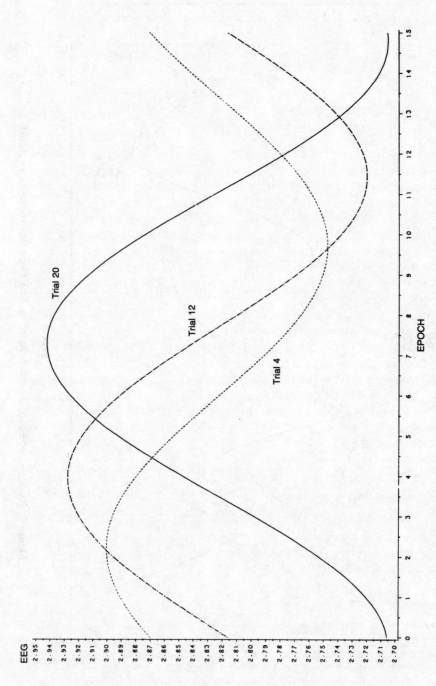

**Figure 8.** Predicted within-trial profiles based on one frequency cosine wave model.

**Table 7.** Likelihood ratio tests of cosine interaction models

| Source | df | $\chi^2$[AR(2)] | Difference in $\chi^2$ |
|---|---|---|---|
| $C4$ | 8 | 25.9** | |
| $C4*TR$ | 17 | 67.9 | 42.0*** |
| $C4*TR^2$ | 26 | 96.5 | 28.6*** |

these cosine terms and the trial number $TR$ are given in Table 7. Here $C4$ denotes the eight terms in (6) with $q = 4$ and $C4*TR$, for example, denotes the 17 terms given by $TR$, $C4$ and all products of $TR$ by each term of $C4$. As in Table 5 the interactions are highly significant.

The predicted mean values of $y$ for values of $EP$ between 1 and 15 and for $TR = 4$, 12 and 20, obtained using maximum likelihood estimates for the model $C4*TR2$, are plotted in Figure 7. Notice that, unlike in Figure 6, the values of $y$ at the beginning of the trial $(EP = 0)$ and at the end of the trial $(EP = 15)$ are now equal. The plots capture more of the shape of the raw data plots in Figure 4. However, there are many peaks and troughs in Figure 7 which are difficult to interpret scientifically and so there is some attraction in using a model with fewer parameters. Since only the term with $q = 1$ was highly significant in Table 6, we also fit the model $C1*TR^2$ with 8 df consisting of $TR,TR2$, the first two terms of (6) with $q = 1$, and the products of these terms with $TR$ and $TR^2$. The predicted values for this model are given in Figure 8. The profiles are, as expected, much smoother and suggest that the decline in EEG becomes more and more delayed as the experiment continues, although the variation in EEG appears to increase. Such a simple model, with its smaller number of parameters, would offer a natural starting point for fitting to data from different subjects to investigate individual differences.

## Acknowledgements

I am grateful to Leila Dehkan and Dave Simon for supplying me with the data in Figures 1 and 2 respectively and to them and Anthony Gale for discussion. Research was supported by grant number HOO 23 2031 from the Economic and Social Research Council.

## References

BARLOW, D.H. & HERSEN, M. (1984). *Single Case Experimental Designs: Strategies for Studying Behaviour Change*, 2nd ed. New York: Pergamon Press.
BOHRER, R.E. & PORGES, S.W. (1982). The application of time series statistics to psychological research: an introduction. In G. Keren (Ed.), *Statistical and Methodological Issues in Psychology and Social Sciences Research*. Hillsdale, N.J.: Erlbaum.

BOX, G.E.P. & JENKINS, G.M. (1976). *Time Series Analysis: Forecasting and Control.* Rev. ed. San-Francisco: Holden-Day.

BOX, G.E.P. & TIAO, G.C. (1975). Intervention analysis with applications to economic and environmental problems. *Journal of the American Statistical Association,* **70,** 70–92.

BRUNSDON, T.M. & SKINNER, C.J. (1987). The analysis of dependencies between time series in psychological experiments. *British Journal of Mathematical and Statistical Psychology,* **40,** 125–139.

CAMPBELL, D.T. & STANLEY, J.C. (1963). *Experimental and Quasi-experimental Designs for Research.* Chicago: Rand McNally.

CHATFIELD, C. (1984). *Analysis of Time Series: An Introduction.* 3rd ed. London: Chapman and Hall.

COOK, T.D. & CAMPBELL, D.T. (1979). *Quasi-Experimentation: Design and Analysis Issues for Field Settings.* Chicago: Rand McNally.

COX, D.R. (1981). Statistical analysis of time series: some recent developments. *Scandinavian Journal of Statistics,* **8,** 93–115.

COX, D.R. (1984). Interaction. *International Statistical Review,* **52,** 1-31.

CROWDER, M.J. (1983). A growth curve analysis for EDP curves. *Applied Statistics,* **32,** 15–18.

CROWDER, M.J. & TREDGER, J.A. (1981). The use of exponentially damped polynomials for biological recovery data. *Applied Statistics,* **30,** 147–152.

DIELMAN, T.E. (1988). *Pooled Cross-Sectional and Time Series Data Analysis.* New York: Marcel Dekker.

EPSTEIN, S. (1980). The stability of behaviour II. Implications for psychological research. *American Psychologist,* **35,** 790–806.

GEWEKE, J. (1977). The dynamic factor analysis of economic time series models. In D.J. Aigner & A.S. Goldberger (Eds), *Latent Variables in Socio-economic Models.* Amsterdam: North Holland.

GLASS, G.V., WILLSON, V.L. & GOTTMAN, J. M. (1975). *Design and Analysis of Time-series Experiments.* Boulder: Colorado Assoc. Univ. Press.

GORSUCH, R.L. (1983). Three methods for analyzing limited time-series (*N* of 1) data. *Behavioral Assessment,* **5,** 141–154.

GOTTMAN, J.M. (1981). *Time-series Analysis: a Comprehensive Introduction for Social Scientists.* Cambridge: CUP.

GOTTMAN, J.M. & RINGLAND, J.T. (1981). The analysis of dominance and bidirectionality in social development. *Child Development,* **52,** 393–412.

GRANGER, C.W.J. & NEWBOLD, P. (1977). *Forecasting Economic Time Series.* New York: Academic Press.

GREGORY, S.W. & HOYT, B.R. (1982). Conversation partner mutual adaptation as demonstrated by Fourier series analysis. *Journal of Psycholinguistic Research,* **11,** 35–46.

GREGSON, R.A.M. (1982). Time series in psychology: a case-study in olfactory psychophysics. In O.D. Anderson (Ed.), *Time Series Analysis: Theory and Practice 1.* Amsterdam: North Holland.

GREGSON, R.A.M. (1983). *Time Series in Psychology.* Hillsdale, NJ: Erlbaum.

GREGSON, R.A.M. (1984). Invariance in time series representations of 2-input 2-output psychophysical experiments. *British Journal of Mathematical and Statistical Psychology,* **37,** 100–121.

HARVEY, A.C. (1981). *The Econometric Analysis of Time Series.* Oxford: Philip Allan.

HUITEMA, B.E. (1985). Autocorrelation in applied behaviour analysis: a myth. *Behavioral Assessment,* **7,** 107–118.

JONES, D., GALE, A. & SMALLBONE, A. (1979). Short-term recall of nine-digit strings and the EEG. *British Journal of Psychology*, 70, 97–119.

JONES, R.H., CROWELL, D.H. & KAPUNIAI, L. E. (1969). Change detection model for serially correlated data. *Psychological Bulletin*, 71, 352–358.

KEPPEL, G. (1982). *Design and Analysis: A Researcher's Handbook*, 2nd ed. Englewood Cliffs, NJ: Prentice-Hall.

LAND, K.C. (1986). Methods for national population forecasts: a review. *Journal of the American Statistical Association*, 81, 888–901.

LARSEN, R.J. (1987). The stability of mood variability: a spectral analytic approach to daily mood assessments. *Journal of Personality and Social Psychology*, 52, 1195–1204.

LEVENSON, R.W. & GOTTMAN, J.M. (1983). Marital interaction: physiological linkage and affective exchange. *Journal of Personality and Social Psychology*, 45, 587–597.

McDOWALL, D., McCLEARY, R., MEIDINGER, E.E. & MAY, R.A. (1980). *Interrupted Time Series Analysis*. Beverly Hills: Sage.

MOLENAAR, P.C.M. (1985). A dynamic factor model for the analysis of multivariate time series. *Psychometrika*, 50, 181–202.

MOLENAAR, P.C.M. & ROELOFS, J.W. (1987). The analysis of multiple habituation profiles of single trial evoked potentials. *Biological Psychology*, 24, 1–22.

OTTER, P.W. (1986). Dynamic structural systems under indirect observation: identifiability and estimation aspects from a system theoretic perspective. *Psychometrika*, 51, 415–428.

PENA, D. & BOX, G.E.P. (1987). Identifying a simple structure in time series. *Journal of the American Statistical Association*, 82, 836–843.

PLEWIS, I. (1985). *Analysing Change: Measurement and Explanation Using Longitudinal Data*. Chichester: Wiley.

PORGES, S.W., BOHRER, R.E., CHEUNG, M.N., DRASGOW, F., McCABE, P.M. & KEREN, G. (1980). New time-series statistic for detecting rhythmic co-occurrence in the frequency domain: the weighted coherence and its application to psychophysiological research. *Psychological Bulletin*, 88, 580–587.

REVENSTORF, D., HAHLWEG, K. & SCHINDLER, L. (1978). Lead and lag in aspects of marital interaction. *Behavior Analysis and Modification*, 2, 174–184.

REVENSTORF, D., KENNERT, H., HAHLWEG, K. & SCHINDLER, L. (1982). The use of cross-correlational and other time-series parameters in clinical analysis. In O.D. Anderson (Ed.) *Time Series Analysis: Theory and Practice 1*, 157–172. Amsterdam: North Holland.

SAS Institute (1984). *SAS/ETS User's Guide, Version 5 Ed.* Cary, NC: SAS Institute Inc.

SIMON, D. (1987). On change, catastrophe and therapy. *Journal of Family Therapy*, 9, 59–73.

TONG, H. & LIM, K. S. (1980). Threshold autoregression, limit cycles and cyclical data (with discussion). *Journal of the Royal Statistical Society, Series B*, 42, 245–292.

TRONICK, E.D., ALS, H. & BRAZELTON, T.B. (1977). Mutuality in mother-infant interaction. *Journal of Communication*, 27, 74–79.

WADE, M.G., ELLIS, M. & BOHRER, R. (1973). Biorhythms in the activity of children during free play activity. *Journal of Experimental Analysis of Behavior*, 20, 155–162.

WING, A.M. (1977). Effects of type of movement on the temporal precision of response sequences. *British Journal of Mathematical and Statistical Psychology*, 30, 60–72.

WING, A.M. & KRISTOFFERSON, A. (1973). Response delays and the timing of discrete motor responses. *Perception and Psychophysics*, 14, 5–12.

WYNN, V.T. (1973). Absolute pitch in humans, its variations and possible connections with other known rhythmic phenomena. In G.A. Kerkut and J.W. Phillis (Eds), *Progress in Neurobiology 1*. Oxford: Pergamon Press.

ZEEMAN, E.C., HALL, C.S., HARRISON, P.T., MARRIAGE, G.H. & SHAPLAND, P.H. (1976). A model for institutional disturbances. *British Journal of Mathematical and Statistical Psychology*, **29**, 66–80.

# 9

# Latent Variable Methods

DAVID BARTHOLOMEW

## SCOPE AND APPROACH

Latent variable methods have been in existence since the introduction of factor analysis at the beginning of the century. They have been through many vicissitudes but have lately re-emerged as useful tools for social scientists. They have shared in the immense growth of applied multivariate analysis consequent upon the widespread availability of cheap computing resources. Analyses which were once embarked upon with fear and trembling can now be undertaken efficiently and quickly even by those who have only a passing acquaintance with the underlying theory. This has brought problems of a different kind in its train and the time has now come to stand back and take stock of the role and usefulness of this battery of techniques in psychological and social science research generally. The primary aim of this chapter is not to describe the methods and models in detail for that has been done elsewhere, in Bartholomew (1987), for example. Its purpose, rather, is to identify some of the important general conclusions about the usefulness of these methods which have emerged from recent research.

A latent variable method is one based on a statistical model which includes random variables which cannot themselves be directly observed. They are, however, assumed to influence variables which can be observed and this enables us, in principle at least, to make some inferences about the latent variables themselves. Psychological theory abounds in such variables. Intelligence was one of the earliest latent variables to receive attention but the whole range of human abilities and attitudes is now included. It is implicit in much theorizing that the 'real' determinants of phenomena underly the observable world which we can directly observe. While the philosophical status of such variables is a matter which can be endlessly debated there is little doubt that their introduction often effectively summarizes and simplifies an otherwise tangled web of interconnected manifest variables.

Broadly speaking there are two ways in which the need for such methods arises in practical research. One is essentially as a measurement problem where the concept is already fairly well defined. The aim then is to find a suitable set of indicators and an optimal way of combining them into a single index whose value can be regarded as a measure of the latent variable in question. Beyond this one might want to investigate the relationships between a set of latent

199

variables. The second way is exploratory in character. Typically we would begin with a large number of measured variables in some area of interest, like views on animals and their welfare. These might, for example, be in the form of answers to items on a questionnaire administered in a social survey. We then ask how many latent dimensions are needed to explain the interdependence among these variables and how these dimensions might be named. By this means we hope to uncover new latent variables which might find a useful role in social theorizing. In reality, of course, few actual studies fall neatly into either category. It is virtually impossible to begin with no preconceptions at all; the act of selecting and framing questions to include in a survey betrays one's half formulated ideas about what the real variables might be. On the other hand even when one has a good idea of what one is trying to measure it is not unusual to discover that some of the chosen indicators are also influenced by other unsuspected latent variables.

## A UNIFIED VIEW

One of the principal advances in recent years has been the recognition that several disparate and apparently unrelated techniques have a common theoretical structure. This has not only served to unify and simplify what was already known but has facilitated the development of new methods and the establishing of links with other multivariate techniques. In this section I shall briefly set out the justification for this remark.

In historical terms the main distinction has been between factor analysis and a collection of methods known as latent structure analysis. The former had its origin in psychology; the latter in sociology. The separation of the two may be, in part, due to their different disciplinary origins but has also been fostered by Lazarsfeld & Henry's (1968) remark that: 'Latent structure analysis is in some ways similar and in many very basic ways different from factor analysis'. This, as we shall see, conceals more than it reveals.

Any latent variable model involves the following elements.

(a) A specification of the observable (manifest) and the unobservable (latent) variables. In the case of the manifest variables this is usually a straightforward matter since their number and level of measurement is often fixed. In the case of the latent variables the question is more complicated. One may have a single nominal level variable or several interval or ratio level variables. In the choice of latent space we may be guided by theory or simply wish to know what measurement level is best supported by the data. For that reason we may wish to try a range of models.

(b) A specification of the joint distribution of the latent variables. In principle this is not necessary since it can (under certain assumptions) be estimated from the data. It is common to assume that they are mutually independent but this is not essential and not always desirable.

(c) A specification of the conditional distribution of the manifest variables given the latent variables.

The last item is crucial since it provides the link between what is observed and what is not. Note that I do not specify directly the distribution of the manifest variables as would be the case in most multivariate models. This follows as a consequence of (b) and (c) taken together. In some cases it is possible to fix the joint distribution of the manifest variables and then make the choice of (b) and (c) subject to that constraint.

The unity of the various existing latent variable models is best seen by noting how their various specifications fit into this framework.

In latent structure analysis the latent space is categorical (that is, nominal) which means that individuals are assumed to belong to one of several latent classes. The term latent class analysis is used to describe the method when the manifest variables are also categorical (often binary). Latent profile analysis refers to the case where the manifest variables are metrical (interval or ratio). Factor analysis refers to the situation when all variables are metrical and usually involves the assumption that each manifest variable has a conditional normal distribution with a mean which is a linear function of the latent variables.

It is thus clear that the essential difference between the various techniques named lies in the level of measurement assumed for the two families of variables involved. The list is obviously not exhaustive and one can easily conceive of various hybrid types of model.

The central element which links the analysis and interpretation of latent variable models is the conditional distribution of the manifest variables. If this belongs to the one-parameter exponential family then there exist sufficient statistics which completely determine the posterior distribution of the latent variables. This is, in fact, the case for all of the commonly used models. In factor analysis the conditional distribution is normal; in the latent trait or latent class model with binary observed variables it is a Bernoulli distribution and with polytomous observed variables it is multinomial. If the canonical parameter of the exponential distribution is chosen to be linear in the latent variables then it turns out that the sufficient statistics are linear combinations of the manifest variables. These linear combinations, called *components*, contain all the information in the data about the latent space. They may be thought of as indices (or measures) of the latent variables and they are used in the same way as factor scores in factor analysis to which they are equivalent. In fact it is easily shown that, for the linear factor models, the components are scalar multiples of the usual factor scores. In Bartholomew (1984) it was argued that one could base the whole interpretation of factor analysis on these components in a way which was exactly equivalent to the more traditional approach. These components also provide a stochastic ordering of individuals in each dimension of the latent space and no higher level of measurement is possible.

## DEFINITIONS AND NOTATION

The diverse origins of latent variable methods have given rise to an equally diverse notation and this has tended to obscure their common structure. We shall therefore adopt a common notation as follows.

Let there be $p$ manifest variables denoted by $x_1, x_2, \ldots, x_p$; these may be scalar values or, for categorical variables, vector valued indicators.

Let there be $q$ latent variables denoted by $y_1, y_2, \ldots, y_q$ and these also may be metrical or categorical.

The object of a latent variable model is to discover whether there exist variables $y$ which explain the inter-correlation of the $x$'s. By 'explain' in this context we mean that variation in the unobservable $y$'s is solely responsible for the observed relationships (correlations) among the $x$'s. This is equivalent to saying that if the $y$'s were held fixed the dependencies among the $x$'s would disappear. A completely general treatment of this problem was given in Bartholomew (1987) as a result of which the 'sufficiency principle' was proposed as a basis for generating a large class of useful models. Initially it will only be necessary to consider three of these in relation to which most of the new work to be reported relates.

(a) *The linear factor model.* This underlies traditional factor analysis for continuous $x$'s and may be expressed by saying that the conditional distribution of $\mathbf{x}$ is $N(\boldsymbol{\mu} + \Lambda \mathbf{y}, \boldsymbol{\psi})$ or, equivalently, that

$$\mathbf{x} = \boldsymbol{\mu} + \Lambda \mathbf{y} + \mathbf{e}, \tag{1}$$

where $\mathbf{y}$ and $\mathbf{e}$ are independent with zero mean. The conditional independence which we seek is contained in the fact that the elements of $\mathbf{e}$ are mutually independent. For some purposes it is necessary to make assumptions about the form of the distributions of $\mathbf{e}$ and $\mathbf{y}$. We denote the variance of $e_i$ by $\psi_i$.

(b) *The logit model.* This is used for binary manifest variables and here the conditional distribution of the $x$'s is

$$x_i \mid \mathbf{y} \cap \text{Bin}(1, \pi_i(\mathbf{y})), \tag{2}$$

where

$$\text{logit } \pi_i(\mathbf{y}) = \alpha_{i0} + \sum_{j=1}^{q} \alpha_{ij} y_j \quad \text{or} \quad \text{logit } \mathbf{\Pi}(\mathbf{y}) = \alpha_0 + \mathbf{A}\mathbf{y}. \tag{3}$$

When $q = 1$ we have the latent trait model. We assume, without loss of generality, that $E(\mathbf{y}) = 0$ and $D(\mathbf{y}) = \mathbf{I}$.

(c) *The latent class model.* This is similar to the logit model but differs in that the latent space is categorical. The conditional distribution may then be written as in (2) but with $y$ taking values in a finite set with specified probabilities. Let the elements of $y$ be numbered 0, 1, 2, . . . , $q$ and let $y$ take the value $j$ with probability $\eta_j$. Other variations are clearly possible and several further models are described in Bartholomew (1987).

## INFERENCE ABOUT THE LATENT SPACE

A prime object of latent variable methods is to learn something about the latent space; about how many dimensions or categories it has, whether they can be related to substantive concepts which it is desired to measure and so forth. It is therefore rather disconcerting to discover that what can be established on this front, even in principle, is severely limited.

A fundamental difficulty, and one not commonly recognized, concerns the distribution of $\mathbf{y}$. The point can be illustrated using the linear factor model. Virtually all methods of fitting this model depend on fitting the theoretical to the sample covariance matrix. However, the covariance matrix for the model (1) does not depend on the form of the distribution of $\mathbf{y}$. This remark holds even if $\mathbf{y}$ is categorical. To take the simplest example of the latter: suppose there is a single $y$ taking just two values. We then have what has been called a latent profile model with two latent classes. But since the covariance structure is exactly the same whatever the distribution of $\mathbf{y}$ there is no empirical means by which that distribution can make its presence felt in the second moments of the data. There will, of course, be some information in the full distribution but very large samples are likely to be needed to extract it.

In general it may be shown that a $(q+1)$-class latent profile model is indistinguishable from a linear factor model with $q$ factors for all practical purposes (see Bartholomew, 1987, p. 36ff). This has very far reaching practical implications. It means that for every linear factor model that has ever been successfully fitted and interpreted with $q$ factors there was an equally well-fitting model with $q+1$ latent classes and vice versa. The ramifications of this simple observation become more serious when we move on to linear structural relations models of the kind that are implemented in the LISREL program. In such a model there are assumed to be linear relationships between the latent variables. If one cannot be sure that continuous latent variables exist there is a serious question to be faced over how far it is useful to talk about relationships between them. This particular problem is further aggravated by the following additional indeterminacy which is revealed by the general approach to latent variable modelling.

Consider what happens if we make a monotonic transformation of a single continuous latent variable. We may write the joint distribution of the $x$'s as

$$f(\mathbf{x}) = \int h(y) \prod_{i=1}^{p} g(x_i \,|\, y) \mathrm{d}y \qquad (4)$$

where $h(y)$ is the prior distribution of $y$ and $g(x_i|y)$ is the conditional distribution of $x_i$ given $y$ ($x$ may be categorical or metrical). If we now make the transformation $z = \phi(y)$ the value of the integral in (4) will not change and so the joint distribution of the **x** is the same even though the distribution of $z$ is different from that of $y$. This means that the distribution of $y$ is quite arbitrary and there is no means of determining it from the data. The only way in which it can be made identifiable is by placing constraints on the form of $\{g(x_i|y)\}$. In the linear factor model, for example, this is done by requiring the regression of $x$ on $y$ to be linear.

The fact that the fit of a model is invariant under monotonic transformations of the latent space means that, on the basis of the data alone, we cannot arrive at more than an ordinal scaling of individuals. Using standard methods we can predict an individual's placing on the latent scale but the scale value assigned will depend on the choice of $h(y)$. If we change $h(y)$ the spacing will change; all that remains invariant is the ordering. (These remarks were formalized in a theorem in Bartholomew, 1987, p. 85.) This conclusion does not mean that all attempts at scaling are futile. There is no objection to adopting a convenient prior distribution, say the normal, as long as it is clear that this choice is no more than a convention. In effect we are then saying that we are choosing a scaling of the latent variable which is such that individuals are normally distributed. For most practical purposes this will be the most convenient distribution to use.

One cannot, of course, exactly transform a metrical latent variable model into a categorical one but, for practical purposes, there is little difference. We illustrate the point in Table 1 which gives the results of fitting a latent trait and a latent class model with two classes to the same set of data. These are taken from Macready & Dayton (1977) and concern four arithmetical items involving multiplication (see Bartholomew, 1987, p. 26). Responses were coded 1 for a correct answer and 0 for a wrong answer. The observed and fitted frequencies for the two models are given in the Table. For interest, the fit of the random effects Rasch model is also included.

For the latent trait model $\chi^2 = 2.35$ with 3 degrees of freedom and for the latent class model $\chi^2 = 2.77$ with 3 degrees of freedom, after grouping and before rounding. On the basis of the goodness of fit test there is little ground for preferring one model to the other; both give an excellent fit. However, the practical implications of the two models are rather different. The latent class model implies that children in this population fall into two classes. If that were the case one would want to identify the classes and, perhaps, treat them differently. The latent trait model, on the other hand, implies a gradation of ability with no clear distinction between the two. In a detailed investigation of this dilemma Wamani (1985) found that the sample size would need to be several thousands before it was possible to distinguish between the two models with any confidence. The Rasch model has $\chi^2 = 12.19$ on 6 degrees of freedom which is clearly a poorer fit but the difference is barely significant.

**Table 1.** Observed and fitted frequencies for Macready & Dayton's (1967) model

| Response pattern | Observed frequency | Fitted frequency (rounded) | | |
|---|---|---|---|---|
| | | Latent trait | Latent class | Rasch |
| 1111 | 15 | 17.9 | 15.0 | 19.2 |
| 1110 | 7 | 4.6 | 6.2 | 4.5 |
| 1101 | 23 | 19.5 | 19.7 | 15.1 |
| 1100 | 7 | 9.5 | 8.9 | 10.1 |
| 1011 | 1 | 1.6 | 4.2 | 3.3 |
| 1010 | 3 | 2.5 | 1.9 | 2.2 |
| 1001 | 6 | 5.5 | 6.1 | 7.3 |
| 1000 | 13 | 13.8 | 12.9 | 12.8 |
| 0111 | 4 | 3.2 | 4.9 | 2.5 |
| 0110 | 2 | 1.9 | 2.1 | 1.7 |
| 0101 | 5 | 6.1 | 6.6 | 6.6 |
| 0100 | 6 | 5.8 | 5.6 | 9.8 |
| 0011 | 4 | 1.3 | 1.4 | 1.2 |
| 0010 | 1 | 4.1 | 1.3 | 2.1 |
| 0001 | 4 | 6.7 | 4.0 | 7.1 |
| 0000 | 41 | 38.2 | 41.0 | 37.5 |
| | 142 | 142.2 | 141.8 | 142.0 |

One further problem about the latent space which has long been recognized is that of fixing the number of dimensions. Since a model with $q$ latent dimensions is a special case of one with more than $q$ dimensions the fit of the model to data necessarily improves as we increase $q$. But the larger $q$ becomes the less explanatory power does the model have. If we have good reason for fixing $q$ in advance there is no difficulty. Otherwise some criterion for deciding on $q$ has to be found. Ideas of goodness of fit are of limited use for the reason already given but a way forward has recently been proposed by Akaike (1983) whose information criterion for model selection in time series is equally applicable to factor analysis.

## ESTIMATION AND GOODNESS OF FIT

Although, in principle, there is no difficulty in applying standard statistical techniques to the various latent variable models there are some unusual features. These have given rise to considerable discussion and raise some important questions of interpretation. The nature of the difficulties has now become much clearer and the aim of this section is to clarify the issues.

Although similar features arise with all methods of estimation the nature of the problem can best be described in relation to maximum likelihood. It has long been known that the likelihood function for the normal factor model may attain its largest value at a boundary point of the parameter space where one or more of the residual variances (the $\psi_i$'s of (1)) is zero. Such occurrences are known as Heywood cases and have been the subject of much debate. There is nothing impossible about a variance being zero, though, since the slope of the likelihood is not zero at such a point, the asymptotic distribution theory of the maximum likelihood estimators will not apply. Nevertheless it rarely seems substantively plausible that any manifest variable should be wholly explained by latent variables alone and so one feels uneasy about such an outcome.

Essentially the same phenomenon arises with other latent variable models and in particular with the latent trait model of (3). Here the analogous behaviour is for one or more of the $\alpha_{ij}$'s ($j>0$) to become large without limit so that the iterative approach to the maximum does not converge. Extensive investigations of the likelihood function in such cases by T. Albanese show that there is no maximum but that there is a ridge on the likelihood surface along which the likelihood increases but at an ever diminishing rate. Very large changes in the $\alpha$ in question will then produce hardly any variation in the likelihood itself. Even when the procedure does converge the asymptotic standard error will be very large if the parameter estimate is large. Since the $\alpha$'s appear as coefficients of the $x$'s in the 'factor scores' (or 'components') the effect of such a large $\alpha$ is to make the associated variable dominant. It virtually divides individuals into two groups; those who respond positively on that variable and those who do not.

From recent research (Fachel, 1986; Boomsma, 1985; Anderson & Gerbing, 1984; van Driel, 1978), it is now clear that this kind of behaviour is a small sample phenomenon. If the sample size is sufficiently large there will be a proper maximum within the parameter space provided that the data have been generated from a *bona fide* latent variable model. Even if a 'Heywood case' is avoided the standard errors of some of the parameters at least are liable to be large thus making inference hazardous. A large sample size in this context means several hundreds at least.

In order to underline how one can easily be mislead I report further on an example first discussed in Bartholomew (1987, p. 165). The data were taken from Mislevy (1985) who had analysed them in a different way. They relate to performance by samples of American youth on the Armed Services Vocational Battery. Four items were taken, all being concerned with arithmetical reasoning ability. The sample was classified according to colour and sex and the comparison to be made is between black and white females. A logit model of the form (3) was fitted to the response pattern frequencies for the case $q=1$ and the estimates in Table 2 were obtained for the estimates of $\{\alpha_{i1}: i=1, 2, 3, 4\}$.

The fit is not good but one could not clearly reject the model in either case. (There is now reason to think that the iteration had not converged in the Black case but that does not affect the point of the discussion.) The point of substantive interest is how one interprets the differences between black and

**Table 2.** Comparison of parameter estimates for black and white females in the latent trait model

| | | $\alpha_{i1}$ | | | |
|---|---|---|---|---|---|
| $i$ | 1 | 2 | 3 | 4 | $\chi^2$ |
| Black (145 cases) | 14.39 | 0.38 | 0.37 | 0.19 | 6.42 (3df) $P = 0.10$ |
| White (228 cases) | 1.04 | 1.24 | 1.00 | 1.44 | 8.39 (6df) $P = 0.21$ |

white females. Why, for example, is item 1 the overwhelmingly important discriminator for black females. The suggestion was made in Bartholomew (1987) that there might be some cultural explanation or possibly that the latent variables being identified were different in the two cases.

This may be so but a further analysis by Albanese strongly suggests that the difference is no more than a sampling aberration which calls for no special explanation at all. There are two approaches which lead to this conclusion. If random samples of size 145 are generated from populations in which the model holds with parameter values as in the Black row of Table 2 then, in an appreciable proportion of cases estimates arise in which the $\alpha$'s are not dissimilar to those in the White row. Conversely, if samples of similar size are drawn when the $\alpha$'s are like those in the White row, sets of estimates with one extreme value like that obtained for the Black sample occur quite often.

In the second approach we test the hypothesis $\alpha_{11} = \alpha_{21} = \alpha_{31} = \alpha_{41}$ against the hypothesis that they are unequal. For this we take the difference between the log likelihood statistics under the two hypotheses and find that the difference is 5.39 which on 3 degrees of freedom is not significant. In other words even the extreme differences observed in this example cannot, on a sample size of 145, be taken as indicating a real difference in the discriminating power of the items. There is no need, therefore, to look for an explanation for the ethnic difference which in all probability does not exist.

We have laboured this point because questions of statistical significance are rarely addressed in factor analysis and latent variable methods generally. Apart from an overall goodness of fit test none of the main statistical packages includes even asymptotic standard errors. Of the more specialized packages LISREL gives standard errors but they are only valid if sample covariances form the input and this is very rarely the case in practice. The reliance on the criterion of 'meaningfulness' without proper regard for statistical significance has undoubtedly led to many false positives in social research. The lack of reproducibility of results, to which critics of such methods often point, probably has more to do with the high sampling variability of the estimates than with the intractable nature of the raw material.

Such problems are more easily prevented than cured. At the planning stage one should aim to have very large samples, hundreds if not thousands. To some extent lack of sample size can be compensated by increasing the number of manifest variables. In an educational test, for example, there should be as many items testing the same skill or ability as can reasonably be attempted by the child without fatigue. The insuperable computing problems to which this would once have given rise have now been largely overcome. The cost of using a large machine like the CRAY for, say, 50 items is not large in comparison with that of collecting the data in the first place. It is arguably as worthwhile as spending a similar amount of computing effort on the structure of a crystal or some similar computation in physics.

## FIXED AND RANDOM EFFECTS MODELS

A considerable proportion of the research in this field is concerned with models which are not, strictly speaking, latent variable models at all but are so closely linked that they must be considered together. The best known is the Rasch model on which there is an enormous and sometimes controversial literature. This originated with Rasch (1960) and may be written

$$\text{logit } \pi_i(j) = \alpha_i + \beta_j \ (i = 1, 2, \ldots, p; j = 1, 2, \ldots, n),$$

where $j$ indexes individuals. A more recent account will be found in Andersen (1980). We call such models fixed effects models because, like their counterparts in the analysis of variance, the ability, say, of a particular individual is treated as a parameter. So far we have regarded an individual's ability as the realized value of the latent random variable. In a fixed effects model it is a parameter to be estimated. The choice between a fixed and random effects model, in general statistical practice, is made by asking whether one is interested in the individuals we happen to have tested or in the population from which they have been sampled. In psychological research it is difficult to find an example where one is interested only in the sampled individuals. In the early post-war period there was some interest in fixed effects models (see, for example, Whittle, 1952, and Anderson & Rubin, 1956) but this quickly died. With the Rasch model this has not been the case and it is instructive to see why.

One obvious drawback of the fixed effects model is that the number of parameters to be estimated goes up in proportion to the sample size and so the consistency of maximum likelihood estimation is lost. This difficulty can be circumvented by using a conditional form of maximum likelihood. There are other desirable statistical properties to do with sufficiency of the item and individual total scores which are also very appealing. They enable one, for example, to estimate item difficulties regardless of which individuals happen to be in the sample.

The random effects version of the Rasch model is the special case of the logit model of (3) with $q = 1$ and $\alpha_{i1} = \alpha_1$ for all $i$. In the fixed effects version the random variable $y$ is replaced by a parameter which takes a different value for each individual. One apparent advantage of this is that it avoids the need to introduce the arbitrary distribution of $y$. This is illusory because any monotonic transformation of the scale on which ability is measured leaves the likelihood unaffected. In other words it does not matter whether the abilities are realized values of a random variable or not, the scale on which they are measured is equally arbitrary. In any event, we have already noted that the form of the distribution of $y$ has little effect on the parameter estimates.

## METHODS FOR MULTI-WAY CONTINGENCY TABLES

The classical latent trait model assumes that the manifest variables are binary responses usually coded 0 or 1. In an educational test, for example, this corresponds to getting the answer right or wrong. In much psychological research responses fall into one of several categories. Sometimes these are ordered as when respondents in a survey are asked to say that they strongly agree, agree, disagree or strongly disagree with a proposition. In other cases responses are not ordered. In either case the response pattern for an individual consists of a list of the categories into which their answers fall. One can then think of the data as constituting a $p$-way contingency table which, in the case of binary data, is a $2^p$ table.

Several latent variable models allowing an arbitrary number of categories are now available for categorical data and these provide another way of analysing multi-way contingency tables. This raises the question of how the latent variable methods relate to other techniques such as log-linear models (Bishop *et al.*, 1975), multiple correspondence analysis (Greenacre, 1984) and Goodman's bilinear models for contingency tables (Goodman, 1981, 1985). Research on these topics is still in the early stages but it is already possible to see interesting connections with other techniques, especially correspondence analysis.

There are two kinds of latent variable model available for multi-way contingency tables. The older one is applicable only to ordered categorical data and has been extensively developed, for example, by Muthén (1978, 1983, 1984). It supposes that the categories of each response are formed by grouping an underlying variable. Responses such as 'agree', 'disagree' and so on are taken to correspond to intervals on a continuous scale of opinion on the issue in question. The assumption has usually been made that these underlying (as distinct from latent) variables have a multi-normal distribution. By positing a normal linear factor model for these underlying variables it has then been possible to bring the analysis of categorical data within the factor analysis framework. The implementation of such a factor analysis requires estimates of the correlation coefficients of the underlying variables to be made from the categorical responses. This is an old problem to which the solution is provided by the polychoric correlation coefficient.

Such a method can be applied, of course, when the responses are binary in which case it might appear to be an alternative to latent trait models of the type given in (3). However, it is easily shown (see Bartholomew, 1987, Section 5.4) that the two kinds of model are then equivalent.

The more interesting case arises when there are more than two categories for each response variable. In this case the two kinds of model are not equivalent. The appropriate generalization of the latent trait model can be derived from the general theory based on the sufficiency principle. The details are given in Chapter 7 of Bartholomew (1987) but it can be defined as follows.

$$\log\{\pi_{is}(\mathbf{y})/\pi_{i0}(y)\} = \alpha_{i0}(s) + \sum_{j=1}^{q} \alpha_{ij}(s)y_j,$$

$$(s = 1, 2, \ldots, c_i - 1; i = 1, 2, \ldots, p). \tag{5}$$

Here $c_i$ is the number of categories on dimension $i$. The category labels are arbitrary and the *reference* category $s = 0$ has no special significance. It is clear that (5) reduces to (3) if $c_i = 2$ for all $i$. The parameters $\{\alpha_{ij}(s)\}$ can be interpreted in several ways: for example, as coefficients of $y_j$ in (5) and as coefficients of the $x$'s in the components

$$X_j = \sum_{i=1}^{p} \sum_{s=0}^{c_i} \alpha_{ij}(s)x_i(s), \tag{6}$$

where $x_i(s)$ is an indicator variable taking the value 1 if an individual falls into category $s$ on variable $i$ and zero otherwise.

The $\alpha$s can also be thought of as scores attached to the categories of the response variables. Thus if $\alpha_{ij}(s)$ is the score for category $s$ of variable $i$ for the $j$th latent dimension then $X_j$ is the individual's total score since the amount $\alpha_{ij}(s)$ is contributed to $X_j$ if, and only if, the individual in question falls into the corresponding category. It is this interpretation which brings out the close connection with multiple correspondence analysis which can also be viewed in precisely that way. The latter is not model-based but aims rather to assign category scores in such a way that in a certain sense, the categories are distinguished as sharply as possible subject to a fixed variability in the total score. It was shown in Bartholomew (1987, p. 149ff) that correspondence analysis provides approximations to the maximum likelihood estimates for the model of (5). The approximation is rather crude but since the origin and scale of the scores is arbitrary what matters is how closely the exact and approximate scores are correlated. In practice these correlations seem to be very high which suggests that the two methods are almost equivalent.

This last fact has important practical implications. Although a program is available for fitting the model (5) by maximum likelihood it is limited in the size of problem with which it can cope. This is a temporary problem and research by Shing On Leung on extending the size of problem and speed of execution is well advanced. Nevertheless, correspondence analysis is much easier to carry out as it requires only the routine solution of an eigenvalue problem. It may therefore be used as a substitute for the latent variable method and the scores to which it leads can then be interpreted in the same way as if they were parameter estimates for the model.

The drawback of a purely data analytical technique such as correspondence analysis is that it provides no basis for inference. There are no standard errors or goodness of fit tests. All of these are available, in principle, for a model-based method. This is particularly important here as perusal of the numerical examples in Chapter 9 of Bartholomew (1987) will show. Our earlier cautions about the need for large sample sizes apply with greater force here since the standard errors of the estimated category scores tend to be uncomfortably large. This warns us of the difficulty of learning anything very precise about the detail of the model.

This conclusion also has implications for the interpretation of multiple correspondence analysis. The fact that the standard errors of the maximum likelihood estimates are large implies that minor variations in the patterns of cell frequencies in the data are liable to produce big variations in the estimated category scores. This implies that the category scores arrived at by correspondence analysis will be sensitive to similar variations in the data. The fact that the data analytic approach avoids all such assumptions does not therefore make it immune to imprecision.

## RELIABILITY

In test theory, considerable attention has been given to the reliability of measures of latent abilities. If on the basis of a test consisting of $p$ items one constructs a measure of some ability then one hopes that it will be precise in the sense that if one were to repeat the measurements one would get much the same answer. It has been common to use the 'number correct' that is,

$$\sum_{i=1}^{p} x_i$$

in the case of binary data though if we use the logit model, $\Sigma \alpha_{i1} x_i$ would be more appropriate. One measure of the reliability is the so-called test–retest correlation, $\rho$, (or its square). In reality this cannot be directly estimated because it is not possible to repeat the test on the same individual since the outcome would be confounded with the possible learning effect. One way out of this difficulty is to compute a bound to the reliability known as Cronbach's alpha. An alternative way is to find a model that fits the data and then use the model to predict what the test–retest correlation would be. The logit model of (3) with $q = 1$ frequently does fit such test data and this can then be used to estimate the reliability.

We have seen that the 'component' $X = \Sigma \alpha_{i1} x_i$ is the natural measure to use for such a model and if $X_1$ and $X_2$ were the values obtained in two replications of the test it may easily be shown that

$$\rho = \operatorname{var}\{E(X\,|\,y)\}/[E\{\operatorname{var}(X\,|\,y)\} + \operatorname{var}\{E(X\,|\,y)\}], \qquad (7)$$

and this holds whatever function of the $x$'s is used for $X$. In any particular case $\rho$ will be a function of the model parameters and hence can be estimated from them. Applications of this measure to data on social life feelings given in Krebs & Schuessler (1988) have been made and it is hoped to publish them shortly.

Research is also proceeding on the following theoretical questions. What function of the $x$'s has the greatest reliability for any particular model? What is the best linear function of the manifest variables? It appears that if the normal linear factor model is appropriate then the most reliable measure is a linear function and that the optimum weights are precisely those which occur in the corresponding component. For the logit model with binary data the optimum linear function is not, in general, the same as the component but the coefficients appear to be very close.

## CONCLUDING REMARKS

This chapter has made no attempt to give an exhaustive account of current research on latent variable methods. Within the limits of space available such a treatment could have been little more than an annotated catalogue of recent papers from journals such as *Psychometrika* and *The British Journal of Mathematical and Statistical Psychology* where much of the material appears. It seemed more important to identify the significant issues which recent research has brought into focus since failure to do this in the past has led to much dissipation of effort and confusion over fundamental statistical questions. My book (Bartholomew, 1987) contains a fairly extensive bibliography. Much of the more recent work has not yet reached publication. Some work in progress by my colleagues and research students (Dr. M. Knott, T. Albanese, J. Fachel and Shing On Leung) has been mentioned in the text but not included in the list of references which follows.

### References

AKAIKE, H. (1983). Information measures and model selection. *Bulletin of the International Statistical Institute*, **50**, Book 1, 277–290.
ANDERSEN, E.B. (1980). *Discrete Statistical Models with Social Science Applications*. Amsterdam: North Holland Publishing Company.

ANDERSON, J.C. & GERBING, D.W. (1984). The effect of sampling error on convergence, improper solutions, and goodness-of-fit indices for maximum likelihood confirmatory factor analysis. *Psychometrika*, **49**, 155–173.

ANDERSON, T.W. & RUBIN, H. (1956). Statistical inference in factor analysis. *Third Berkeley Symposium on Mathematics, Statistics and Probability*, **5**, 111–150.

BARTHOLOMEW, D.J. (1984). The foundations of factor analysis. *Biometrika*, **71**, 221–232.

BARTHOLOMEW, D.J. (1987). *Latent Variable Models and Factor Analysis*. London: Griffin.

BISHOP, Y.M.M., FIENBERG, S.E. & HOLLAND, P.W. (1975). *Discrete Multivariate Analysis: Theory and Practice*. Philadelphia: The MIT Press.

BOOMSMA, A. (1985). Nonconvergence, improper solutions, and starting values in LISREL maximum likelihood estimation. *Psychometrika*, **50**, 229–242.

DRIEL, O.P. van (1978). On various causes of improper solutions in maximum likelihood factor analysis. *Psychometrika*, **43**, 225–243.

FACHEL, J.M.G. (1986). *The C-type Distribution as an Underlying Model for Categorical Data and its use in Factor Analysis*. PhD Thesis, University of London.

GOODMAN, L.A. (1981). Association models and canonical correlation in the analysis of cross-classifications having ordered categories. *Journal of the American Statistical Association*, **76**, 320–334.

GOODMAN, L.A. (1985). The analysis of cross-classified data having ordered and/or unordered categories: association models, correlation models, and asymmetry models for contingency tables with or without missing entries. *Annals of Statistics*, **13**, 10–69.

GREENACRE, M.J. (1984). *Theory and Applications of Correspondence Analysis*. London: Academic Press.

KREBS, D. & SCHUESSLER, K. (1988). *Sociale Empfindungen*. Frankfurt/New York: Campus Verlag.

LAZARSFELD, P.F. & HENRY, N.W. (1968). *Latent Structure Analysis*. New York: Houghton-Mifflin.

MACREADY, G.B. & DAYTON, C.M. (1977). The use of probabilistic models in the assessment of mastery. *Journal of Educational Statistics*, **2**, 99–120.

MISLEVY, R.J. (1985). Estimation of latent group effects. *Journal of the American Statistical Association*, **80**, 993–997.

MUTHÉN, B. (1978). Contributions to factor analysis of dichotomous variables. *Psychometrika*, **43**, 551–560.

MUTHÉN, B. (1983). Latent variable structural equation modelling with categorical data. *Journal of Econometrics*, **22**, 43–65.

MUTHÉN, B. (1984). A general structural equation model with dichotomous ordered categorical, and continuous latent variable indicators. *Psychometrika*, **49**, 115–132.

RASCH, G. (1960). *Probabilistic Models for Some Intelligence and Attainment Tests*. Copenhagen: Paedagogiske Institut.

WAMANI, W.T. (1985). *An Empirical Study of Latent Class Models; Application to Criterion-Referenced Tests*. PhD Thesis, University of London.

WHITTLE, P. (1952). On principal components and least square methods of factor analysis. *Skandinavisk Aktuarietidskrift*, **35**, 223–239.

# 10

# Compositional Data Analysis

JOHN AITCHISON

Compositional data, consisting of vectors whose components represent the proportions of some whole or unit, occur in many disciplines. Some typical examples from psychology and the social sciences are the following.

*Education.* In educational research there may be interest in how a lesson for listening to English language is divided by a student teacher into four mutually exclusive and exhaustive activities of: (1) equipment, (2) organization, (3) listening, (4) checking; and in the extent to which the variability in the resulting set of four proportions is dependent on school form level (Coleman & Lee, 1988).

*Psychology.* In a psychological study of supervisory behaviour the unit period of confrontation between the supervisor and supervisee may be divided into activities such as commanding, demanding, expository and faulting, with interest in how the pattern of the four proportions may vary with supervisee and over time (Aitchison, 1986*a*, Section 1.6).

*Human geography.* The object of a study may be to describe the nature of the variability in the use of agricultural land from region to region through the recorded proportions of the land allocated to different uses such as corn, wheat, oats, soybeans and hay (Evans & Jones, 1981).

*Economics.* In household expenditure studies we may wish to study the household budget pattern, the proportions in which a household allocates its total expenditure to different commodity groups and how such allocations relate to income and type and size of household (Working, 1943; Aitchison, 1986*a*, Section 1.7).

*Politics.* In an election, the proportions of the electorate in a constituency voting (1) Conservative, (2) Labour, (3) Liberal, (4) Nationalist, (5) other party and (6) abstaining, form a six-part composition and we may be interested in studying the nature of the variability of these compositions in different regions (Johnston, 1978).

In general a composition of $D$ parts, labelled $1, 2, \ldots, D$, is a vector $(x_1, \ldots, x_D)$ of proportions or positive components $x_1, \ldots, x_D$, subject to the unit-sum constraint

$$x_1 + \ldots + x_D = 1. \tag{1}$$

214

In particular applications the parts will have more meaningful labels but in our development of the appropriate statistical analysis it is convenient to have them simply numbered in sequence.

To provide motivation for the development of concepts, principles and methodology introduced we shall use the following data set, which has been kept to the minimum size needed for expository purposes but which is sufficiently general in nature to demonstrate how more elaborate analyses may be conducted.

### *Example.* ACTIVITY PATTERNS OF UNIVERSITY TEACHERS

Each of 28 randomly selected university teachers was asked to keep a diary over a week allocating time to the five activities

*1* teaching,
*2* administration,
*3* research,
*4* recreation, defined as all other wakeful activities,
*5* sleep.

Each row of Table 1 records for a university teacher the proportions of time spent in these five activities, together with the status, professor (P) or other rank (O), and the age in years. Each set of five proportions forms a five-part composition $(x_1, \ldots, x_5)$, an activity pattern, and there is clearly considerable variability in these compositions between teachers. Obvious questions are how we can describe this variability and whether the patterns are dependent in any way on status and age. We might also be interested in more specific questions such as whether the pattern within the working parts of the week is dependent on the pattern within the non-working parts.

### A LITTLE HISTORY

Compositional data analysis has a sad history of wishful and muddled thinking, misdirected energy and ignoring of a fundamental perception. The battery of so-called standard multivariate statistical techniques, designed for the analysis of unconstrained vectors, has been ruthlessly applied to the constrained vectors of compositional data sets. 'Ignore the constraint or drop out one of the components and go ahead'. has been the general attitude. For example, the geological literature abounds in studies which place substantial trust in the interpretation of the product-moment correlations between components of geochemical compositions. That such correlations are essentially uninterpretable has been pointed out repeatedly by a number of scientists, particularly in geology starting with Chayes (1948, 1960); see Evans & Jones (1981) for similar warnings in the context of social sciences. The reason for the

**Table 1.** Weekly activity patterns of 28 university teachers

| Teacher | Proportion in activity | | | | | Rank | Age |
|---|---|---|---|---|---|---|---|
| | teach | admin | resch | recr | sleep | | |
| 1 | 0.247 | 0.209 | 0.043 | 0.170 | 0.332 | O | 33 |
| 2 | 0.232 | 0.162 | 0.074 | 0.208 | 0.326 | O | 34 |
| 3 | 0.191 | 0.082 | 0.186 | 0.210 | 0.332 | P | 40 |
| 4 | 0.248 | 0.167 | 0.065 | 0.229 | 0.291 | P | 52 |
| 5 | 0.268 | 0.189 | 0.047 | 0.281 | 0.216 | O | 45 |
| 6 | 0.202 | 0.096 | 0.154 | 0.209 | 0.340 | P | 43 |
| 7 | 0.259 | 0.316 | 0.015 | 0.179 | 0.231 | O | 44 |
| 8 | 0.237 | 0.140 | 0.087 | 0.212 | 0.323 | O | 39 |
| 9 | 0.237 | 0.237 | 0.034 | 0.155 | 0.336 | O | 31 |
| 10 | 0.181 | 0.073 | 0.219 | 0.272 | 0.255 | P | 63 |
| 11 | 0.259 | 0.220 | 0.038 | 0.228 | 0.263 | O | 58 |
| 12 | 0.219 | 0.097 | 0.145 | 0.244 | 0.294 | P | 44 |
| 13 | 0.246 | 0.173 | 0.063 | 0.242 | 0.277 | O | 29 |
| 14 | 0.217 | 0.122 | 0.115 | 0.209 | 0.337 | P | 35 |
| 15 | 0.179 | 0.062 | 0.213 | 0.172 | 0.374 | P | 50 |
| 16 | 0.231 | 0.117 | 0.111 | 0.292 | 0.249 | O | 40 |
| 17 | 0.216 | 0.161 | 0.082 | 0.245 | 0.295 | O | 49 |
| 18 | 0.278 | 0.232 | 0.028 | 0.195 | 0.266 | O | 30 |
| 19 | 0.254 | 0.169 | 0.060 | 0.283 | 0.234 | O | 51 |
| 20 | 0.223 | 0.159 | 0.081 | 0.241 | 0.295 | P | 46 |
| 21 | 0.245 | 0.188 | 0.051 | 0.195 | 0.320 | P | 45 |
| 22 | 0.199 | 0.085 | 0.174 | 0.291 | 0.251 | P | 47 |
| 23 | 0.239 | 0.277 | 0.025 | 0.172 | 0.287 | O | 27 |
| 24 | 0.218 | 0.141 | 0.096 | 0.229 | 0.316 | O | 37 |
| 25 | 0.233 | 0.198 | 0.047 | 0.162 | 0.368 | O | 29 |
| 26 | 0.239 | 0.219 | 0.045 | 0.267 | 0.238 | O | 60 |
| 27 | 0.235 | 0.161 | 0.072 | 0.233 | 0.299 | O | 40 |
| 28 | 0.210 | 0.113 | 0.121 | 0.220 | 0.336 | P | 40 |

impossibility of any meaningful interpretation of such correlations has been variously expressed but the source of the difficulty lies in the constraint and the impossibility of defining any concept of independence in terms of the crude components: if one component increases then at least one of the other components must decrease.

Awareness of the inappropriateness of the standard methods did not, however, lead to their discarding but to increasing effort to obtain more detailed descriptions of their pathology in misapplications, somewhat akin to continuing with a discredited medicine and trying to live with the side effects rather than searching for a new therapy. During much of this effort it has often been correctly perceived that a composition provides information only about the relative magnitudes of the components of the real entity, but there seems to have been a reluctance to build on this perception. The reader wishing to obtain more details of the nature of these misapplications and lost opportunities will find a self-contained account in Aitchison (1986a, Chapter 3). Rather than spend time on how not to analyse compositional data we now turn our attention to an account of an appropriate methodology.

## SUBCOMPOSITIONS AND TERNARY DIAGRAMS

The concept of a subcomposition is an important one in compositional data analysis and is the counterpart of a marginal distribution in the study of unconstrained variability. If in the example we wish to focus attention on the activity pattern only of the working part of the week we may find it convenient to rescale the relevant teaching, administration and research components $x_1$, $x_2$ and $x_3$, by division by the total working proportion $x_1 + x_2 + x_3$ to form a *subcomposition* $(s_1, s_2, s_3)$ with components

$$s_i = x_i/(x_1 + x_2 + x_3), \qquad (i = 1, 2, 3) \tag{2}$$

satisfying the unit-sum constraint $s_1 + s_2 + s_3 = 1$. For teacher #1 of Table 1 this subcomposition provides the proportions (0.495, 0.419, 0.086) of the working week spent on teaching, administration and research. Such subcompositions can be considered and analysed as three-part compositions in their own right and the concept generalizes in an obvious way to any subset of parts of a composition. An important feature of the formation of a subcomposition is that any ratio $s_i/s_j$ of components within the subcomposition remains the same as the corresponding ratio $x_i/x_j$ within the full composition.

A simple diagrammatic representation of three-part compositions or subcompositions can be provided in a ternary diagram, a kind of triangular frame of reference. The triangle of Figure 1a with vertices 1, 2, 3 is equilateral and has unit altitude. For any point $P$ within the triangle the perpendiculars $x_1$, $x_2$, $x_3$ from $P$ to the sides opposite 1, 2, 3 satisfy

$$x_i > 0, \qquad (i = 1, 2, 3), \qquad x_1 + x_2 + x_3 = 1. \tag{3}$$

Moreover, corresponding to any vector $(x_1, x_2, x_3)$ satisfying (3), there is a unique point in the triangle with perpendicular values $x_1$, $x_2$, $x_3$. There is therefore a one-to-one correspondence between three-part compositions and points within the triangle, and so we have a convenient frame of reference for compositions. Figure 1b shows for the 28 teachers of Table 1 the representational points of the three-part subcompositions for the working part of the week as discussed above. In such a ternary diagram the larger a component $x_i$ is, the farther the representational point is away from the side opposite the vertex $i$ and so, roughly speaking, the nearer the point is to the vertex $i$. Moreover, compositions with a fixed ratio of two components, say $x_2/x_3$, are represented by points on a ray through the vertex 1, so that we can judge the range of any particular ratio by the amount of the sweep of such a ray required to cover the whole data set.

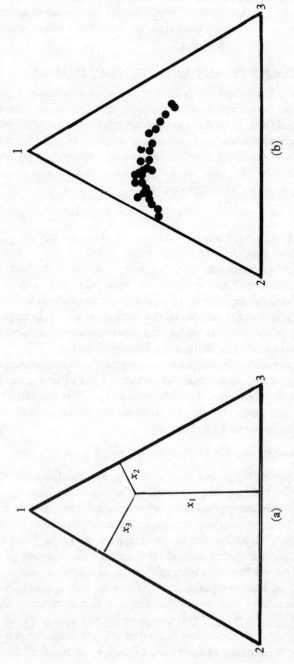

**Figure 1.** (a) Representation of a three-part composition $(x_1, x_2, x_3)$ in the reference triangle 123. (b) Ternary diagram for the (1) teaching, (2) administration, (3) research subcompositions for the 28 teachers of Table 1.

## THE SIMPLEX AS SAMPLE SPACE

In statistical terminology the ternary diagram of Figure 1a plays the role of a sample space for problems involving three-part compositions and highlights the special nature of compositional data. It would indeed be surprising if statistical methodology, developed for an unconstrained real space, could be applied directly to such very different sample spaces. The generalization of the ternary diagram defined by (3) to $D$-part compositions is termed the simplex and is defined by

$$\{(x_1, \ldots, x_D): x_i > 0, \quad (i = 1, \ldots, D), x_1 + \ldots + x_D = 1\}. \quad (4)$$

Figure 2 shows this space for the case $D = 3$ within three-dimensional space. If we lift out the simplex of Figure 2 and lay it flat on the two-dimensional page we have its more amenable form, the ternary diagram of Figure 1. Note that, because of the unit-sum constraint, the effective dimension of the sample space for $D$-part compositions is $d = D - 1$.

Awareness of the special constrained nature of such sample spaces, the inevitable starting point in the statistical modelling of any kind of variability, raises two obvious questions. What classes of distributions do we know that

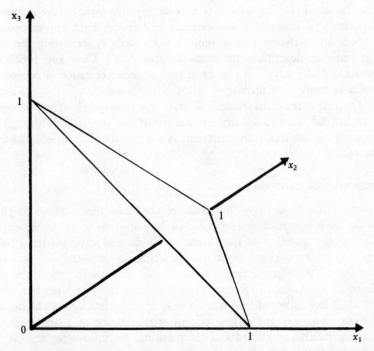

**Figure 2.** The simplex sample space for three-part compositions $(x_1, x_2, x_3)$ as a subset of three-dimensional space.

describe variability within a triangle or simplex? Certainly not the popular multivariate normal class. Are there any special requirements of compositional data analysis which may lead us to appropriate concepts on which to build a sensible statistical methodology for the study of compositional variability? In addressing and resolving this second question we shall find a reasonable answer to the first.

# REQUIREMENTS OF A METHODOLOGY FOR COMPOSITIONAL DATA

## Scale invariance

Any statistical method applied to compositions, such as those of Table 1, should lead to the same inference whatever units are used to record the components, whether proportions of a week (as in Table 1), in hours, minutes or seconds. In other words, two analysts, one using $D$-part compositions $(x_1, \ldots, x_D)$ and the other using $(cx_1, \ldots, cx_D)$, where $c > 0$, must agree in their conclusions. This is a requirement of *scale invariance* and recognizes the fact that compositions provide information only about the relative magnitudes of their components. (From this viewpoint we see that an alternative to the simplex as sample space would be the set of rays from the origin in the positive orthant (the subset with all components positive) of $D$-dimensional real space. Each ray represents a composition, the different points along a ray simply representing the use of different units in describing the same composition.) Thus any problem in compositional data analysis can be expressed in terms of ratios of components and confining analysis to the use of ratios, such as $x_1/x_D, \ldots, x_d/x_D$, where $d = D - 1$, ensures scale invariance. Within this framework of ratios there is clearly no special need to specify the nature of the constraint although it is convenient to use the unit-sum constraint as a reminder of the special nature of the data vector.

## Subcompositional coherence

An important requirement of any sensible statistical methodology is that it should provide *subcompositional coherence* in the following sense. In the example suppose that the question of the extent to which the activity pattern of the working parts may depend on status is being investigated by two social scientists, A and B. Suppose that A has collected information about the whole week, in other words the full five-part compositions, from each teacher. On the other hand, B has collected information only on the working part of the week from the same teachers, and so has concentrated attention on a subcomposition involving the relative magnitudes of the teaching, administrative and research parts only. In other words, B has available the 1, 2, 3 subcompositions formed from the full compositions by rescaling the first three components to add to 1.

Thus for the first academic, B has the subcomposition (0.495, 0.419, 0.086). Suppose now that both A and B apply the available methodology to their respective data sets. Then they must draw the same conclusions. This requirement of subcompositional coherence is not met by the application of standard multivariate analysis to the crude components $x_1, \ldots, x_D$ of compositions (Aitchison, 1986a, pp. 54–56), but can be easily met by other simple considerations. To ensure scale invariance we must work with ratios of components and we have seen that ratios within a subcomposition are the same as within the full composition. Hence we meet both requirements of scale invariance and subcompositional coherence by the simple perception that we must study compositions in terms of relative magnitudes or ratios.

## FROM RATIOS TO LOGRATIOS

The realization that the motto of the compositional data analyst should be 'think ratios' suggests a first requirement of any attempt at defining summary characteristics of a pattern of variability of compositional data. At a minimum we would want to be able to estimate the mean and variance of each possible ratio $x_i/x_j$, namely $E(x_i/x_j)$ and $\mathrm{var}(x_i/x_j)$. We then immediately face a major technical problem in that there are no exact, and not even simple, approximate relationships between the means and variances of a ratio $x_i/x_j$ and the reciprocal ratio $x_j/x_i$. This awkwardness can easily be removed, and a great bonus in ease of interpretation obtained, by using the logarithms of ratios instead of the ratios themselves. The simple relationships, stemming from the fundamental property of logarithms that

$$\log(x_i/x_j) = \log x_i - \log x_j,$$

can be expressed as follows:

$$\xi_{ij} = E\{\log(x_i/x_j)\} = -E\{\log(x_j/x_i)\}$$
$$= E\{\log(x_i/x_D)\} - E\{\log(x_j/x_D)\}, \tag{6}$$

$$\tau_{ij} = \mathrm{var}\{\log(x_i/x_j)\} = \mathrm{var}\{\log(x_j/x_i)\}. \tag{7}$$

It is easily seen that these relationships reduce the number of characteristics to $d = D - 1$ for the logratio or relative means $\xi_{iD}$ $(i = 1, \ldots, d)$ and to $\frac{1}{2}dD$ for the logratio or relative variances $\tau_{ij}$ $(i = 1, \ldots, d; j = i + 1, \ldots, D)$, a total of $\frac{1}{2}d(d+3)$, the same as are required for the specification of a $d$-dimensional multivariate normal distribution. Thus we have apparently as parsimonious a set of characteristics as we may reasonably expect. Moreover all the kinds of covariances between logratios that we may require can be expressed in terms of the $\tau_{ij}$. The general relationship is

$$\mathrm{cov}\{\log(x_i/x_h), \log(x_j/x_l)\} = \frac{1}{2}(\tau_{il} + \tau_{hj} - \tau_{ij} - \tau_{hl}). \tag{8}$$

Hence, in the example, if we are interested in whether the ratio of research $x_3$ to teaching $x_1$ is uncorrelated with the ratio of sleep $x_5$ to recreation $x_4$, knowledge of the $\tau_{ij}$ will allow us to study whether $\text{cov}\{\log(x_3/x_1), \log(x_5/x_4)\}$ is close to zero.

## THE RELATIVE VARIATION ARRAY

The set of logratio means and variances or, alternatively, the relative standard deviations $\delta_{ij} = \sqrt{\tau_{ij}}$, can be conveniently set out in a relative variation array with the relative means displayed below and the relative standard deviations above the diagonal line as follows.

|   | 1 | 2 | 3 | ... | d | D |
|---|---|---|---|---|---|---|
| 1 | . | $\delta_{12}$ | $\delta_{13}$ | | $\delta_{1d}$ | $\delta_{1D}$ |
| 2 | $\xi_{12}$ | . | $\delta_{23}$ | | $\delta_{2d}$ | $\delta_{2D}$ |
| 3 | $\xi_{13}$ | $\xi_{23}$ | . | | $\delta_{3d}$ | $\delta_{3D}$ |
| . | | | | | | |
| . | | | | | | |
| . | | | | | | |
| d | | | | | . | $\delta_{dD}$ |
| D | $\xi_{1D}$ | $\xi_{2D}$ | | | $\xi_{dD}$ | . |

This relative variation array for the activity pattern data of Table 1 is shown in Table 2, where the standard sample estimates of logratio means and variances are computed in the familiar way from the corresponding sets of logratio values.

It is worth emphasizing here that since the use of logratios ensures subcompositional coherence the relative variation array contains direct information

**Table 2.** Relative variation array for the activity patterns

|   | teach | admin | resch | recr | sleep |
|---|---|---|---|---|---|
| teach | . | 0.318 | 0.778 | 0.221 | 0.221 |
| admin | 0.415 | . | 1.084 | 0.500 | 0.476 |
| resch | 1.153 | 0.738 | . | 0.631 | 0.648 |
| recr | 0.041 | −0.374 | −1.112 | . | 0.301 |
| sleep | −0.245 | −0.659 | −1.397 | −0.286 | . |

about any particular subcomposition of interest. For example, if we wish to focus on the activity pattern of the working week, namely the subcomposition (teaching, administration, research), we simply pick out the relevant subcompositional array from the teaching, administration, research rows and columns of the array. The summarizing ability of a relative variation array can be seen by a comparison of this subcompositional array and the pattern of subcompositional variability, as depicted in Figure 1b. From the logratio means we see that on average the teaching component is somewhat larger than the administrative component and that both are substantially larger than the research component, agreeing with the location of the pattern in the ternary diagram. Moreover, the ranking of the logratio standard deviations, namely $\delta_{23} > \delta_{13} > \delta_{12}$, agrees with the variation we see in Figure 1b when we recall that the extent of the variability of a ratio such as $x_2/x_3$, or the corresponding logratio, depends on the amount of sweep that a ray through the vertex 1 requires to cover all the compositional points.

## THE RELATIVE VARIATION DIAGRAM

Despite the summarizing power of the relative variation array we may still find it difficult to obtain insights into the nature of the pattern of compositional variability from such a set of numbers, particularly when faced with the novelty of having to formulate ideas in terms of logratios. Fortunately we can obtain excellent graphical representations of compositional variability which provide not only a clear picture of how, in the example, the components of teaching, administration, research, recreation and sleep relate to each other but also highlight differences between teachers in these activities. This graphical approach requires the adaptation (Aitchison, 1990) of the biplot technique (Gabriel, 1971, 1981) to the special features of compositional vectors. The biplot method for unconstrained vectors is based on the use of a second order approximation to the data matrix provided by the singular value decomposition (Eckart & Young, 1936) of the data matrix. For compositional data all that is required is a simple initial adjustment of the $N \times D$ compositional data matrix $\mathbf{X} = [x_{ri}]$, where $x_{ri}$ denotes the $i$th component of the $r$th composition. Each element of the data matrix is first replaced by its logarithm and then from each of these logarithms the row average of the logarithms is subtracted (thus producing logratios in which the divisor is the geometric mean of the components) and subsequently the column average of these logratios is also subtracted yielding a 'centred' logratio data matrix $\mathbf{Z}$ with typical element

$$z_{ri} = \log x_{ri} - D^{-1} \sum_{i=1}^{D} \log x_{ri} - N^{-1} \sum_{r=1}^{N} \log x_{ri} + (ND)^{-1} \sum_{r=1}^{N} \sum_{i=1}^{D} \log x_{ri}. \quad (9)$$

For the use of the relative variation diagram in compositional data analysis it is sufficient to know that the singular value decomposition expresses $\mathbf{Z}$ as the product of three matrices

$$\mathbf{Z} = \mathbf{UKV}, \tag{10}$$

with $\mathbf{U}$ of order $N \times R$, $\mathbf{K}$ a diagonal $R \times R$ matrix with its positive diagonal elements or *singular values* $k_1, \ldots, k_R$ in descending order of magnitude and $\mathbf{V}$ of order $R \times D$, where $R$ is the rank of the $\mathbf{Z}$ matrix. The columns of $\mathbf{U}$ and the rows of $\mathbf{V}$ also have the special property of being orthonormal, that is, each column (row) is of unit length and every pair of columns (rows) is orthogonal, with the sum of products of corresponding components equal to zero. In this respect the decomposition is directly related to the special form of principal component analysis appropriate to compositional data, where the usual linear combinations are replaced by logcontrasts of the components of the form $v_{i1} \log x_1 + \ldots + v_{iD} \log x_D$, with $v_{i1} + \ldots + v_{iD} = 0$. In this form of analysis the rows of $\mathbf{V}$, as the notation indicates, play the role of logcontrast principal component vectors with corresponding eigenvalues equal to $k_i^2/(N-1)$. There are excellent algorithms in many software packages for the computation of such singular value decompositions. In practice $R$ is usually equal to $d = D - 1$ and for diagrammatic purposes we use the singular value decomposition approximation of second order, namely

$$\mathbf{Z} \approx \mathbf{U}_2 \mathbf{K}_2 \mathbf{V}_2, \tag{11}$$

where $\mathbf{U}_2$ consists of the first two columns of $\mathbf{U}$, $\mathbf{V}_2$ the first two rows of $\mathbf{V}$, $\mathbf{K}_2$ the leading submatrix of order $2 \times 2$ of $\mathbf{K}$. For the activity patterns of Table 1 this singular value decomposition approximation is

$$
\begin{bmatrix}
0.152 & -0.232 \\
0.007 & -0.105 \\
-0.277 & -0.129 \\
0.038 & 0.034 \\
0.119 & 0.367 \\
& \cdots
\end{bmatrix}
\begin{bmatrix}
4.104 & 0 \\
0 & 1.104
\end{bmatrix}
\begin{bmatrix}
0.197 & 0.587 & -0.785 & -0.014 & 0.143 \\
0.059 & -0.029 & -0.032 & 0.706 & -0.704
\end{bmatrix},
$$

$$\tag{12}$$

where the matrix $\mathbf{U}$ has been curtailed for economy of space. The singular values are 4.104, 1.104 (shown in $\mathbf{K}_2$ above) and 0.2780, 0.0670.

The construction of the relative variation diagram or biplot for compositional data is then straightforward. In a two-dimensional diagram (Figure 3) with origin $O$ we plot, corresponding to each part $i$ (activity in the example), a *vertex i* with coordinates $(k_1 v_{1i}, k_2 v_{2i})/(N-1)^{1/2}$ and term the join of $O$ and $i$ the *ray Oi* and the join of two vertices $i$ and $j$ the *link ij*. Corresponding to the $r$th composition (activity pattern associated with the $r$th teacher in the example) we plot a *compositional marker r* with coordinates $(N-1)^{1/2}(u_{r1}, u_{r2})$.

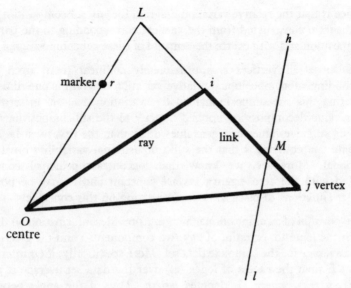

**Figure 3.** Construction of a relative variation diagram.

For such diagrams we can now list the main properties which are useful in the interpretation of the pattern of variability of the compositional data set; for further details see Aitchison (1990, in press). These properties are stated as if they were exact but, of course, they depend on the degree to which the diagram provides a satisfactory approximation to the pattern of variability.

(*a*) The proportion of the total compositional variability which is retained by the relative variation diagram is

$$(k_1^2 + k_2^2)/(k_1^2 + \ldots + k_R^2).$$

This is a property similar to that associated with the first two principal components in standard unconstrained principal component analysis.

(*b*) The length of $|ij|$ of a link $ij$ is the estimate of the logratio standard deviation $\delta_{ij}$. A consequence of this property is that two nearly coincident vertices correspond to a nearly constant ratio of two components.

(*c*) If links $ij$ and $hl$ intersect at $M$ then $\cos(iMh)$ is the correlation between the two logratios $\log(x_i/x_j)$ and $\log(x_h/x_l)$. A consequence of this property is that any two links $ij$ and $hl$ which intersect at right angles indicate uncorrelated logratios.

(*d*) The origin or *centre* $O$ of the relative variation diagram is the centroid of all the vertices $1, \ldots, D$. A consequence of this property and subcompositional coherence is that the relative variation diagram for any subcomposition consists of the diagram constructed from the vertices corresponding to the parts of the subcomposition and with centre the centroid of these subcompositional vertices.

(e) If a subset of vertices is approximately collinear then, from (d), the corresponding subcompositional relative variation diagram is one-dimensional. Interpreting this subcompositional relative variation diagram in terms of the singular value decomposition applied directly to the subcompositions, we see that all its singular values or eigenvalues other than the first must be zero. An immediate consequence is that the subcompositional variability must be one-dimensional. Moreover, we know that logcontrast principal components associated with the zero eigenvalues are constant and it may be possible in particular situations to place some interpretation on this constancy.

(f) The position of a compositional marker $r$ provides information on the extent to which the logratio, or ratio, of any two components $i$ and $j$ is greater or less than the average for the complete data set. More specifically, if $Or$ intersects the link $ij$ at $L$ then the excess of $\log(x_i/x_j)$ over the data set average is given by $|Or||ij|\cos(rLi)$, where $|.|$ denotes length. Thus if the angle between the directed vectors $Or$ and $ji$ is acute (obtuse) we have an excess (deficit) with respect to average, and for a fixed angle the greater the length of $Or$ the greater the discrepancy from average.

From the interpretational viewpoint it is clear that the basic elements of the relative variation diagram are the links $ij$ and not the rays $Oi$. Since, however, the number of links increases rapidly with the number $D$ of parts it is best, for $D$ greater than 4, to omit the links and to move a ruler around or depend on the eye when interest is in particular links.

## THE RELATIVE VARIATION DIAGRAM FOR TEACHERS' ACTIVITY PATTERNS

Figure 4 shows the relative variation diagram for the activity patterns of the 28 teachers of Table 1. From (a) the proportion of the total compositional variability which is retained by the relative variation diagram is 0.996 so that we have in this case an excellent representation of the pattern of compositional variability. From (b) the lengths of the links represent the standard deviations of the logratios and since we have already computed estimates of these in Table 2 we can easily judge the efficacy of the relative variation diagram. From the longest link 23, corresponding to the largest logratio standard deviation 1.084 of the parts administration and research, to the smallest links 14 and 15, corresponding to the smallest logratio standard deviations 0.221 of the teaching/recreation and teaching/sleep ratios, we have a consistent ordering. We can next use (c) to obtain an interesting insight into the correlations of logratios. Each of the links 12, 13 and 23 are approximately at right angles to the link 45 and so we

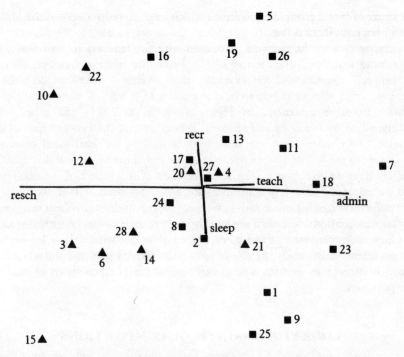

**Figure 4.** Relative variation diagram for the activity patterns of the 28 teachers of Table 1. Key: Professors ▲, other ranks ■.

can conclude that the patterns of the working and non-working parts of the week are independent of each other. We shall see in the next section how such a hypothesis of independence can be tested. We also observe that the vertices 1, 2, and 3 are almost collinear so that we can infer from (d) and (e) that the subcomposition associated with the working weekly pattern is almost one-dimensional. Such a one-dimensional pattern is, of course, confirmed for the case of this three-part subcomposition, from the ternary diagram already constructed in Figure 1b. If we were to identify, as in (e), the one logcontrast associated with the zero singular value in a full singular value decomposition of these three-part subcompositions, we would be able to express the constancy property described in (e) as approximately

$$7\log x_1 - 5\log x_2 - 2\log x_3 = \text{constant}.$$

It seems doubtful whether any useful interpretation can be placed on this academic 'law', but the interpretation can be highly successful in other situations: see Aitchison (in press) for a relative variation diagram approach to the study of blood group compositions which leads to rediscovery of the Hardy-Weinberg equilibrium law.

Turning now to the markers associated with the teachers we can note some interesting features from the use of (*f*). From the relative variation diagram we can see immediately, for example, that teacher 7 seems to do a lot of administration relative to research, that teacher 15 is high on sleep and research relative to other activities. In Figure 4, with professors and other ranks distinguished by triangles and squares, it is clear that the two groups fall into roughly two clusters with the separation mainly in the horizontal direction, professors to the left and other teachers to the right; in the vertical direction the clusters have similar ranges. The interpretation of this aspect of the diagram is that the ratios of research to administration and of research to teaching are larger for professors than for other ranks, whereas their recreation to sleep ratios have similar distributions. We shall see later how these aspects can be formally tested and how such relationships can be expressed more quantitatively. Also we have not yet attempted to study the role of age on the activity patterns of the teachers. This will emerge as we turn now towards more analytical methods of studying compositions.

## LOGRATIO ANALYSIS OF COMPOSITIONS

So far our discussion of the patterns of variability of compositional data has been confined to characteristics associated with first and second moments of the underlying distribution, equivalent to confining attention to the sample mean and standard deviation in the study of unconstrained univariate observations. For detailed statistical analysis it is often highly desirable to have available a parametric class of distributions on the sample space, which is rich enough to describe many patterns of variability and which allows the formulation and testing of detailed hypotheses within the class. One simple way of providing such a class and ensuring both scale invariance and subcompositional coherence is:

(*a*) to use a one-to-one transformation between *D*-part compositions **x** in the *d*-dimensional simplex and unconstrained *d*-dimensional vectors in real space ($d = D - 1$), involving ratios or logratios of components;

(*b*) to allow the rich class of *d*-dimensional normal distributions to induce through this transformation an equally rich class of distributions on the simplex.

One such simple transformation from the simplex to real space is the logratio transformation

$$y_i = \log(x_i/x_D) \qquad (i = 1, \dots, d), \tag{13}$$

with inverse transformation from real space to the simplex the generalized logistic transformation

$$x_i = \exp(y_i)/\{\exp(y_1) + \ldots + \exp(y_d) + 1\} \quad (i = 1, \ldots, d),$$

$$x_D = 1/\{\exp(y_1) + \ldots + \exp(y_d) + 1\}. \tag{14}$$

The technique here is basically the same as that involved in the 'invention' of the lognormal class by the transformations $y = \log x$ and $x = \exp(y)$ between the positive real line and the whole real line.

The class of distributions on the simplex derived by the above process has been termed the additive logistic normal class by Aitchison & Shen (1980). For the practical analysis of compositional data its adoption is simple: formulate the compositional problem in terms of ratios and, *a fortiori*, logratios; transform each composition x to its logratio vector y, and apply standard normal multivariate techniques to these unconstrained logratio vectors. Thus, hypothesis testing and estimation within such techniques as multivariate analysis of variance, discriminant analysis, canonical correlation analysis, are all readily available. Since the transformation (13) uses one of the components as common divisor in forming logratios, a question which is commonly posed is whether two analysts using different orderings of the compositional parts would arrive at the same inference. Technically the question here is one of invariance of procedures under the group of permutations of the parts; however, it can be shown that the invariance property holds (Aitchison 1986a, Section 7.1). It should also be noted that the assumption of multivariate normality of the logratio vectors can be studied through standard tests, as for example in Aitchison (1986a, Section 7.3). Moreover, we are not confined to the particular transformation (13), (14) between the simplex and real space for the purposes of analysis. Indeed we shall see that for the analysis of the example another transformation is perhaps better suited to investigating the relevant questions.

For the teachers of the example we can ask whether any teacher's activity pattern appears atypical of the distribution of patterns assessed from the other teachers. In fact we can assign to each teacher an atypicality index (Aitchison, 1986a, p. 175) which is, roughly speaking, an estimate of the proportion of compositions which, based on the experience of the other teachers, we would expect to be more typical than the considered composition. Such atypicality indices will lie between 0 and 1, with higher indices signifying greater atypicality. Only one teacher, #15, with atypicality index 0.9999 has an index greater than 0.95; the reasons for this are probably those already identified in Figure 3, namely the very high proportions of sleep and research relative to other activities.

## LOGRATIO ANALYSIS OF TEACHERS' ACTIVITY PATTERNS

We first address the question of the extent, if any, to which the teachers' activity patterns are dependent on status and age. As our model in which to study

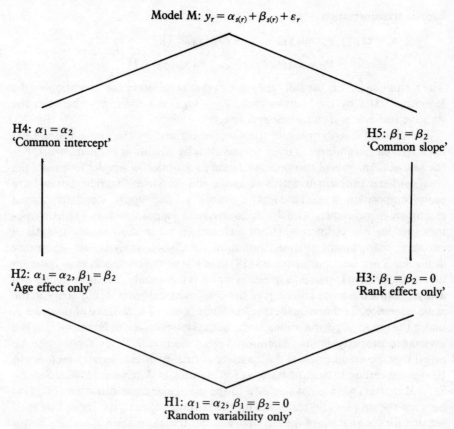

Model M: $y_r = \alpha_{s(r)} + \beta_{s(r)} + \varepsilon_r$

H4: $\alpha_1 = \alpha_2$
'Common intercept'

H5: $\beta_1 = \beta_2$
'Common slope'

H2: $\alpha_1 = \alpha_2, \beta_1 = \beta_2$
'Age effect only'

H3: $\beta_1 = \beta_2 = 0$
'Rank effect only'

H1: $\alpha_1 = \alpha_2, \beta_1 = \beta_2 = 0$
'Random variability only'

**Figure 5.** Lattice for hypothesis testing of dependence of teachers' activity patterns on status and age.

**Table 3.** Means of logratios $\log(x_i/x_j)$ for professors (first entry) and for other ranks (second entry) separately

|        | teach  | admin  | resch  | recr   |
|--------|--------|--------|--------|--------|
| admin  | 0.764  |        |        |        |
|        | 0.246  |        |        |        |
| resch  | 0.507  | -0.167 |        |        |
|        | 1.570  | 1.423  |        |        |
| recr   | -0.070 | -0.744 | -0.577 |        |
|        | -0.112 | -0.134 | -1.457 |        |
| sleep  | -0.391 | -1.065 | -0.898 | -0.321 |
|        | -0.149 | -0.395 | -1.718 | -0.261 |

various hypotheses we may take the following

$$y_{r1} = \log(x_{r1}/x_{r5}) = \alpha_{1s(r)} + \beta_{1s(r)}z_r + \varepsilon_{r1},$$

$$y_{r2} = \log(x_{r2}/x_{r5}) = \alpha_{2s(r)} + \beta_{2s(r)}z_r + \varepsilon_{r2},$$

$$y_{r3} = \log(x_{r3}/x_{r5}) = \alpha_{3s(r)} + \beta_{3s(r)}z_r + \varepsilon_{r3},$$

$$y_{r4} = \log(x_{r4}/x_{r5}) = \alpha_{4s(r)} + \beta_{4s(r)}z_r + \varepsilon_{r4},$$

(15)

where $s(r)$ denotes the status, 1 for professor, 2 for other rank, and $z_r$ denotes age of the $r$th teacher ($r = 1, \ldots, 28$) and the four-dimensional error vector $\varepsilon_r$ denotes the usual error vector in multivariate regression analysis. We can then set out in a lattice (Figure 5) various hypotheses of interest which are specializations of the model. Note that, in the specification of hypotheses within this lattice, hypotheses which set $\alpha_1 = \alpha_2$ or $\beta_1 = \beta_2$ correspond to no difference between ranks whereas the hypothesis $\beta_1 = \beta_2 = 0$ corresponds to an absence of an age effect. Standard multivariate regression software allows us to test each of the possible hypotheses within the model, and in this multiple-hypotheses situation we adopt the simplicity postulate of preferring a simple explanation of variability to a more complex one. We thus start at the bottom of the lattice, progressing upwards only on the rejection of hypotheses at each level, and stop as soon as we fail to reject a hypothesis, considering such a hypothesis as a kind of working model within which to quantify effects. In the present problem we reject H1, the hypothesis of no status or age effect, with significance probability $P = 0.005$; we reject H2, the hypothesis of an age effect only, with $P = 0.02$; but do not reject H3, the hypothesis of a rank effect only since its $P$-value is 0.11.

For the working model $y_r = \alpha_{s(r)} + \varepsilon_r$ we can obtain the estimates of the two four-dimensional vectors $\alpha_1$ and $\alpha_2$, which in this simple situation will clearly be the means of the four logratios $\log(x_1/x_5), \ldots, \log(x_4/x_5)$ for professors and other ranks separately. We can extend the expression of the differences here by providing in Table 3, as in a relative variation array, these means for all the possible logratios.

These results simply reflect what we have already seen in the relative variation diagram of Figure 3; for example, the ratio of administration to research is much larger for other ranks than for professors, the ratio of research to sleep is appreciably smaller for professors, whereas the ratio of recreation to sleep is somewhat similar for the two groups.

## A PARTITION ANALYSIS OF THE TEACHERS' ACTIVITY PATTERNS

We saw above one transformation (13), (14) between the simplex sample space and real space involving logratios which allowed a straightforward statistical analysis. There are clearly many such transformations and some may be more appropriate for particular problems. For example, in the study of the teachers' activity patterns one of the questions posed is concerned with a natural division of the unit of the week into the working and non-working parts. As an illustration of the flexibility of such transformations we now seek one which directs attention to the two subcompositions formed from the full composition by the division $(x_1, x_2, x_3 | x_4, x_5)$ and the *amalgamation* $(x_1 + x_2 + x_3, x_4 + x_5)$ which records the total proportions for the division of the week into working and non-working parts. It is easy to devise such a one-to-one transformation which will select relevant logratios:

$$y_1 = \log(x_1/x_3), \quad y_2 = \log(x_2/x_3), \quad y_3 = \log(x_4/x_5),$$

$$y_4 = \log\{(x_1 + x_2 + x_3)/(x_4 + x_5)\},$$

with a unique inverse which is of no direct interest to us here. With this transformation we can then easily address questions of independence, for example, whether it is reasonable to suppose that the working and non-working activity patterns are independent. To answer this, all we require is to test whether $(y_1, y_2)$ is independent of $y_3$. This requires a simple standard test of whether the appropriate submatrix of the covariance matrix of $(y_1, y_2, y_3, y_4)$ is the zero matrix: see Aitchison (1986a, Section 10.3) for details of this and other tests related to the partition of a composition. For the teachers' activity patterns such tests provide the following conclusions.

(a) The working and non-working activity patterns are independent of each other.

(b) The non-working activity pattern, in effect the ratio of recreation to sleep, is independent of the way in which the week is divided into total working and non-working parts, whereas the working activity pattern and this division are dependent.

## EXTENSIONS AND DISCUSSION

The biplot can be extended in a great variety of ways to highlight special aspects. For example, for each electoral region in a country we may have available one composition consisting of the proportions of the electorate in different occupational categories and a second composition consisting of the voting pattern at an election. Interest may then be in how the voting pattern is associated with the occupational patterns. It is possible either to devise a biplot to describe the joint variability of the two compositions or to emphasize within the biplot the role of the occupational pattern as a potential compositional explanatory factor for the variability in the voting patterns. Again, in the example, we have age playing the role of a possible covariate in the explanation of the variability of the teachers' activity patterns. Such covariates can be incorporated into the relative variation diagram. For further details, see Aitchison (1990).

A major limitation of the above analysis is that it has not allowed consideration of a compositional data set in which some of the components of some compositions are zero. There is no single answer to the problem of zeros where logarithmic transformations are concerned. Where the zeros are in the nature of undetected traces then some form of sensitivity analysis may be the appropriate approach, seeing to what extent conclusions may be sensitive to replacements of the zeros by different small amounts. In other situations the zeros may be absolute, for example in a household budget study where households may divide into two categories, those with and without purchases of 'alcohol and tobacco'. If there is interest in whether the two types of household differ in the pattern over the other commodity groups there is no real zero problem. We would simply test the hypothesis that the budget patterns of the two types are the same for the subcompositions involving commodities other than alcohol and tobacco. For further discussion of such zero problems, see Aitchison (1986a, Sections 11.5 and 11.6).

PC software for most of the analyses of this paper is available in Aitchison (1986b). An updated version of this software is available from the author.

## References

AITCHISON, J. (1986a). *The Statistical Analysis of Compositional Data*. London: Chapman & Hall.

AITCHISON, J. (1986b). *CODA: A Microcomputer Package for the Statistical Analysis of Compositional Data*. London: Chapman & Hall.

AITCHISON, J. (1990). Relative variation diagrams for describing patterns of compositional variability. *Mathematical Geology*, 22, 487–512

AITCHISON, J. (in press). On decompositions of compositions. *Applied Statistics*.

AITCHSION, J. & SHEN, S.M. (1980). Logistic-normal distributions: some properties and uses. *Biometrika*, 67, 261–272.

CHAYES, F. (1948). A petrographic criterion for the possible replacement origin of rocks. *American Journal of Science*, 246, 413–429.

CHAYES, F. (1960). On correlation between variables of constant sum. *Journal of Geophysical Research*, 65, 4185–4193.

COLEMAN, S.Y & LEE, S. (1988). Compositional data analysis of activities in a typical lesson. *Educational Research Journal* (A publication of the Hong Kong Research Association), 3, 98–103.

ECKART, C. & YOUNG, G. (1936). The approximation of one matrix by another of lower rank. *Psychometrika*, 1, 211–218.

EVANS, I.S. & JONES, K. (1981). Ratios and closed number systems. In N. Wrigley & R.J. Bennett (Eds), *Quantitative Geography: A British View*. Andover: Routledge & Kegan.

GABRIEL, K.R. (1971). The biplot-graphic display of matrices with applications to principal component analysis. *Biometrika*, 58, 453–467.

GABRIEL, K.R. (1981). Biplot display of multivariate matrices for inspection of data and diagnosis. In V. Barnett (Ed.), *Interpreting Multivariate Data*. New York: Wiley.

JOHNSTON, R.J. (1978). *Multivariate Statistical Analysis in Geography*. London: Longman.

WORKING, H. (1943). Statistical laws of family expenditure. *Journal of the American Statistical Association*, 38, 43–56.

# 11

# A Short History of Statistics in Twentieth Century Psychology

SANDY LOVIE

## A LITTLE LIGHT HISTORIOGRAPHY

It may seem somewhat perverse to include a chapter on the *past* of a subject in a book which purports to reveal aspects of its modern face, but I believe that there are several good reasons why the history of statistical psychology should be included in such a survey. First, mainstream statistics has long shown a minor but constant interest in its past, even to the extent of sponsoring a long running series of papers on historical topics in the prestigious journal *Biometrika*. The story of the past of statistics, in other words, has now gained the imprimatur of the statistical establishment. These papers, moreover, are no mere recycling of the accepted or received views of the history of statistics. On the contrary, most bear impressive tribute to the growing scholarship and independence of mind of many historians of statistics.

This brings me rather neatly to my second reason for including a history chapter in this book, which is that we are actually very ignorant or, at the very best, extremely confused about the past of psychological statistics. In other words, one can, paradoxically, say entirely new things about the past or offer new interpretations of issues that were thought long settled. It is in this sense, therefore, that new findings in the history of statistics in psychology can have a place in a text devoted to contemporary matters in psychological statistics.

And, of course, no historian, whatever their area of scholarship, would ever support the proposition that the past could ever be entirely known territory. History, like any area of active endeavour, is forever changing, forever re-examining its assumptions and conclusions in the light of altered attitudes and novel findings. It would be foolish to expect anything less in psychology and related areas of social science.

Of course, the amount of research today into the history of psychological statistics is modest, but there is enough to allow us to produce an outline of several of the major strands in this century's developments. This is equally the case whether we are considering central areas of substantive importance such as the analysis of variance or factor analysis, or tracing changes in methodology which have direct implications for statistics such as the gradual (and lockstepped) switch from the use of individual to group data in empirical studies in psychology.

Nor can we ignore fundamental changes in the philosophical base of psychology during the latter part of the nineteenth century which ushered in the commitment to psychology as a natural science with all the implications for data handling that were smuggled in with it. Equally, one cannot ignore the significance for the history of psychology of the novelties emerging from the field of statistics itself. Some of these were inspired by psychology and in consequence were incorporated into the subject fairly rapidly, while others were thought of as being so relevant or so important that a home had to be found for them in psychology, even though they had originally been developed to solve the problems of other disciplines.

My final reason for including this chapter is that the history of an area often provides a useful introduction to the topic itself. Thus my treatment should supply some of the historical background to certain of the topics in the present text, particularly factor analysis (and variants), analysis of variance (ANOVA), and the design and analysis of experiments.

I will conclude this section with one or two remarks on the more technical problems that face any historian when attempting to account for the past, that is, on issues of historiography. In particular, my decision to operate cut-offs around 1900 and 1950 is entirely arbitrary and merely reflects the space limitations imposed by the length of the chapter. In other words, I do not believe for one moment that the nineteenth century had no impact on the statistical developments of this century, or that there was nothing of interest to psychological statistics after 1950. Nor would I want to lay down arbitrary positions in time when such and such a technique was first used in psychology; that kind of grand-standing cannot be justified today.

Equally firmly, I would not argue for a hermetically sealed approach to statistics, that most socialized and most ideologically committed area of applied mathematics. For example, Charles Spearman's espousal of the single factor, hierarchical model of factor analysis owed as much to Galton and nineteenth century establishment beliefs about the nature and structure of intelligence and society as it did to either the tractability or simplicity of the mathematics that underlay the approach (see Norton, 1979, on the historical context of Spearman's ideas).

Furthermore, the monograph by MacKenzie (1981) has provided many examples from within the mainstream of late nineteenth and early twentieth century statistics of the social construction of the statistical process. Such a contextualized account of the subject seems increasingly to be one of the major hallmarks of modern historical scholarship in the sciences. The rest of this chapter is devoted to brief but meaty sketches of some three or four major areas in psychological statistics this century, beginning with the analysis of controlled laboratory studies from the early part of the century.

## BETTER BY DESIGN – AND ANALYSIS

It will no doubt come as something of a shock for modern experimental psychologists to find just how statistically sophisticated were their turn of the century colleagues. For example, in a paper on reaction times published in the *Psychological Bulletin* of 1904, Yerkes discusses a range of statistical measures of spread, particularly those which will enable researchers to equate stimulus intensity values across modalities in terms of homogeneity of reaction time variability. Thus, Yerkes lists the conventional standard deviation and the average (unsigned) deviation, and two measures derived from them, the coefficient of variation (which is given as the SD divided by the mean) and what the author terms the 'relative variation', that is, the average deviation divided by the mean. Yerkes also discusses the relative merits of the median and the mode as alternatives to the arithmetic mean.

Furthermore, in a note in the same year and in the same journal, Yerkes draws attention to the prevalent decision rule for judging whether comparisons between means were important, that is, the ratio of the difference between means (or other measures of central tendency) and a measure of their shared variability. Here, the suggestion is that the ratio should exceed a critical value before deciding that the difference is worth considering seriously.

This decision rule was neither particularly novel in 1904 (see Gigerenzer & Murray, 1987, for a reference to much earlier work on this topic), nor was it very difficult to calculate because of the extensive computational aids available to the researcher (see Thorndike's widely used text, first published in 1904, with a second edition in 1913, for a list of short cut methods and useful calculation tables). As a consequence, the ratio rule could be worked out fairly rapidly and accurately even for large data sets or for experiments which generated many samples. There was, however, some variation in how the components of the ratio were calculated and what constituted the critical value for the ratio, although the latter problem has not gone away with more recent and more sophisticated analyses!

Thus, for Thorndike (1904 and 1913), the variability of a sample could be calculated in several, equally legitimate, ways. For example, there were the methods which trimmed off a percentage of the sample, a procedure long favoured by nineteenth century workers because of the protection that it afforded against outliers (see Lovie, P., 1986).

More importantly for our purposes, however, are the measures of spread based on deviations from measures of location, that is, from the median, mode and arithmetic mean. Here Thorndike separates out the Average or Mean (unsigned) Deviation (AV or MV) from the Mean Square Deviation (of which the conventional Standard Deviation is an instance). However, Thorndike does not distinguish further between the measures of variability except to note that the trimmed estimators are not as precise as location based ones.

Consequently, when he deals with the assessment of differences between both measures of location and spread, there seems to be a willingness to accept a wide range of definitions of variability. Even in Thorndike's chapter on the reliability of the various measures given in the text (including differences between measures of location) variability is still expressed as deviations from *any* of the indices of location. This is also true for the case where Thorndike, in effect, develops a sampling distribution for the difference between any pair of measures.

Interestingly, Thorndike, in discussing the single most widely used measure of variability for the ratio rule, that is, the Probable Error (PE), defines this as the *median* of the unsigned deviations of a set of readings from its measure of location. This is to be contrasted with its more recent definition as a simple function of the standard error which was in turn based on the conventional standard deviation.

Although I am not attempting a complete history of the rise and fall (and variation in meaning) of the PE in experimental psychology and its role in statistical inference, it is reasonably clear that modern views on the latter issue had generally become accepted by the end of the 1930s. This was probably due to the increasing penetration of the work of Gosset and Fisher on small sample analyses (see Garrett, 1937; also Woodworth, 1938, p. 396, on the psychophysical methods), while by 1940 Chambers could brusquely dismiss the calculation of the Probable Error (of the mean) as a 'practice which has little to recommend it' (1952 edition, p. 36).

However, in the early years of this century, psychology seemed to have begun with an ambiguously defined ratio rule. The same, unfortunately, can also be said for the range of critical values against which this ratio was compared. For example, in 1916, Burtt suggested that this should be 1.5, while in the same year (and the same journal) Woodrow would only accept ratios which were equal to or greater than 3.0. This latter value was also used by Froeberg in 1920. However, Cason (1921), in a move remarkably like that contained in Thorndike's earlier treatment of the same problem, gave a 'chance out of hundred' criterion to use as a test for the usual (difference/PE) ratio. In addition, Boring, in a note published in 1926, describes linked ratio and probability based criteria, for example, that the (difference/PE) ratios should exceed three, four or even six before a result was declared 'significant', and that such critical values could, therefore, be equated to arbitrarily selected probabilities that the results could not be ascribed to chance alone.

By the early and middle 1930s, small sample *t*-tests for both independent and correlated group data were beginning to appear in psychology and the related area of education (see, for example, the expository accounts of the matched pairs *t*-test by Lindquist and Wilks, both in 1931), although a quick survey, for example, of the *Journal of Experimental Psychology* over this period still reveals widespread use of the ratio rule, with the PE progressively being replaced by the

SE. However, even as late as 1940, it is possible to find the *t*-test referred to as a statistical method 'which is not yet in general use in the field of education' (quote from Shen in the *Journal of Educational Psychology*, 1940, p. 347). Nevertheless, by the late 1930s, many of the ingredients of contemporary two-sample analysis were in place in psychology and in so far as the *t*-test could be viewed structurally and interpretationally as a less ambiguous, small sample version of the ratio test, so its incorporation into psychology proceeded without major trauma (see also Chambers, 1940).

There was, however, other much richer fare associated with the new statistics which our long term dalliance with oldstyle data analysis (as exemplified by the ratio test) prevented us from swallowing. In particular, there was the problem of the Neyman-Pearson conception of statistics as decision making in uncertainty which dates from as early as 1928 (see Neyman & Pearson, 1928) and which provided a much more logically complete analysis of statistical hypothesis testing, for example, by pointing to the consequences of mixing probabilistic with deductive inference.

The difficulty should be a familiar one to cognitive psychologists, *viz.*, the wish to discover only positive and affirming results, to see only the expected or the wished for in data. Thus, the emphasis which the ratio test placed on simple rules for deciding when there were significant results suited such affirmation seeking behaviour down to the ground, particularly as many experiments, then as now, were run in order to highlight such differences. Warnings about whether you could actually draw such a positive conclusion even when the ratio exceeded the critical value or perversely that you could be wrong in asserting that there really was no difference even though the ratio did *not* exceed the critical value, would both have seemed highly counterintuitive.

Chambers' description in 1940 (repeated in 1952) of a two sample *t*-test as a device that allowed one to decide whether the samples came from one or two parent populations, demonstrates both the resistance to the Neyman-Pearson analysis and the clear historical link with the critical ratio approach. On the other hand, the second edition of McNemar's *Psychological Statistics* (1955) contained the conventional Type I and Type II error analysis of statistical hypothesis testing, but not its extension to power and sample size analysis.

Again, the treatment was incomplete enough to allow McNemar to concentrate on the detection of differences even in situations where the test statistic had not exceeded the critical value, but not to consider the flip side which would question the confident rejection of the null hypothesis if the critical value were exceeded. Although, with hindsight, such an analysis follows reasonably easily from the definition of Type I and II errors, the continuing wish to positively affirm had clearly coloured even McNemar's treatment of the material. I would even suggest that such a wish is part of the hidden agenda of the recent work on the power of a test (see Singer *et al.*, 1986), since it could be interpreted as a way of overcoming (in a Neyman-Pearson analysis) the last logical obstacle to the confident detection of differences.

Finally, the rise of interest in Bayesian analysis post 1960 meant that the whole business of hypothesis testing was once again under scrutiny. But that is another story!

It is worth ending this section by noting a group of papers from the 1910s and 1920s, particularly associated with the name of Boring, which some have seen as anticipations of much of the later discussion of the Neyman-Pearson school of statistical inference (see Fernberger, 1916 and 1917; Boring, 1916, 1917, 1919 and 1926; and Kelley, 1923). Specifically, these writers have pointed to Boring's distinction between mathematical and scientific significance. This, they argue, shows that Boring was aware of such issues as sample size/power effects and the need to place any statistical analysis in a scientific context in order to give it meaning and generalizability.

In a way, such commentators have a point, in the sense that it is possible to find off the cuff remarks by Boring on such topics as the relationship between the effective sample size and the extent of the (expected) difference between conditions (Boring, 1916, p. 316), and the requirement to consider just how representative is the sample of the population before generalizing from it (Boring, 1919, p. 337; also 1926, p. 304). This never, however, amounted either to a systematic new form of statistical inference or a rigorous and sustained attack on current statistical practice in psychology, but the questionings of an experimental psychologist unhappy with his colleagues' uncritical acceptance of contemporary statistical methods.

Such unease, particularly when it is linked to problems of the substantive meaning of a particular statistical analysis, has surfaced many times this century as quantitative methods have grown ever more powerful and pervasive. I would point, for example, to the debates in the 1950s and 1960s on the issue of scales of measurement and the relevance of Bayesian statistics to psychology. Boring is clearly in good company!

## INTERLUDE: DESIGN AND ANALYSIS

There is a strongly rooted view in psychology that, following Fisher's dictum, design and analysis go hand in hand, and that this must also be true historically. Thus one can often read in textbooks, even ones published as late as the 1930s and 1940s, that the typical experiment in psychology controlled all variables except one which was then systematically explored by means of appropriate one or two sample tests (see, for example, Underwood, 1949).

However, in a survey of the history of ANOVA in psychology, I found that psychology had employed multifactor experimental structures as early as the 1920s, including repeated measure designs of the group by trials variety; all this, of course, without the benefit of ANOVA (Lovie, 1979). Let me re-emphasize this point by citing other early experimental papers which also utilized complex designs. For example, in 1916 Strong investigated the effects of repetition and times between exposure of items on newspaper advertising by means of a fully crossed two factor design. Strong's analysis of the experiment is essentially qualitative in that the argument is supported by drawing the readers' attention to various aspects of the graphs and tables in the paper. However, the author attempts a more sophisticated analysis of the data by fitting a model of the attention-value of an advert as a function of the square root of its printed area.

In 1921, Wells *et al.* published a study linking reaction time and attention which employed a three factor fully crossed design with factors of stimulus modality, foreperiod interval (time between the warning signal and the stimulus) and experimental interval when the foreperiod was varied. Their analysis of the data is a mixture of qualitative description and the calculation of a series of variances.

Boring (1926) also cites a study by Murchison & Gilbert (1925) of the IQ scores of some of the inhabitants of the Maryland State Penitentiary which forms a fully crossed $2 \times 2$ design (black versus white, and married versus unmarried prisoners). The analysis of this design (by Boring) employs an exhaustive series of two sample ratio tests on both 'main' and 'interaction' effects, for example, married versus unmarried, white unmarried versus black married.

Since these studies have been picked almost at random in the sense that I really did not have to work very hard or selectively to come across them, so these would seem to bear out my original, 1979, thesis that pre-ANOVA psychology was quite happy to utilize complex experimental designs, and to employ essentially piecemeal and qualitative analyses of the results (see also the many extra experiments cited in Lovie, 1979). This is not, however, to argue that these experiments were necessarily badly or haphazardly designed, rather there seemed to be a fairly self-conscious attempt to run studies that had a degree of balance in the way that the factors were crossed, and also to employ some kind of control or comparison group where appropriate.

Nevertheless, much more research is needed to see just how well founded are these latter remarks in the generality of experimental work in psychology, and to chart in more detail the various inferential strategies, formal or informal, that were used in the decades prior to 1940 (see Danziger, 1985 and 1987, for a pioneering study of the growth of group based data analysis from the latter part of the nineteenth century to the beginning decades of the present one).

## ANALYSIS OF VARIANCE: THE EXPERIMENTAL CORNUCOPIA AT LAST?

Another myth that seems to have haunted the history of psychological statistics for many years is that ANOVA did not appear in psychology until well after the Second World War. Thomson, for example, summed up the views of many commentators when he wrote that Fisher's methods, including ANOVA, 'did not influence psychology until after the Second World War' (1968, p. 343), while in Hearnshaw we read that a major reason for this neglect was the excessive use of agricultural terms (1964, p. 226). Yet others have elaborated on this general theme by pointing to the extreme slowness with which Fisher's work on ANOVA became incorporated into psychology (see, for example, Garrett & Zubin, 1943 and Lindquist, 1940). It is also worth noting that the first edition of Fisher's influential treatise *The Design of Experiments* only appeared in 1935, while *Statistical Methods*, Snedecor's widely cited exegesis of Fisher, was published in 1937.

Shrewd readers will, by now, have begun to smell a rat as they compare the dates of my references. In actuality, the passage of as complex a technique as ANOVA into psychology was accomplished with commendable speed. What difficulties that were experienced were predictable from my earlier remarks on the history of two sample design and analysis in psychology while, as we have also seen earlier, our long standing addiction to complex experiments guaranteed that for psychology at least ANOVA has never been viewed as a cure in search of a disease.

In support of my various points, it will be seen from my paper in 1979 and the review by Rucci & Tweney (1980) that the earliest works on ANOVA in psychology appeared as early as the mid 1930s (see, for example, Reitz, 1934), while the decade's most important pair of papers (by the learning theorists Crutchfield and Tolman) were published in 1938 and 1940. (I am discounting the statistically sophisticated but psychologically backward looking work from 1937 by Gaskill & Cox.)

Although Tolman and Crutchfield's use of ANOVA was both naive and partial (the overlap with older forms of analysis is painfully obvious in Crutchfield's clear dependence on an informal eye-balling of his graphs; see 1938), their espousal of the analysis of interactions as the Royal Road to model building in psychology pointed to the growing awarness of what ANOVA could do for complex multifactor designs. This theme was quickly taken up and considerably extended by Baxter, who was a lively member of the University of Minnesota's coven of ANOVA worshippers (1940, 1941 and 1942). Interestingly, Baxter's main area was the analysis of multifactor designs by methods that had only very recently been discussed by Yates (1937) – no evidence of a long historical delay there either.

Other pioneers worthy of mention include Palmer O. Johnson (also from Minnesota) who had spent a year in the late 1930s in London studying with both Fisher and Neyman (Johnson & Tsao, 1944, 1945), while Hackman (1940), in a clearly transitional paper, mixed both ANOVA and traditional methods in his analysis of a visual target detection task. A final paper worthy of mention here is by Helson (1942) which shows a sophisticated appreciation of the concept of interaction, even going so far as to predict one of the beastly things. (It will, of course, be recalled that Helson, during the 1920s, was an important figure in the introduction to America of Gestalt psychology, with its emphasis on inter-related structures – perhaps it is also no coincidence that Tolman was similarly inclined!)

Perhaps some of the most important innovations for psychology lay in methods for analysing data from investigations where the subject is observed either on many occasions under the same treatment condition, or on several different treatment conditions. These widely employed designs are, of course, known as repeated measure or within-subject studies.

In a detailed analysis of a small number of key papers from the 1940s (Lovie, 1981), it appeared that the main conceptual theme was the separation of experimental treatments into the substantive ones of particular interest to the researcher, and subjects. When this was achieved, then the ANOVA could also be split along similar lines, that is, into between subject and within subject analyses, with separate error terms for each part. Thus the approach was essentially univariate, with the implicit acceptance that some factors were not of the same intrinsic interest or value as the others. This can be traced fairly easily to Fisher (1935) who had distinguished between randomly selected agricultural sites and pre-determined treatments, for example, types of fertiliser or strains of wheat.

As a consequence of all this effort, Garrett & Zubin (1943) were able to cite over thirty papers and books in psychology and education which used analysis of variance, or one of its variants and extensions. Although this was by no means an exhaustive survey, it shows that the technique had a growing band of supporters, some of whom, like Tolman and Lindquist, were acknowledged leaders in their respective fields.

A further straw in the wind is that the first edition of A. L. Edwards' influential text book on design, published a scant seven years after the Garrett & Zubin review, contains at least double the number of psychological references to ANOVA in its bibliography (1950). This list included papers on independent and repeated measures designs, analysis of covariance, variance components, interactions as error terms in mixed effects models, tests of trend using orthogonal polynomials and the analysis of Latin squares. In other words, by 1950 the full range of ANOVA technology had been wheeled into place.

## FACTOR ANALYSIS AS THE ANSWER TO ALL OUR PROBLEMS

In William Brown's short tract on quantitative psychology entitled *Mental Measurement* (1911), we find him extolling the virtues of correlation as the only method for developing complex descriptions of the psychological universe. Further, for Brown, factor analysis (then, as now, a considerable provoker of unseemly bouts of fisticuffs amidst the groves of academe) formed a vital part of this movement to dominate the psychic world, with Charles Spearman as its founder and ever vigilant defender.

However, it is my thesis that early factor analysis was not as substantively neutral a technique as Brown (and later generations) viewed it, but had been developed to prove the existence of a previously postulated psycho-social reality. For Spearman and his numerous followers factor analysis was there to give the scientific and statistical cachet to the idea that intelligence was hierarchical in nature. It was not, therefore, a device for uncovering any old structure in the data, but a means of demonstrating a particular one. Factor analysis, in other words, began its life as a deductive, confirmatory technique and only gradually became the inductive engine of the 1940s and 50s. The partial irony, of course, is that because of the model testing problems attendent upon such an atheoretical use of the method, there is today a return to factor analysis as a test of the *a priori*.

In 1904 Spearman published two papers which launched factor analysis onto an unsuspecting world. The first (1904*b*) was on single factor analysis itself, (which Spearman refers to here as both the common faculty and as 'General Intelligence', and which he later, somewhat confusingly, renamed as the theory of the Two Factors), while the second was on some correlational novelities (1904*a*).

It is important to see the relationship between these two papers since it is Spearman's discovery of and solution to the so-called 'accidental and systematic deviations' which beset simple correlations that allowed him to demonstrate his major point that there is indeed a common faculty. These methods enabled him both to evaluate (through the calculation of probable errors) the mass of raw correlations thrown up by his own and other people's work, and to correct them for attenuation and the other manifold errors that correlations are heir to. The 1904*a* paper also contains a discussion of the qualitative determinants of correlation. This analysis was used by Spearman in 1904*b* to account for the failure of earlier work to reveal a common faculty (but see Fancher, 1985, for a contradictory re-analysis of Spearman's own data).

For Spearman, the immediate intellectual source of the common faculty theory was Galton, although the idea can be traced at least as far back as Aristotle. Galton's hereditarian views made him seek for variations in this common faculty in differences in social and economic success, and to find them. Commentators have also pointed to the way that he drew parallels between a hierarchically arranged society and the wrangler system that characterized the degree of success in the Cambridge examinations of Galton's day (Forrest, 1974).

Not surprisingly, Spearman, who came from the same social milieu as Galton and had been a long term career soldier at a time when the British Army was still amongst the country's most conservative institutions, embraced with alacrity the ideological and hierarchical message of his mentor (Norton, 1979). One has only to look at the terms in which he cast his three competing theories of intelligence (monarchic, oligarchic and anarchic) and the value-loaded way with which he dealt with them to see which way the social land lay (Spearman, 1927; no prizes for guessing which of the three came nearest to Spearman's own version of intelligence). It is also no coincidence that Spearman defended his quasi-monarchic theory against Godfrey Thomson's onslaught (which was pursued over the three decades from 1916) by savagely dismissing the latter's position as providing a theory not of intelligence or ability, but merely one of random, unstructured 'sampling' (see, for example, Spearman, 1938).

Earlier attacks on the theory of the Two Factors (a term coined not by Spearman himself but by Sancti de Sanctis – see Spearman, 1914) were also tinged by the clash of ideologies. For example, Thorndike's connectionist position, which was elaborated in a series of books and papers in the 1900s (see, for instance, Thorndike *et al.*, 1909), was dismissed by Spearman as one of the anarchic theories of intelligence (Spearman, 1927). The ideological contrast between the new and old world's view of the body psychic (and its connection with the body politic) could be no clearer.

It is somewhat ironic, given Spearman's essentially hypothetico-deductive use of factor analysis, that neither he nor his many students were really able to assemble a larger body of empirical applications of the methods, particularly outside the rather limited area of test theory and construction. There were, however, some attempts to establish the value of the approach in mainstream experimental psychology, for example, in the work by McQueen (1917) on what would today be termed divided attention. Here, factor analysis was used to see if there were any real differences in the amount of general factor ('$g$') that people would draw on when tackling single and dual tasks. The short answer is apparently 'no'.

Another body of Spearman's work, only marginally related to psychometrics, was that inspired by his attempt to link his interesting if only partly formulated theory of cognition ('noegenesis') to the theory of the Two Factors. However, because the programme of research on noegenesis was so fragmentary and Spearman's commitment to the theory such an intellectual handicap, so the undoubtably ambitious aims of the project (Spearman was wont to describe the 'laws' of noegenesis as 'ultimate') were never even remotely realized (see Lovie, 1984).

What Spearman, in fact, devoted his considerable ability and energy to was academic jousting. Although I will not list his various tourney partners, or indeed the grounds for their various encounters, it is fair to say that he broke lances with some of the best of this century's tiltyard heroes. For example, I have already mentioned Thorndike and his unstructured views on intelligence. Spearman's answer was to show, *au contraire*, that some of Thorndike's own data could be modelled by a hierarchy (see, for instance, Hart & Spearman, 1912).

Thomson's early claim that it was possible to demonstrate a hierarchy without a general factor (see 1916 and 1919) was dismissed by Spearman partly as irrelevant to 'real world' factor analysis and partly as, in fact, lending support to the theory of the Two Factors. Non-psychologists were also to be found in the mêlée, for example, the statisticians Truman Kelley and Edwin Wilson threw down weighty gages, the former over the existence of group factors (see Kelley, 1928), the latter over the fundamental problem of factor indeterminacy (see Steiger & Schönemann, 1978, and Lovie & Lovie, 1989).

But towering head and shoulders above all of these was the doughty champion Louis Thurstone, with his all-conquering method of factor rotation to a 'simple structure'. Although he had, in his own words, written down the equations for a non-hierarchical, multifactor approach to intelligence as early as 1922 (Thurstone, 1952), he was only in serious contention in 1935 with the publication of *The Vectors of Mind*, the first edition of the better known *Multiple Factor Analysis* (1947). Interestingly, the emphasis in both books was on the development of flexible, content-free technology, with little space devoted to the specifically psychological interpretation of factor analysis. Indeed, the psychological speculations seem positively medieval in that Thurstone described his new style factors as old style faculties (Thurstone, 1935, p. 53; see also Lovie, 1983).

This inductive, atheoretical and structure seeking approach to factor analysis, which also seemed (unlike that of Spearman) to be comparatively free of controversy, very quickly replaced the tailored solutions of this latter figure, even to the extent of seducing at least two of Spearman's North American students (Slocombe and Line) into Thurstone's camp. There was, however, Holzinger, the one important exception to this almost complete American rout, although even he was more unambiguously softer on group factors than Spearman.

Why had this reverse in Spearman's fortunes happened so swiftly? The reasons, I think, are to be found in the pragmatic, egalitarian and optimistic atmosphere of American psychology of the 1930s and 40s. This was coupled with the realization of American psychology's increasing intellectual dominance and its concomitant ability (and need) to offer new, essentially American-based ideas.

There also seemed to be a parallel realization that psychology (particularly the psychometric variety) needed, on the one hand, to develop a set of analytical tools which matched the perceived complexity of its subject matter without, on the other, making the commitment to a specific (and limiting) psychological theory. If you followed Spearman, however, and his slightly sinister approval of the medieval Schoolmen with their appeal to established (and ancient) order, one bought a specific theory of how the mind worked (tied to the suspect neurophysiology of 'mental energy') and a methodology to demonstrate its truth – not exactly the recipe for a forward-looking and open-ended technology.

The attacks upon Spearman had, therefore, a kind of poetic and historical symmetry about them in so far as they were, at base, as much about the psychological reality of his Two Factors as they were about the statistical methodology (see, for example, Thomson, 1938, and Thurstone, 1940). In other words, if you dismantled Spearman's substantive framework then what you can now do is indeed test for any old structure. The change was clearly complete when Wolfle in his major review of factor analysis from 1928 to 1940 was able to write that 'the first objective of factor analysis is simplifcation' (Wolfle, 1940, p. 1). This was followed in the review by a commentary which in effect questioned the reality of factors separate from their mathematical definition (see, in addition, Dunlap, 1938). In the company of such radical Young Turks, even Thurstone appeared dangerously deductive.

Of course, what we also saw in the 1930s and 40s was a speeding up of mathematical invention, for example, Lawley's development of maximum likelihood factor analysis (see, for example, Lawley, 1943), and Hotellings' ditto of principal components (1933), while the older workers such as Thomson were busily refining their systems into structures of an almost Euclidian beauty and abstraction (Thomson, 1954). Towards the end of the period it is also possible to detect the first gropings toward latent variable analysis, that more respectable offspring of factor analysis (Lazarsfeld, 1950).

There were, of course, some attempts to reclothe factor analysis in the respectable raiment of other branches of statistics, in particular multiple regression (see, for example, Ledermann, 1939); while Burt (1948) affected to see a link between his passenger-on-the-Clapham-omnibus version of factor analysis and analysis of variance. However, there has always been something a little magical, if not piratical, about factor analysis which should guarantee its continuing independent existence in some form or other.

## CODA - SELF CRITICISM OF WHAT HAS GONE BEFORE

This chapter has ranged so far and wide, and in so small a compass, that the whole enterprise might seem both too fragmentary and lacking in detail. However, what I hope I have done is put psychological statistics into a broad-brush historical setting and sequence, whilst at the same time pointing out that there is a slowly growing but respectable body of modern historical scholarship dealing with the topic. I also hope that I might have stimulated you into considering a test of the water: please do – there is plenty of room for everyone.

### References

BAXTER, B. (1940). The application of factorial design to a psychological problem. *Psychological Review*, **47**, 494–500.
BAXTER, B. (1941). Problems in the planning of psychological experiments. *American Journal of Psychology*, **54**, 270–280.

BAXTER, B. (1942). A study of reaction time using a factorial design. *Journal of Experimental Psychology*, **31**, 430–437.

BORING, E.G. (1916). The number of observations upon which a limen may be based. *American Journal of Psychology*, **27**, 315–319.

BORING, E.G. (1917). On the computation of the probable correctness of differences. *American Journal of Psychology*, **28**, 454–459.

BORING, E.G. (1919). Mathematical vs. scientific significance. *Psychological Bulletin*, **16**, 335–339.

BORING, E.G. (1926). Scientific induction and statistics. *American Journal of Psychology*, **37**, 303–307.

BROWN, W. (1911). *The Essentials of Mental Measurement*. Cambridge: Cambridge University Press.

BURT, C. (1948). A comparison of factor analysis and analysis of variance. *British Journal of Psychology, Statistical Section*. **1**, 3–26.

BURTT, H.E. (1916). The effect of uniform and non–uniform illumination upon attention and reaction times, with especial reference to street illumination. *Journal of Experimental Psychology*, **1**, 155–182.

CASON, H. (1921). The conditional eyelid reaction. *Journal of Experimental Psychology*, **4**, 153–196.

CHAMBERS, E.G. (1940). *Statistical Calculation for Beginners*, 1st ed. Cambridge: Cambridge University Press. (2nd ed., 1952).

CRUTCHFIELD, R.S. (1938). Efficient factorial design and analysis of variance illustrated in psychological experimentation. *Journal of Psychology*, **5**, 339–346.

CRUTCHFIELD, R.S. & TOLMAN, E.C. (1940). Multiple-variable design for experiments involving interaction of behavior. *Psychological Review*, **47**, 38–42.

DANZIGER, K. (1985). The origins of the psychological experiment as a social institution. *American Psychologist*, **40**, 133–140.

DANZIGER, K. (1987). Statistical method and the historical development of research practice in American psychology. In G. Gigerenzer, L. Kruger & M. Morgan (Eds), *The Probabilistic Revolution: Ideas in Modern Science, Vol. II*. Cambridge: MIT Press.

DUNLAP, J.W. (1938). Recent advances in statistical theory and applications. *American Journal of Psychology*, **51**, 558–571.

EDWARDS, A.L. (1950). *Experimental Design in Psychological Research*. New York: Rinehart & Co.

FANCHER, R.E. (1985). Spearman's original computation of $g$: A model for Burt? *British Journal of Psychology*, **76**, 341–352.

FERNBERGER, S.W. (1916). The effects of practice in its initial stages in lifted weight experiments and its bearing upon anthropometric measurements. *American Journal of Psychology*, **27**, 261–272.

FERNBERGER, S.W. (1917). Concerning the number of observations necessary for the determination of a limen. *Psychological Bulletin*, **14**, 110–113.

FISHER, R.A. (1935). *The Design of Experiments*. Edinburgh: Oliver and Boyd.

FORREST, D.W. (1974). *Francis Galton: The Life and Work of a Victorian Genius*. London: Elek.

FROEBERG, S. (1920). Effects of smoking on mental and motor efficiency. *Journal of Experimental Psychology*, **3**, 334–346.

GARRETT, H.E. (1937). *Statistics in Psychology and Education*, 2nd ed. New York: Longmans, Green & Co.

GARRETT, H.E. & ZUBIN, J. (1943). The analysis of variance in psychological research. *Psychological Review*, **40**, 233–267.

GASKILL, H.V. & COX, G.M. (1937). Patterns in emotional reactions: I. Respiration;

the use of analysis of variance and covariance in psychological data. *Journal of General Psychology*, **16**, 21–38.

GIGERENZER, G. & MURRAY, D.J. (1987). *Cognition as Intuitive Statistics*. Hillsdale: Erlbaum.

HACKMAN, R.B. (1940). An experimental study of variability in ocular latency. *Journal of Experimental Psychology*, **27**, 546–558.

HART, C. & SPEARMAN, C.E. (1912). General ability: Its existence and nature. *British Journal of Psychology*, **5**, 51–84.

HEARNSHAW, L.S. (1964). *A Short History of British Psychology. 1840–1940*. London: Methuen.

HELSON, H. (1942). Multiple–variable analysis of factors affecting lightness and saturation. *American Journal of Psychology*, **55**, 46–57.

HOTELLING, H. (1933). Analysis of a complex of statistical variables into principal components. *Journal of Educational and Psychological Measurement* **24**, 417–441, 498–520.

JOHNSON, P.O. & TSAO, F. (1944). Factorial design and the determination of differential limen value. *Psychometrika*, **9**, 107–144.

JOHNSON, P.O. & TSAO, F. (1945). Factorial design and covariance in the study of individual educational development. *Psychometrika*, **10**, 133–162.

KELLEY, T.R. (1923). Principles and technique of mental measurement. *American Journal of Psychology*, **34**, 408–432.

KELLEY, T.R. (1928). *Crossroads in the Mind of Man: A Study of Differential Mental Abilities*. Stanford: Stanford University Press.

LAWLEY, D.N. (1943). The application of maximum likelihood method to factor analysis. *British Journal of Psychology*, **33**, 172–175.

LAZARSFELD, P.F. (1950). The logical and mathematical foundation of latent structure analysis. In S.A. Stouffer, L. Guttman, E.A. Suchman, P.F. Lazarsfeld, S. A. Star & J.A. Clausen, (Eds), *Measurement and Prediction*. Princeton: Princeton University Press.

LEDERMANN, W. (1939). On a shortened method of estimation of mental factors by regression. *Psychometrika*, **4**, 109–116.

LINDQUIST, E.F. (1931). The significance of a difference between 'matched' groups. *Journal of Educational Psychology*, **22**, 197–204.

LINDQUIST, E.F. (1940). *Statistical Analysis in Educational Research*. Boston: Houghton Mifflin.

LOVIE, A.D. (1979). The analysis of variance in experimental psychology: 1934–1945. *British Journal of Mathematical and Statistical Psychology*, **32**, 151–178.

LOVIE, A.D. (1981). On the early history of ANOVA in the analysis of repeated measure designs in psychology. *British Journal of Mathematical and Statistical Psychology*, **34**, 1–15.

LOVIE, A.D. (1983). Images of Man in early factor analysis – psychological and philosophical aspects. In S. Bem, H. Rappard & W. van Hoorn, (Eds), *Studies in the History of Psychology and the Social Sciences, Vol. I*. Leiden: University Press.

LOVIE, A.D. (1984). Aspects of noegenesis: Spearman's system of cognition and applied psychology. In S. Bem, H. Rappard & W. van Hoorn, (Eds), *Studies in the History of Psychology and the Social Sciences, Vol II*. Leiden: University Press.

LOVIE, A.D. & LOVIE, P. (1989). Spearman and Wilson on the elusive general factor. Paper given to the eighth meeting of Cheiron, Europe.

LOVIE, P. (1986). Identifying outliers. In A.D.Lovie (Ed.), *New Developments in Statistics for Psychology and the Social Sciences*. London: The British Psychological Society and Methuen.

MacKENZIE, D.A. (1981). *Statistics in Britain, 1865–1930: The Social Construction of Scientific Knowledge*. Edinburgh: Edinburgh University Press.

McNEMAR, Q. (1955). *Psychological Statistics*, 2nd ed. New York: Wiley.

McQUEEN, E.I. (1917). *The Distribution of Attention*. Cambridge: Cambridge University Press.

MURCHISON, C. & GILBERT, R. (1925). Some marital concomitants of negro men criminals. *Pedagogical Seminary*, 32, 652–656.

NEYMAN, J. & PEARSON, E.S. (1928). On the use and interpretation of certain test criteria for purposes of statistical inference, Parts I and II. *Biometrika*, 20a, 175–240, 263–294.

NORTON, B.J. (1979). Charles Spearman and the General Factor in intelligence: Genesis and interpretation in the light of sociopersonal considerations. *Journal of the History of the Behavioral Sciences*, 15, 142–154.

REITZ, W. (1934). Statistical techniques for the study of institutional differences. *Journal of Experimental Education*, 3, 11–24.

RUCCI, A.J. & TWENEY, R.D. (1980). Analysis of variance and the 'Second Discipline' of scientific psychology. *Psychological Bulletin*, 87, 166–184.

SHEN, E. (1940). Experimental design and statistical treatment in educational research. *Journal of Experimental Education*, 8, 346–353.

SINGER, B.R., LOVIE, A.D. & LOVIE, P. (1986). Sample size and power. In A. D. Lovie (Ed.), *New Developments in Statistics for Psychology and the Social Sciences*. London: The British Psychological Society & Methuen.

SNEDECOR, G.W. (1937). *Statistical Methods*. Ames: Collegiate Press.

SPEARMAN, C.E. (1904a). The proof and measurement of the association between two things. *American Journal of Psychology*, 15, 72–101.

SPEARMAN, C.E. (1904b). 'General Intelligence' objectively determined and measured. *American Journal of Psychology*, 15, 202–293.

SPEARMAN, C.E. (1914). The theory of two factors. *Psychological Review*, 21, 101–115.

SPEARMAN, C.E. (1927). *The Abilities of Man*. London: Macmillan.

SPEARMAN, C.E. (1938). Proposed explanations of individual differences of ability by 'sampling'. *British Journal of Psychology*, 29, 182–191.

STEIGER, J.H. & SCHÖNEMANN, P.H. (1978). A history of factor indeterminacy. In S. Shye (Ed.), *Theory Construction and Data Analysis in the Behavioral Sciences*. San Francisco: Jossey Bass.

STRONG, E.K. (1916). The factors affecting a permanent impression developed through repetition. *Journal of Experimental Psychology*, 1, 319–338.

THOMSON. G.H. (1916). A hierarchy without a general factor. *British Journal of Psychology*, 8, 271–281.

THOMSON. G.H. (1919). The hierarchy of abilities. *British Journal of Psychology*, 11, 337–344.

THOMSON, G.H. (1939). *The Factorial Analysis of Human Ability*. London: London University Press.

THOMSON, G.H. (1954). *The Geometry of Mental Measurement*. London: University of London Press.

THOMSON, R. (1968). *The Pelican History of Psychology*. Harmondsworth: Penguin.

THORNDIKE, E.L. (1904). *An Introduction to the Theory of Mental and Social Measurements*, 1st ed. New York: Teachers College, Columbia. (2nd ed., 1913).

THORNDIKE, E.L., LAY, W. & DEAN, P.R. (1909). The relation of accuracy in sensory discrimination to general intelligence. *American Journal of Psychology*, 20, 364–369.

THURSTONE, L.L. (1935). *The Vectors of Mind*. Chicago: University of Chicago Press.

THURSTONE, L.L. (1940). Current issues in factor analysis. *Psychological Bulletin*, 37, 189–236.

THURSTONE, L.L. (1947). *Multiple Factor Analysis*. Chicago: University of Chicago Press.

THURSTONE, L.L. (1952). Autobiography. In E.G. Boring, H.S. Langfeld, H. Werner & R.M. Yerkes, (Eds), *A History of Psychology in Autobiography, Vol IV*. Mass.: Clark University Press.

UNDERWOOD, B.J. (1949). *Experimental Psychology*. New York: Appleton-Century Crofts.

WELLS, F.L., KELLEY, C.M. & GARDNER MURPHY (1921). Attention and simple reaction time. *Journal of Experimental Psychology*, 4, 391–398.

WILKS, S.S. (1931). The standard error of the means of 'matched' samples. *Journal of Educational Psychology*, 22, 205–208.

WOLFLE, D. (1940). *Factor Analysis to 1940*. Chicago: University of Chicago Press.

WOODROW, H. (1916). The faculty of attention. *Journal of Experimental Psychology*, 1, 285–318.

WOODWORTH, R.S. (1938). *Experimental Psychology*. New York: Holt.

YATES, F.C. (1937). *The Design and Analysis of Factorial Experiments*. Harpenden: Imperial Bureau of Soil Science.

YERKES, F. (1904). Variability of reaction time. *Psychological Bulletin*, 1, 137–176, and 370.

# Index

Note: Multiauthored works are generally indexed by first author only.

Aitchison, J. 214, 217, 221, 223, 225, 227, 229, 232, 233
Akaike, H. 205, 212
analysis of variance (ANOVA)
  early history in psychology 240–2
  time series 185
  unbalanced *vs* balanced designs 135, 138, 138–9, 141, 143, 146–7
Andersen, E.B. 208, 212
Anderson, J.C. 206, 213
Anderson, T.W. 208, 213
Applebaum, M.I. 140, 141, 152, 153
Atkinson, A.C. 75, 77, 79, 102, 115, 118, 132

Barlow, D.H. 180,195
Barnard, G. 77, 79
Barnett, V. 98, 101, 132
Bartholomew, D.J. 29, 30, 47, 199, 201, 202, 203, 204, 206, 207, 210, 211, 212, 213
Bartlett, M.S. 147, 152
Batchelder, W.H. 79
Baxter, B. 241, 246, 247
Becker, R.A. 77, 79
Belsley, D.A. 100, 101, 103, 104, 118, 122, 125, 126, 132, 133
Benard, A. 7, 18
Bishop, Y.M.M. 209, 213
Blair, R.C. 152
BMDP 34, 132, 147, 172
Bohrer, R.E. 183, 195, 197
Boomsma, A. 206, 213
bootstrap xi, 49, 50, 52–6, 59–69, 76, 77, 78, 
  bias 61–4, 75–6
  and classification trees 88
  confidence intervals 64–9
  definition 52–3
  difference in location 59–60
  location measures 52–3, 55–6
  procedure 52–6
Boring, E.G. 237, 239, 240, 247
Box, G.E.P. 160, 163, 172, 179, 181, 182, 183, 184, 196, 197
box plots 20–3, 100
  effect and box plot error display 40–1
  notched 22–3
  multiple 20–1, 34, 36, 39
Bratko, I. 82, 93
Breiman, L. 81, 82, 86, 87, 88, 93
Brown, W. 242, 247

Brunsdon, T.M. 184, 196
Buck, S.F. 148, 152
Burt, C. 246, 247
Burtt, H.E. 237, 247

Campbell, D.T. 158, 172, 180, 196
Carlson, J.E. 139, 153
Carroll, R.J. 118, 133
Cason, H. 237, 247
Chambers, E.G. 237, 238, 247
Chambers, J.M. 20, 27, 30, 32, 34, 45, 47, 77, 79
Chatfield, C. 183, 196
Chatterjee, S. 100, 101, 102, 103, 104, 118, 130, 133
Chayes, F. 215, 233
Chernoff, H. 45, 47
Clark, P. 82, 93
classification trees xi, Chapter 4, *passim*
  alternatives 81
  applications 81–2, 90–2
  basic method 83–85 (see pruning, shrinking, splitting and stopping rules)
  highly correlated branched 89 (*see also* regression diagnostics)
  many-branched trees 89–90
  missing data 89
Cleveland, W.S. x, xv, 27, 30, 43, 47, 48
Cochran, W.G. 8, 18, 78, 79
Cole, J.W.L. 164, 172
Coleman, S.Y. 214, 233
Collier, R.O. 164, 172
collinearity detection
  condition index 125–6, 128, 130, 132
  graphical methods 127, 128–30, 131
  $R^2$ 124, 132
  variance decomposition proportion (VDP) 125–6, 128
  variance inflation factor (VIF) 124, 125, 126, 128, 132
combined S test 2–3
compositional data analysis xiii–xiv, Chapter 10, *passim*, (*see also* multifactor and multivariate displays, singular value decomposition)
  additive logistic normal distributions 228–9
  centred logratio data matrix 223–4, 227–8
  composition 217, 228–9

examples 214–5
logratio 221–2, 223, 226
and multivariate regression 229–31
partitioning 231–2
past misuses 215–17
relative variation array 222–3
relative variation diagram 223–4, 225–6
scale invariance 220
simplex 219–20
subcomposition 217–8, 220–1, 227
subcompositional coherence 220–1
ternary diagrams 217–8
zero components 233
computationally intensive methods x–xi,
    Chapter 3, *passim*, (*see also* bootstrap,
    jackknife, randomization tests, Monte
    Carlo tests)
    estimation 52–69
    testing 69–76
Conover, W.J. 151, 153
Cook, N.R. 41, 48
Cook, R.D. 47, 48, 77, 79, 101, 102, 103, 104,
    133
Cook, T.D. 180, 196
Cowan, T.M. 73, 79
Cox, D.R. 182, 196
Cramer, E.M. 140, 141, 152, 153
Crowder, M.J. 182, 196
Crutchfield, R.S. 241, 247

Daniel, C. 16, 18, 114, 116, 133
Danziger, K. 240, 247
Diaconis, P. 49, 79
Diciccio, T.J. 69, 79
Dielman, T.E. 178, 196
Draper, N.R. 16, 18, 114, 116, 118, 130, 132,
    133
van Driel, O.P. 206, 213
Dunlap, J.W. 246, 247
Durbin, J. 9, 18

Eckart, C. 223, 233
Edgington, E.W. 70, 71, 72, 73, 79
Edwards, A.L. 242, 247
Efron, B. 49, 52, 55, 60, 62, 65, 69, 76, 77,
    78, 79, 88, 93
van Elteren, P. 7, 9, 18
Emerson, J.D. 115, 118, 133
Epstein, S. 180, 196
Erickson, B.H. 23, 48
Evans, I.S. 214, 215, 233
extreme 98–99 (*see also* outlier)

Fachell, J.M.G. 206, 213
Fanscher, R.E. 243, 247
Fernberger, S.W. 239, 247
Fielding, A. 81, 93

Fisher, R.A. 81, 93, 155, 167, 172, 241, 242,
    247
Forrest, D.W. 243, 247
Friedman test
    one reading per cell 5–6
    *m* readings per cell 7
    balanced incomplete blocks 7–9
Froeberg, S. 237, 247

Gabriel, K.R. 223, 233
Garrett, H.E. 237, 241, 242, 247
Gaskill, H.V. 241, 247
GAUSS 132, 134
Geisser, S. 164, 172
Geweke, J. 184, 196
Gigerenzer, G. 236, 248
Glass, G.V. 135, 153, 180, 183, 184, 196
Goldman, L. 91, 93
Goodman, L.A. 209, 213
Gorsuch, R.L. 184, 196
Gottman, J.M. 176, 179, 181, 183, 184, 196,
    197
Gower, J.C. 20, 48
Granger, C.W.J. 174, 196
graphical methods x, Chapter 2, *passim*, (*see
    also* box plots, multifactor and
    multivariate displays, quantile plots,
    scatterplots, stem and leaf display)
    computer packages 47, 132
    dynamic graphics 47
    and exploratory data analysis 19–20
    and transformations 34–9, 112–6
Gray, J.B. 104, 133
Greenacre, M.J. 209, 213
Greenhouse, S.W. 164, 172
Gregory, S.W. 176, 196
Gregson, R.A.M. 176, 179, 181, 184, 196

Hackman, R.B. 241, 248
Hall, A.V. 82, 93
Hall, P. 69, 78, 79
Hand, D.J. 81, 88, 93, 94, 167, 173
Hardyck, C.D. 32, 33, 48
Hart, C. 244, 248
Harvey, A.C. 186, 196
Hearnshaw, L.S. 241, 248
Helson, H. 241, 248
Hettmansperger, T.P. x, xv, 1, 9, 15, 16, 18,
    151, 153
Hinkley, D.V. 77, 78, 79
history of statistics in psychology xiv, Chapter
    11, *passim*, (*see also* analysis of variance
    (ANOVA), latent variable methods,
    repeated measures)
    correlation and factor analysis 242–3
    early ANOVA 240–2
    factor analysis before 1940 242–6

historiographic considerations 234–5
measures of location and spread 236–7
multifactor theory 245–6
pre-ANOVA experimental design 239–40
ratio test *vs* *t*-test 236–8
two factor theory 243–4
two sample comparisons 236–9
Hoaglin, D.C. 28, 48, 100, 101, 102, 118, 133
Hodges-Lehmann aligned rank test one
    treatment 3–6
    *k* treatments 6–7
Hotelling, H. 246, 248
Howell, D.C. 139, 140, 153
Huber, P. 100, 133
Huitema, B.E. 136, 149, 153, 184, 196
Huynh, H. 162, 164, 173

influence measures (*see also* residuals)
    Cook's distance 102–3, 105–6, 109, 112
    CVR 104, 105–6, 109, 112
    DFBETAS 103–4, 105–6, 109, 112
    DFFITS 103, 105–6, 109, 112
    for subsets 104

jackknife xi, 49, 50, 56–69, 76, 77, 78,
    bias 61–4
    confidence intervals 64–9
    definition 56–7
    difference in location 59–60
    location measures 57–9
    procedure 57–9
Johnson, N. 62, 79
Johnson, P.O. 241, 248
Johnson, R.E. 151, 153
Johnston, R.J. 214, 233
Jones, B. 31, 48
Jones, D. 176, 185, 197
Jones, R.H. 180, 197

Kelley, T.R. 239, 245, 248
Kempthorne, P.J. 102
Kenward, M.G. 31, 48, 167, 173
Keppel, G. 180, 181, 197
Keselman, H.J. 164, 173
Krebs, D. 212, 213

Land, K.C. 174, 197
Larsen, R.J. 176, 181, 197
Larsen, W.A. 118, 133
latent variable methods xiii, Chapter 9,
    *passim*, (*see also* latent variable model)
    alternatives 209, 211
    components of latent space 201, 210, 212
    for contingency tables 209–11
    definition and notation 199–200, 202–3
    estimation 205–8
    for exploratory work 200

and factor analysis 200–1, 207, 209–10
goodness of fit 205–8
indeterminacy 203–5
inference 203–5, 207–8
for measurement problems 199–200
reliability 211–2
sample size and Heywood cases 206–8
latent variable model
    fixed and random effects 208–9
    latent class 202–3, 204–5
    latent trait 204–5, 210
    linear factor 202
    logit 202, 206, 211–2
    model specification 200–1
    Rasch 204–5, 208–9
Lawley, D.N. 246, 248
Lazarsfeld, P.F. 200, 213, 246, 248
Leach, C. x, xv, 1, 2, 3, 10, 12, 15, 18
Ledermann, W. 246, 248
Lehmann, E.L. x, xv, 1, 2, 5, 6, 18
Levenson, R.W. 181, 184, 197
leverage 100 (*see also* influence measures) hat
    values 100–12, 128, 130–1
    and influential observations 102
    plot 105, 107–8, 131
Lewis, P.A.W. 77, 78, 79, 80
Li, G. 118, 133
Lillard, L. 150, 153
Lindquist, E.F. 237, 241, 248
Little, R.J.A. 148, 150, 153
Loh, W-Y, 82, 85, 87, 89, 94
Lord, F.M. 141, 149, 153
Lovie, A.D. ix, xv, 238, 239, 242, 244, 245,
    248, 249
Lovie, P. 21, 34, 35, 39, 48, 98, 133, 236, 238,
    240, 245, 248, 249

Mabbett, A. 81, 87, 90, 94
MacKenzie, D.A. 235, 249
Macrae, A.W. 141, 153
Macready, G.B. 204, 213
Mauchly, J.W. 163, 173
McCullagh, P. 118, 132, 133
McDowall, D. 184, 197
McNeil, D.R. 30, 48
McNemar, Q. 238, 249
McQueen, E.I. 244, 249
Mead, R. 73, 80
mean square error (MSE) 99, 101
    deletion MSE 101, 103, 106, 109, 112
Meddis, R. 1, 2, 18
Miller, R.G. 56, 77, 78, 80
Milligan, G.W. 135, 148, 150, 153
Milliken, G.A. 164, 173
MINITAB 15, 16–7, 47, 48, 77, 132, 134
Mislevy, R.J. 206, 213
Mitzel, H.C. 162, 173

Molenaar, P.C.M. 184, 197
Monte Carlo tests xi, 49, 50, 73–6, 77, 79
    and bootstrap and jackknife 75–6
    limitations 76
    an parametric analyses 73
    procedures 73–5
Montgomery, D.C. 101, 116, 118, 132, 133
Moore, D.S. 20, 21, 48
Morgan, B.J.T. 77, 80
Morgan, J.N. 81, 94
Morse, L.E. 82, 94
Mosteller, F. 20, 48, 49, 53, 57, 59, 64, 76,
    78, 80, 115, 118, 133
multifactor and multivariate displays 39–46
    biplot (relative variation diagram) 223–8
    casement 43–4
    Chernoff faces 43, 45–6
    cube 111–2, 121–2, 127
    draughtsman's 41–3, 110
    effect and box plot error 40–1
    trees 82–84, 90–93
multivariate repeated measures 164–7, 168
    Wilks Λ 165
    Lawley-Hotelling $T^2$ 165–6
    Roy's largest root 166
    Pillai's trace 166–7
multivariate sign test, one sample 10–12
multivariate signed-rank test, two samples
    12–15
Murchison, C. 240, 249
Murdock, B.B. 79, 80
Muthén, B. 209, 213

NCSS 47, 48, 132, 134
Neave, H.R. 1, 18
Neyman, J. 238, 249
nonparametric methods x, Chapter 1, *passim*,
    (*see also* combined S, Hodges-Lehmann
    aligned rank, Friedman, multivariate
    sign, and multivariate signed-rank tests;
    and Chapter 3)
    block designs 1–9
    multivariate tests 9–15
    rank tests in linear models 15–18
Norton, B.J. 235, 243, 249

O'Brien, R.G. 140, 153
Olson, C.L. 161, 173
Osborn, J.F. 116, 133
outlier 98–9, 101–2 (*see also* regression)
Otter, P.W. 184, 197
Overall, J.E. 139, 140, 153

Pankhurst, J.R. 82, 94
Payne, R.W. 82, 94
PC-ISP 132, 134
Pena, D. 184, 197

Plewis, I. 155, 173, 178, 197
Porges, S.W. 183, 184, 195, 197
Potthoff, R.F. 164, 173
Pregibon, D. 88
pruning rules 85, 87–8

quantile 32
quantile plots 32–9
    empirical quantile quantile (EQQ) 32–4
    normal probability 35–8, 114–6, 117
    quantile quantile (QQ) 34–9
    symmetry 34–5, 37–8
Quenouille, M.H. 52, 56, 76, 80
Quinlan, J.R. 82, 94

Raj, B. 49, 80
randomization tests xi, 49, 50, 69–73, 77, 78
    and bootstrap 69
    definition 70
    and nonparametric tests 70
    as permutation tests 70–2
    procedure 70–3
Rasch, G. 208, 213
Rasmussen, J.L. 64, 73, 80
regression
    adding new variables 118–9
    ordinary least squares (OLS) method 95,
        96–7
    other alternatives to OLS 118, 130–1
    outlier 98
    rank 15–8
regression diagnostics xi–xii, Chapter 5,
    *passim*, (*see also* collinearity detection,
    influence measures, leverage, outlier,
    residuals, scatterplots)
    collinearity 119–32
    influential data 98–112, 128–30
    model checking 112–9
Reitz, W. 241, 249
repeated measures xii, Chapter 7, *passim*, (*see
    also* univariate and multivariate repeated
    measures; and Chapter 8)
    carryover effects and crossover designs
        157–8
    design considerations 157–61
    early history in psychology 242
    Gompertz model 168, 169–71
    groups × occasions interaction 158–60
    multivariate methods 164–7, 168
    as observations over time 155–6, 180
    response curve approaches 167–9
    serial correlation 156–7
    univariate methods 161–4, 168
residuals (*see also* influence measures,
    scatterplots)
    and outliers 101
    raw 97, 100, 118, 128–9

standardized 101
studentized 101–9, 112, 113–5, 117, 131
Revenstorf, D. 176, 184, 197
Ripley, B.D. 53, 76, 77, 80
Robertson, C. 73, 75, 80
Rosenbaum, P.R. 31, 48
Rouanet, H. 163, 173
Rousseeuw, P.J. 118, 133
Rucci, A.J. 241, 249
Ryan, B.F. 77, 80

S 47, 48, 77
SAS 132, 134, 147, 172, 186, 197
SC 132, 134
SMTBPC 77
scatterplots 23–39, 98 (*see also* residuals,
    leverage, collinearity detection, quantile
    plots, smoothing)
  added variable 118–9
  difference-average 31
  index 24–5, 27, 100, 101
  residual 24–5, 105–8, 112–9, 129–30
  sunflower 26–8
  smoothed 28–31
Scheffé, H. 141, 153
Schluchter, M.D. 149, 153
Seber, G.A.F. 165, 173
Seheult, A. 20, 48
Shen, E. 238, 249
Shen, S.M. 229, 233
shrinking rules 88
Siegel, S. x, xv, 1, 18, 151, 153
Simon, D. 176, 197
Singer, B.R. 238, 249
singular value decomposition 132, 224
Skinner, C.J. 184, 196
smoothing 28–31
  lowess 29–30
  median 28–31
  reasons for 28
  smoothing window 28
Snedecor, G.W. 241, 249
Snee, R.D. 168, 173
Spearman, C.E. 243, 244, 248, 249
splitting rules 83–7
  Gini index 87
  orthogonal and non-orthogonal splits 88–9
  purity 83, 84, 85–6
  resubstitution error rate 86
Sprent, P. x, xv, 1, 18, 59, 70, 71, 77, 78, 80
SPSS 132, 134, 147, 172
Steiger, J.H. 245, 249
stem and leaf display 76, 100, 101
Sternberg, R.J. 69, 80
Stewart, G.W. 122, 132, 133
Still, A.W. 72, 73, 80, 151, 154
stopping rules 85, 87

Strong, E.K. 240, 249
Sturt, E. 81, 87, 89, 91, 94
SYSTAT 132, 134

Tabachnick, B.G. 149, 154
Thomson, G.H. 244, 245, 246, 249
Thomson, R. 240, 241, 249
Thorndike, E.L. 236, 244, 249
Thurstone, L.L. 245, 246, 250
Tiao, G.C. 183, 184, 196
time series xii–xiii, 116, Chapter 8, *passim*, (*see
    also* time series models)
  analysis of variance 185
  data analytic approaches 181–2
  individual *vs* aggregate (macro-level) 174,
    176–9
  likelihood ratio tests for main and
    interactions effects 187, 189–92
  likelihood ratio tests for order 186–7
  likelihood ratio tests for sine and cosine
    wave models 192–5
  models 182–4
  objectives for studying 179–81
  quasi-experiments 158, 180
  serial correlation 186
  single subject, $n=1$ 180–1
  time fundamental to study 181
  time incidental to study 180–1
time series models 182–4
  alternative analysis 184
  ARIMA 182–3
  frequency domain 181
  intervention 183–4
  polynomial 189–92
  sine and cosine wave 192–5
  time-domain 181
  transfer function 183–4
Todman, J.B. 69, 80
Tong, H. 181, 197
Tronick, E.D. 176, 197
Tufte, E.R. 27, 45, 48
Tukey, J.W. ix, xv, 19, 20, 21, 28, 30, 48, 49,
    53, 57, 59, 64, 76, 77, 78, 80, 115, 118,
    133

unbalanced designs xii, Chapter 6, *passim*, (*see
    also* analysis of variance)
  data missing at random only within
    treatment (MROWT) 147, 149–50
  data missing completely at random (MCAR)
    147
  equally weighted means (EWM) analysis
    139–40, 141, 142, 143–5, 146–7, 151–2
  equally weighted observations (EWO)
    analysis 139, 140–1, 142–5, 146–7, 149,
    152
  experiment *vs* group studies 136–7

missing data 147–50
observations sampled completely at random
    (OSCAR) design 136, 137, 142–5, 146,
    148–9, 151, 152
partial confounding 137–8
randomly only within treatment (ROWT)
    design 136, 137, 141–5, 146, 151, 152
recommendations 141–2
robustness of analyses 150–1
role of assumptions 151–2
statistical tests 138–41
two way designs 142–5

Underwood, B.J. 239, 250
univariate repeated measures 161–4, 168
    Box's correction factor 160–1, 163, 164
    homogeneity of variance-covariance matrix
        160–1
    mixed models 162
    sphericity of variance-covariance matrix
        162–4, 168–9
    split plot design and analysis 161–2
    'three-step procedure' 164
Upton, G.J.G. xiv, xv

Velleman, P.F. 28, 48, 100, 102, 103, 118,
    132, 133

Vinod, H.D. 49, 80

Wade, M.G. 181, 197
Wallenstein, S. 164, 173
Wamani, W.T. 204, 213
Weisberg, S. 47, 48, 77, 79, 101, 102, 103,
    104, 114, 118, 133, 134
Wells, F.L. 240, 250
Wetherill, G.B. 132, 134
Whittle, P, 208, 213
Wilks, S.S. 237, 250
Winer, B.J. 40, 41, 48, 147, 154
Wing, A.M. 181, 197
Wing, J.K. 91, 94
Wolfle, D. 246, 250
Wood, F.S. 16, 18, 114, 116, 118, 133, 134
Woodrow, H. 250
Woodward, W.A. ix, xv
Woodworth, R.S. 237, 250
Working, H. 214, 233
Wynn, V.T. 176, 198

Yates, F. 162, 173, 241, 250
Yerkes, F. 236, 250
Young, A. 78, 80

Zeeman, E.C. 176, 181, 198